VILLAGES
OF EDINBURGH

To my daughter
Ingrid
In the year of her 21st birthday

VILLAGES
OF EDINBURGH
Volume 1

MALCOLM CANT

Foreword by
ALAN R. DEVEREUX C.B.E.
Chairman of the Scottish Tourist Board

JOHN DONALD PUBLISHERS LTD
EDINBURGH

ISBN 0 85976 131 2 (Paper)
ISBN 0 85976 147 9 (Hardback)

Exclusive distribution in the United States of
America and Canada by Humanities Press Inc.,
Atlantic Highlands, NJ 07716, USA.

Phototypesetting by H.M. Repros Ltd., Glasgow
and printed by Clark Constable (1982) Ltd., Edinburgh.

Foreword

For those in search of the secrets of old Edinburgh, here is a fascinating time-machine tour of the capital's villages, exploring their misty and sometimes turbulent past, tracing their recent history and relating it to modern landscaping and development.

It is a timely publication. Modern conurbations tend to swallow their individual villages. Over the centuries, Edinburgh's concern for conservation has slowed this process down and reduced the pace of visible change, but the speed of technological progress in transport and building techniques has sadly tended to submerge the identities of distinctive communities in the grey anonymous suburban sprawl. Despite this urban erosion, however, the basic fabric of each village — with its church, school, rows of cottages, inns, hostelries and graveyard — is still discernible, and Mr Cant treats each village as a separate study, tracing its distant origins and modern development in a way that provides guidance and interest to the visitor.

This is not a gazetteer of nostalgia. The detailed and authentic accounts of personalities and landmarks are the result of meticulous research, and the book provides the international traveller and the resident with a lively guidebook to the past, and the historian, architect and social worker with a useful textbook on village life and society in bygone days.

Mr Cant couples his enthusiasm for accuracy with a readable and lively style that enlivens the text with anecdote and humour to bring out the facts and the legends of the villages. Restalrig for example was an unscheduled landing ground for James Tytler when he made the first manned British hot-air balloon ascent in Edinburgh in 1784. Many villages grew up around a lifestyle dominated by one trade, including the millers in Dean village, the fishermen in Newhaven, and the miners in Newcraighall. Edinburgh's Dean village is a fine example in Britain of the conservation of an old village; its ancient buildings have been modified by modern society into housing flats but the old mills retain their distinctive architectural status as rare examples of a bygone style.

Many tourists visit Scotland to find their roots, and this book will help them to interpret a key part of Scotland's heritage. It will have a wide readership among overseas visitors, and it has much to offer the Scots themselves who will find that, as Mr Cant says, 'although much has changed there is still plenty of opportunity to inspect, to ponder, and to speculate on the meaning of what remains'.

ALAN R. DEVEREUX, C.B.E.,
CHAIRMAN OF THE SCOTTISH TOURIST BOARD

Contents

Introduction

Villages of Edinburgh was an idea which emerged during my recent study of the district of Marchmont. I discovered that the very old villages of Newcampbeltown and Westerhall had been almost completely destroyed in the Victorian tenement building era of the late nineteenth century. Whilst it is perhaps naive to think that Newcampbeltown and Westerhall could have been saved intact, nevertheless there have been many, much larger, communities in Edinburgh which have come under similar threat, particularly in the first half of the twentieth century. Fortunately, the tide of destruction has turned, with the result that many new housing developments now make a conscious effort to retain at least some part of the original fabric. Full-scale demolition is no longer the first and only choice.

Having discovered that many Edinburgh villages had survived, my first problem was to decide the way in which they should be selected and portrayed. The simplest selection was by geographical area. I have therefore devoted this first volume to those villages located in what might be referred to as the northern hemisphere of the City. Having established the area to be covered, there remained the much more difficult question: when is a village not a village? Taken to its ultimate conclusion, the answer might well be 'when the last inhabitant dies', but that criterion was unsuited to my purpose. By and large, I have selected those communities which have retained a distinct physical entity, not seriously diluted by the suburban area around it. I did not want to point to a sea of semi-detached houses and say 'once upon a time...' I wanted to be able to go and see what was left: to see what had happened to the old village street; to trace the varied occupation of the dominant buildings; to see why the village had grown up in the first place; and, above all, to experience what village life and atmosphere was still coveted by the indwellers. Of necessity my selection will fall short of some expectations, because Edinburgh has many inhabitants who know their own district far better than I ever will. To them my promise must be in the future: having unearthed a few gems in the first quick sweep, I might return to dig a little deeper.

CORSTORPHINE. My thanks go to the Corstorphine Trust collectively and to individual members: Dr. Ernest Cormack, T.D; W.G. Dey, F.R.I.B.A., F.R.I.A.S., A.M.T.P.I; and Miss A.S. Cowper; also to Joanne Soroka, Artistic Director of the Edinburgh Tapestry Company Limited.

CRAMOND. I acknowledge considerable assistance from the Cramond Association and the Cramond Heritage Trust. In practical terms this was provided, unsparingly, by Barclay S. Fraser, M.A., and Mrs N. Dean who kindly read through my script and contributed useful material. I also received guidance from George Jamieson on Cramond Tower.

DAVIDSON'S MAINS. I derived assistance from many sources — Davidson's Mains and Silverknowes Association, residents, traders, churches and schools. My special thanks must go to A.W. Bannerman, M.A; Albert Black; Barclay S. Fraser, M.A; Mrs Freda McIntyre; and James McKenzie. Guidance on Craigcrook Castle was given by H.H. Macdonald, F.R.I.B.A., F.R.I.A.S., and on Lauriston Castle by David Scarrat, B.A., A.M.A., F.R.S.A., F.S.A. (Scot).

DEAN. I extend my thanks to the Dean Village Association, particularly to Dorothy L. Forrester, M.A.(Edin)., M.A.(Essex); and to John W. Fyfe, D.A.(Edin)., R.I.B.A., A.R.I.A.S., of the Bamber Gray Partnership; Philip Taylor, General Manager of the Dragonara Hotel; J. Campbell Reid of Whytock and Reid; and Lawrence Walker of Bell's Mills House.

DUDDINGSTON. The present appearance of the village owes much to the Society for the Preservation of Duddingston Village whose members were most helpful to me. I acknowledge assistance and encouragement from Rev. William Ramsay; H.G.C. Roger; W.G. Cruikshank; Sheriff D.B. Smith; Colin McLean of the Scottish Wildlife Trust; and the National Museum of Antiquities of Scotland.

NEWCRAIGHALL. Many residents and ex-residents helped in my research, too numerous to mention by name. My special thanks, though, go to Mr and Mrs J. McFarlane. I am also indebted to the National Coal Board, the school, churches, clubs, *Craigmillar*

Festival News, Councillor David Brown, David Spence, George Montgomery and Bill Douglas, the film producer. The section on Newhailes was completed with the assistance of Lady Antonia Dalrymple and the National Library of Scotland.

NEWHAVEN. My initial approach was to Newhaven and District Community Association which led to further contact with the church, the school and the Society of Free Fishermen. I also received information on particular aspects from Robert Allan, Bill and Margaret Gibbs, William K. Ritchie, and the Peacock Hotel.

RESTALRIG. Invaluable assistance was derived from Rev. W. Carmichael, B.Sc., F.L.S; H.G. Lindley of Kinloch Anderson; Charles A. Kemp; A.S. Cowper; and Mr & Mrs Smith of Dunira. On particular topics, information was also received from Simmers Bakery and George Wimpey & Co. Ltd.

STOCKBRIDGE. A lot of interest in my research was shown by various members of the schools and churches. I thank particularly: L.E. Ellis, M.A., Rector of the Edinburgh Academy; John Miller, Headmaster of Donaldson's School for the Deaf; and Mrs Barbara A. Cant, widow of John K. Cant, M.A., former Headmaster at Donaldson's School; Miss May M. Beattie, Headteacher at Stockbridge Primary School; the Very Rev. Malcolm A. Clark of St. Vincent's Church; Rev. A. Ian Dunlop, T.D., B.D., of St. Stephen's Church; and Rev. John Munro of St. Bernard's Church. Additional information was gladly supplied by many residents, traders, and Theatre Workshop.

GENERAL. I derived assistance from a wide range of people, perhaps much wider than I first imagined was necessary. My final acknowledgements go to the small group of people whose help was not confined to any one village. Leader in the field was undoubtedly the staff of the Edinburgh Room of Edinburgh Central Library, followed closely by Malcolm Liddle who undertook reproduction of many old photographs and also slides for my Extra-Mural class at Edinburgh University. I extend my thanks to Basil Skinner, M.A., F.S.A., Director of Extra-Mural Studies, and to the various members of the class, many of whom I never knew by name.

I also appreciate the interest shown by the Scottish Tourist Board. The Chairman, Alan R. Devereux, C.B.E., has kindly written the Foreword, and the External Relations Director, John A. Stuart, also showed great interest in the project from inception.

I have tried to keep the text as accurate as possible, but inevitably mistakes will have arisen. In accordance with tradition, and good sense, I accept responsibility now: the errors would have been much greater had it not been for the very careful proof reading done by Morag Sinclair.

Finally, I thank my wife Phyllis for typing the script, occasionally twice, often at short notice, and even sometimes when she had other things to do. To Phyllis, and to our family, who always waited 'patiently' for their tea, I would only say 'watch out for volume two'.

MALCOLM CANT

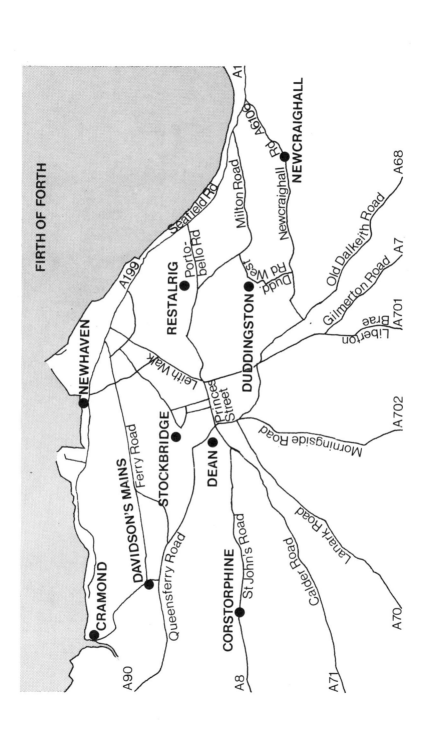

CHAPTER 1

Corstorphine

The name Corstorphine is applied to one of Edinburgh's largest suburbs, extending from Saughtonhall, westwards to the city boundary. The modern suburb contains all manner of houses, businesses and hotels, but the old village of Corstorphine was little more than a cluster of cottages to the north of the narrow isthmus separating Gogar Loch from Corstorphine Loch. Gogar Loch was by far the smaller of the two. It extended westward from the village, for a distance of approximately a mile and a half, over the district of South Gyle. Corstorphine Loch, on the other hand, extended eastwards in a long narrow plain before widening out to cover the present districts of Balgreen and Roseburn. On the strategically important strip of land between the two lochs, the ancient family of Forrester built the impregnable defence, Corstorphine Castle, in the late fourteenth century. The original village grew up close to the protection of the castle, and became known over the years as the low village to distinguish it from the high village which developed at the end of the eighteenth century and the beginning of the nineteenth century along the line of St. Johns's Road. Improved communication between the city and Corstorphine during the nineteenth and twentieth centuries resulted in a plethora of villas, bungalows, flats and businesses which go to make up the present district of Corstorphine.

The origin of the name Corstorphine can be traced back to the year 1128 when it appeared as 'Crostorfin', suggesting Thorfin's crossing, although the identity of Thorfin has never been satisfactorily explained.

The Forresters of Corstorphine

The early development of Corstorphine is synonymous with the ancient family of Forrester. Prior to 1376 Adam Forrester lived in Forrester's Wynd on the south side of the High Street, near the present George IV Bridge. He was a man of ability and ambition whose first public appointment was that of Justice Clerk in 1362. A

1

The Forrester Tomb, Corstorphine Church, with the armorial bearings of
the three buffaloes' horns stringed.
From Grant's *Old and New Edinburgh.*

few years later he acquired land near Whitburn, and in 1373 he
became Provost of Edinburgh, and later Deputy-Governor of
Edinburgh Castle. His first involvement in Corstorphine was in 1374
when he acquired the lands of Corstorphine from Gilchrist More,
brother of Sir William More of Abercorn. In later life he held the
positions of Auditor of Public Accounts and Keeper of the Great Seal
of Scotland. Towards the end of his life he obtained permission from
the Abbot of Holyrood to build, beside the already established parish
church of St. Mary, a votive chapel where he was buried in 1405.
Sometime in the latter part of the fourteenth century he built
Corstorphine Castle as the seat of the Forrester family. On the death
of Adam Forrester the estates went to his son John who continued the
work on the chapel and established a collegiate church at
Corstorphine, which was confirmed by Pope Eugenius in 1429.

When George, the tenth head of the Forrester family, was created a
peer in 1633, he took the title Lord Forrester of Corstorphine, but
little did he know that his elevation was to prove a turning point in the
history of the family. Although he had five daughters, his only son
had predeceased him without issue, and he therefore decided to
resolve the matter of his succession during his own lifetime. Tempted

by the natural desire to maintain the family house and name, George made the fatal mistake of favouring one child at the expense of the others. He relinquished his title, and handed the barony to James Baillie, the husband of Joanna his fourth daughter. On the death of George, in 1654, James Baillie became the second Lord Forrester of Corstorphine, but he was not equal to the task. He neglected the estates; he incurred heavy debts; he drank too much and too often at the Black Bull Inn; and he engaged in extra-marital relationships, principally with Christian Nimmo, his first wife's niece. From the seeds of debauchery he was later to reap a dismal harvest. His first wife Joanna died very young, as did William their only child. His second marriage in 1661 was to Janet Ruthven, daughter of the Earl of Forth and Brentford, but when Janet died also, he lost all purpose in life. During one of his bouts of drinking he supposedly doubted the morality of Christian Nimmo with whom he had been associating. When she heard the gossip she came to Corstorphine Castle on the night of 26th August 1679 only to be told that James was still at the Black Bull Inn. A messenger was sent to bring him home, and Christian set out to meet him. When they met at the famous Corstorphine sycamore tree (at the east end of Dovecot Road), there was a violent quarrel during which James repeated his accusations. Incensed by the slur on her character and smarting from his refusal to marry her, Christian drew the sword from his scabbard and ran the blade through her drunken paramour. Leaving Lord Forrester dead, she fled to the castle where she was captured and taken to Edinburgh Tolbooth. She escaped from the Tolbooth Jail but was recaptured at Fala Mill and was executed in Edinburgh on 12th November 1679. On the death of James the second Lord Forrester, so great was the trauma that his brother, heir to the estate, did not take the title of third Lord Forrester. The brother's son William became fourth Lord in 1684, by which time the estate was burdened with debts. It was sold in 1698 to Hugh Wallace W.S. of Ingliston, and then in 1713 to Sir James Dick of Prestonfield, in whose family it remained for the next century and a half.

To this day the Corstorphine sycamore remains. It is protected by a Preservation Order of 1955, and in 1970, it was gifted to the Corstorphine Trust along with a small piece of ground round the tree. Inevitably its great antiquity has given rise to some imaginative stories. On moonlight nights the ghost of Christian Nimmo is said to appear holding a bloody sword in her hand and moaning and wailing beneath the branches of the old sycamore. G. Upton Selway, writing in 1890, also relates the legend that Lord Forrester is supposed to have buried treasure beneath the tree and that at least one villager was frightened off by hearing a voice from beneath the tree commanding him to stop digging — a legend perhaps, but still a warning to anyone tempted to excavate too near its hallowed roots.

Corstorphine Castle and Dovecot; Dovecot Studios

Nothing remains of Corstorphine Castle. In relation to modern street names it stood on ground now occupied by bungalows in Castle Avenue to the south of the Dovecot Road entrance to St. Margaret's Park. When the castle was built in the fourteenth century it occupied a most important position in the western defences of Edinburgh. It was protected on the east by Corstorphine Loch, on the west by Gogar Loch, on the south by a wide expanse of bogland, and on the north by the rising ground of Corstorphine Hill. It featured prominently in the fortunes of the Forrester family for several generations until it was sold in 1698. The last person to reside there may have been Margaret Crauford relict of John Forbes of Knaperine as sub-tenant of Lord Cullen, who used it for several years during vacations of the Court of Session.

In its heyday the castle was a most impressive fortress, surrounded by a moat, with an interior courtyard protected by solid curtain walls one hundred feet long and massive towers twenty-one feet in diameter on each corner. There was an approach from the east which was later lined with trees, one of which is the Corstorphine sycamore. By 1721 the castle had become ruinous, and the records of the Kirk Session state that Sir James Dick 'allows to take what stones are needful for building the churchyard dykes and two offering houses out of the old mansionhouse of Corstorphine'.

In more modern times one or two small artefacts have been unearthed by people with garden ground near where the castle stood. By far the most important relic, however, is the fireplace lintel bearing the carved armorial shields of the Forrester and Preston families. It contains three raised shields commemorating the marriage of Henry Forrester to Helenor Preston of Craigmillar. The centre shield bears the initials H.P. and the three unicorns of the Preston family, while the outer shields bear the initials H.F. and the three hunting horns of the Forrester family. Around 1750 the lintel was built into a fireplace at Amulree House at the north-west end of Corstorphine High Street and remained there until the house was demolished in the 1950s, when the lintel was removed to its present location at 199 St. John's Road.

Corstorphine Dovecot, dating from the sixteenth century, is not quite as old as the castle but undoubtedly was closely associated with it. It stands near the Corstorphine sycamore, at the north-east end of Dovecot Road, its great bulk rising high above the boundary wall of the Dovecot Studios. Like many similar dovecots, its preservation probably owes much to the old Scottish superstition that destruction of a dovecot meant death, within a year, of the lady of the house. Many Scottish dovecots are rectangular in shape, but the Corstorphine Dovecot, like that at Lochend, is circular, rather like a gigantic beeskep. It is divided horizontally by three string courses and has six entrance holes in the south wall, above the middle course. The walls are about four feet thick at the base, with twenty eight tiers providing more than a thousand nesting places. The entrance is on the north side, the door being embellished by ornamental ironwork.

The Corstorphine Dovecot stands in the garden of the Edinburgh Tapestry Company which was founded as the Dovecot Studios in 1912 in Dovecot Road. The dovecot was the insignia woven into each tapestry in the early days of the studio, while today its symbol is a flying dove. The studio was founded by the fourth Marquess of Bute, with the first two master weavers, Gordon Berry and John Glassbrook, coming from William Morris' famous studio at Merton Abbey. The large, historical and finely woven tapestries of this era were destined for the walls of the many Bute family homes.

The Company closed for the duration of the Second World War, as all the weavers had enlisted. When the Company re-opened, the members of the Bute family decided on a change of emphasis from large tapestries to smaller panels designed by well-known artists, intended for sale, and now the studio is entirely a commercial venture concentrating on commissioned work. In 1980 the studio had a major retrospective exhibition entitled 'Master Weavers' during the Edinburgh International Festival. The studio's work is known around the world, and it has translated the work of the best known British and American artists into tapestry.

Corstorphine Church, 1817 (after an etching by James Skene of Rubislaw), showing the beacon light niche in the gable on the extreme left. From Grant's *Old and New Edinburgh*.

Corstorphine Church

The parish church of St. John, with its stone roof and irregular roofline, is perhaps Corstorphine's most distinctive building, parts of which date from as early as 1404. Its long and eventful history prompted D.M. Thomson to observe in *The Corstorphine Heirloom* that 'it bears the marks of having been more than once rudely handled in times of national crises, although the finger of time has smoothed out most of these scars'.

At first sight the history of the church is somewhat confusing. The first definite record is of a parish church of St. Mary, in a charter dated 1128 of King David I who founded the Abbey of Holyrood. It survived until 1646 when it was absorbed into the north aisle of the church. St. Mary's therefore had no separate existence after 1646.

The present church of St. John began as a very modest votive chapel, constructed in 1404 by Sir Adam Forrester as a place of burial for himself and his family. Whether Sir Adam ever intended the chapel to be the foundation of a greater ecclesiastical building is a matter of conjecture, but after his death in 1405 his son Sir John

Forrester installed two choir boys and increased the number of chaplains to five. This was the basis of the collegiate church in 1429, but it was not until 1443 that its status was confirmed by Pope Eugenius. Sir John did not, however, wait for official approval before going ahead with the necessary additions to the church. In 1429 he made several improvements and additions which gave the church its basic shape for many years to follow. Starting with the original votive chapel (which is now at the east end of the church), he built westwards to form the nave with a south transept, and then further westward for the bell tower and the inner porch. In 1646 the adjacent parish church of St. Mary was demolished to allow the construction of the north transept, the porch being constructed from the ruins of St. Mary. In the early eighteenth century a gallery was built with access to it from an outside stair, the cost of this being met by Sir Andrew Myrtoun of Gogar House.

In the early part of the nineteenth century the population of Corstorphine had grown to such an extent that the seating arrangements in the church were inadequate, to say nothing of being very uncomfortable. Several suggestions were mooted, and in 1828 the matter was put in the hands of the architect William Burn of Hermiston House. Although the parishioners and heritors declared themselves delighted with the result, their enthusiasm for Burn's work has not been shared by later generations. In fact it is generally considered that much of his restoration work was very insensitive. Burn's restoration reorientated the whole church by repositioning the main door below the east window of the chancel, but when further restoration was done in 1905, the door was re-sited at the west end.

The very distinctive square tower dates from 1429. There are finials on each corner of the wallhead, and the squat stone steeple is divided into three tiers. The bell has an interesting inscription: SIR JAMES FORRESTER GIFTED ME TO THIS KIRK ANNO 1577 AND THE HERETORS OF CORSTORPHINE ME RENEUED ANNO 1728 R M FECIT EDR. R.M. of Edinburgh may have been either Robert Meikle or Robert Maxwell, both of whom were well known bell-founders.

At the opposite end there is an equally interesting feature, also designed to draw people in the direction of the church. It is the beacon light niche dating from 1429 and kept in regular use until 1769. In the days when the ground around Corstorphine was covered by the loch and marshland, it had become the duty of the priests to raise a burning lamp on a pulley into the niche on the east gable, to give direction to anyone travelling by land or by water. The cost of maintaining this service was financed by the endowment of 'the lamp acre', a piece of ground near Coltbridge, now commemorated in Lampacre Road in Corstorphine. The 'lamp acre' was that piece of triangular-shaped ground at the foot of Ormidale Terrace lying between the south side of Corstorphine Road and the north bank of the Water of Leith, and extending westward to a point opposite the south end of Murrayfield Road.

The interior of the church is also famous for the recumbent effigies of the Forrester family. The tombs of the founder Sir John Forrester and his wife are on the north wall of the present chancel. Sir John's effigy wears a fifteenth-century helmet and plate armour, whilst Lady Forrester wears a dress with an embroidered belt and is surmounted by a cloak. A short distance from the founder's tomb is that of his son, also named John, and his wife. In the south transept there is the effigy of Sir Adam Forrester.

The 'Low' Village

The old village of Corstorphine extends along the High Street, from Corstorphine Church at the east end to Ladywell Road at the west end. It is here that the remaining vestiges of village life can be seen, or imagined, largely unaffected by the hustle and bustle of St. John's Road. Few people, however, would pretend that the village has remained unscathed. There are no thatched cottages; there is no smiddy; the old street signs and house names are noticed only by historians and by inquisitive strangers, and even in this age of conservation the dangers from commercial development are ever present.

An estate plan of the district, dated 1777, shows the village well established with the position of the main streets not greatly different to the present day. By 1777 the Forrester family had long since fallen from grace, and their mighty fortress lay in ruins a few hundred yards south of the main street. Corstorphine Loch had been drained and Gogar Loch had been greatly reduced in size by deepening the Stank ditch to the north. Agricultural potential was being discovered in the morass which had protected the Forresters of old. By the middle of the nineteenth century a thriving agricultural community had grown up and there were definite commercial links with the city of Edinburgh. The village consisted of about four hundred people, mostly employed on the neighbouring farms, but there were other occupations which gave the village its sense of independence. The tradesmen included a drystone mason, a thatcher, several weavers, a blacksmith, a quarryman, two shoemakers, and four master tailors. The shopkeepers consisted of two bakers and three grocers, whilst the professions were represented by an architect, a minister, two doctors and a teacher. Another interesting aspect of the population was the number of Irish labourers who took accommodation in the village whilst working firstly on the construction of the Union Canal and then the Edinburgh to Glasgow railway. After the line was completed, many of the Irish families stayed on and formed a small community of their own at the east end of the village which came to be known as Irish Corner.

Irish Corner was that part of Kirk Loan near its junction with North Saughton Road. The old cottages which stood opposite the library were demolished in 1928, and in the following year the War Memorial was resited there from its original position in Station Road. The east end of the High Street, near the church, is an obvious starting point for any study of the old village. The most prominent building is the turreted red sandstone facade of Corstorphine Public Hall. The main section to the west with the twin turrets is the original Public Hall built in 1891. Above the doorway there is a most interesting pediment containing the Forrester hunting horn in the tympanum, and a Scottish thistle on the apex flanked by two clinging reptiles. The smaller section to the east was added in 1903 and has a similar doorway, except that the tympanum contains an open book, as befitted its intended use as the public library. In 1920, when Corstorphine was brought within the city boundary, control of the library passed from Corstorphine Parish Council to Edinburgh Corporation. Later the library outgrew its accommodation in the wing of the Public Hall, and Paddockholm Cottage, immediately to the east, was acquired and demolished to allow the construction of the present library.

Opposite the Public Hall the short section of roadway leading to Saughton Road North is named Hall Terrace, but only two of the row of single-storey cottages now remain. They do, however, help to consolidate the historical importance of this corner which includes the former Black Bull Inn at which Lord Forrester took courage before

Free Church picnic outing c.1900, passing Gladstone Place in the Low Village. Courtesy of W.G. Dey.

his encounter with Christian Nimmo at the sycamore tree. G. Upton Selway, writing in 1890, refers to the building as 'The Camps' and indicates that it had long since ceased to be an inn. At the beginning of the present century the building was renovated and a stone plaque was added on the projecting east gable, 'Ye Olde Inne Oakland 1904'. The embellishments also appear to contain the date 1561 and the initials C D B.

The Parish Church Hall is on the north side of the High Street adjacent to the lane giving access to the churchyard. It is by no means a building of architectural significance but it occupies the site of the house of the provost of the collegiate church, built around 1550. When the old house was demolished in the 1880s, the inscribed skewstones were preserved and built into the gable of the church hall. Also on the north side of the High Street the three-storey tenement block with the date 1910 over the entrance marks the approximate location of the Tron Tree at which a market was at one time held for the sale of farm produce, including the celebrated delicacy Corstorphine Cream. The *Old Statistical Account of Scotland* records the mystery of its preparation:

> They put the milk, when fresh drawn, into a barrel or wooden vessel, which is submitted to a certain degree of heat, generally by immersion

Manse Road looking north towards St. John's Road, before the days of the Astoria Picture House.

> in warm water, this accelerates the stage of fermentation. The serous is separated from the other parts of the milk, the oleaginous and coagulable; the serum is drawn off by a hole in the lower part of the vessel; what remains is put into the plunge-churn and after being agitated for some time, is sent to market as Corstorphine Cream.

Although it is many years since Corstorphine Cream was sold at the Tron Tree, other processes of fermentation have lost little to history: the Corstorphine Inn with its famous skittle alley is the only remaining hostelry in the 'low' village.

Beside Albyn Cottage on the north side of the road a small lane gives access to a feu of ground acquired by the Corstorphine United Free Church in 1930. At the Union of the United Free Church and the Church of Scotland in 1929 those of the Free congregation who were opposed to the Union formed a congregation of their own and worshipped in the Masonic Hall for the first few months. The reasons for not joining the Established Church are worth recalling: 'The minority of the United Free Church believing that the obstacles to union had not been removed and that the Church of Scotland as a State-privileged and State-endowed institution was handicapped in its work of spreading the Gospel, has endeavoured from that date, to maintain the testimony and continue the life of the Church from which it began'. When the new Church Hall was opened for worship on 5th June 1930, there was a membership of fifty-one, but by 1935

11

the congregation was sufficiently established to call its first minister of full status, Rev. Robert Waugh. In the years that followed the congregation increased substantially and set up a Sunday School, Choir, Prayer Union and Temperance Association.

Beyond Corstorphine Inn the High Street is bisected by Manse Road to the north and Orchardfield Avenue to the south. Manse Road was once named Bernard's Slap or Bernard's Vennel, and the short section of the High Street to the west was known as Gladstone Place. The name is still cut into the corner stone of the cottages erected in 1880 by a parliamentary supporter of Gladstone. Further to the west the single tenement, Nos. 56–60 Corstorphine High Street, was erected by supporters of the Earl of Dalkeith, son of the Duke of Buccleuch, and named Buccleuch Place. At that time the High Street was very much narrower, but in 1929 it was widened on the south side along the line of St Margaret's Park. This entailed the repositioning of the elegant gate pillars and ironwork leading to the Dower House.

The Dower House, built by one of the Lords Forrester, sits in the north-east corner of St. Margaret's Park and dates from the mid-seventeenth century, although it has been altered on several occasions since. It is now a three-storey building with crowstepped gables and entrance on the north wall. The exterior is harled with the corner stones exposed, the skewputs still jutting out at a lower level indicating that the wallhead has probably been raised at some time in the past to form another storey. Internally the house has been modernised but there are several rooms with moulded fireplaces and original wall panelling. At one time the house was known as Gibson Lodge after Dame Henrietta Watson, Lady Gibson (of Pentland) who owned it. In recent years it was used for a time as a Retired Men's Club.

In the road-widening programme of 1929 all but one of the old Cross Cottages were demolished. The remaining one was used as the Scout Hall up to the Second World War when it was destroyed by fire despite being used at the time as an Air Raid Precaution station! The Scout Hall, built on the foundations of the old cottage, is the last very tenuous link with the famous Cross of Corstorphine. The Cross was a group of five old elm trees arranged in a square with one in the centre which stood about opposite the present school. It was here that Corstorphine's larger market was held for the sale of cattle, pigs and horses. Although there have been no elms at the Cross for many years, they are clearly depicted in the old colours of the Corstorphine Friendly Society, constituted in August 1789.

The land lying to the south of the old Cross is now occupied by St. Margaret's Park, gifted to the Parish Council in 1915 by the Honourable Christopher Douglas Brown of Arizona whose wife Margaret Dixon came from a long-established Corstorphine family. The gate pillars at the north entrance record the event for posterity:

ST. MARGARET'S PARK   ST. MARGARET'S PARK
PRESENTED BY   OPENED BY
C. DOUGLAS BROWN   MARGARET DOUGLAS
                            BROWN
JULY 1915   JULY 1915

(LEFT HAND PILLAR)   (RIGHT HAND PILLAR)

It is Christopher Douglas Brown's initials 'C D B' which appear on the Oakland plaque of 1904 built into the old Black Bull Inn at the east end of the village.

The history of the west end of the village is closely associated with the ancient Physic Well which was famed for its medicinal qualities. The site of the Physic Well is still marked by several large flat stones in the wooded area to the south-east of Dunsmuir Court. In its heyday in the mid-eighteenth century, such was the attraction of the well for the people of Edinburgh that a coach ran specially between the city and Corstorphine, making eight or nine journeys each weekday and four journeys on a Sunday. In 1750 the number of visitors to Corstorphine had reached such proportions that a Leith wood merchant decided to build fairly substantial accommodation for overnight guests. Unfortunately the deepening of the Stank ditch to improve drainage resulted in interruption of the water supply to the well, and his investment, like the water, showed little or no return. The old 'hotel', variously named throughout its life as Irelands Block, Amulree House and the Mansion House, was eventually demolished in 1952. Thanks to the interest taken by local historians the old fireplace lintel with the coats of arms of the Forrester and Preston families was rescued from one of the rooms and refitted in The Cedars in St. John's Road. Another spring at the west end of the village was Our Lady's Well which earned the reputation of never running dry and must therefore have been of considerable practical value to the villagers.

On leaving the village at its west end there is one last stone worthy of mention. It lies among mature trees to the left of the pavement leading from Ladywell Road to Dunsmuir Court, and contains the following inscription which is now barely visible:

5
MILES FROM THE
GENERAL POST OFFICE
EDINBURGH

ERECTED TO REGULATE
THE POST HORSE DUTIES
PAYABLE
BY HACKNEY COACHES
1824

Its function is clear but it is not five miles from the General Post Office. Moreover it is not placed in such a position as to be visible from any main road, particularly in 1824. Apparently the stone was first erected much nearer to the Maybury roundabout but was removed many years ago and used ornamentally in the grounds of Dunsmuir House. The house was built around 1850 and modernised by Pringle Taylor in 1900. Ironically, it was badly damaged by fire during the Second World War whilst occupied by those best equipped to deal with such eventualities, the Auxiliary Fire Service. Shades of the A.R.P. at the Scout Hall! When Dunsmuir was demolished in the 1950s, the milestone was preserved and incorporated in the modern housing development built on the site.

Corstorphine School

The earliest record of a school in the village is 1646. It was established by George the first Lord Forrester in rather humble surroundings near Albyn Cottage at the east end of the High Street. James Chalmers the schoolmaster was paid a salary of one hundred merks by the heritors and, through Lord Forrester, was provided with 'ane house and yards within the toun of Corstorphine, lying betwixt the minister's manse on the east and John Aitken, mason on the west, together with ane aiker and half of land lying above the smiddie upon the cast side of the walk that goes to Cramond, and an aiker of land lying bewest the Cowes brigge upon the south side of the little house that stands by the wayside, commonly called the Lamp Aiker, within the parochine of St. Cuthberts'. Seventeenth-century methods of land cultivation, and the additional responsibility of being precentor and session clerk at the parish church, obviously placed a heavy burden on anyone taking the post of local schoolmaster. The degree of probity expected of the incumbent was seriously breached in 1698 when John Cunningham the village schoolmaster was found drunk on the roadway between Edinburgh and Corstorphine, 'tottering south and north on the causey'. When the Kirk Session found him guilty of several offences, he resigned in October 1698 and commenced legal action for moneys due to him for past services. As a precentor he was judged to be lacking in both repertoire and intonation, the Kirk Session alleging that he had only two tunes and 'neither doth he sing these aright'. It was also said that he was given to haunting ale houses, and in consequence was unable to keep the minutes, and that he neglected the mortcloth list.

According to an interesting inset in the Corstorphine School Logs the Committee of Heritors decided on 3rd April 1819 that a new school was to be built on ground occupied by cottars on the north side of the Cross of Corstorphine. A second meeting a few weeks later confirmed that the trees forming the Cross were to be sold and that Alexander Simpson, the headmaster, was to plant other trees in the same formation 'upon the south-east angle of the land now belonging to the schoolmaster'. There is no evidence that these trees were ever planted, but the small single-storey school was constructed in 1819. In its early years the school did not have adequate resources to meet local needs. The wife of Dr. Robert Morehead founded a small private school for girls in 1829 because 'the girls of the village were rough and neglected and neither taught morals nor manners, nor sewing and knitting for in those days there was no female teacher in the parish schools'.

A fine new school was, however, built on the present site in 1848, a commemorative plaque being built into the east gable — ERECTED 1848 — J.M.W. ARCH. The first meeting of the School Board of Corstorphine met on 26th April 1873, and within three years there was talk of further expansion. But this did not take place until 1894, when the present building was erected with a plaque on the south facing frontage — REBUILT 1894. Thus the smart, orderly appearance of Corstorphine Primary School, now under the control of Lothian Regional Council, belies a history of less enlightened

times. The elm trees were never planted to re-form the Cross of
Corstorphine, but at least today's schoolboys have the advantage of a
gigantic horse chestnut tree which dominates the playground on the
north side of the High Street.

The 'High' Village

Corstorphine is in the unique position of having two villages,
separated at one time by a degree of rivalry, if not of jealousy. The
indwellers of the 'low' village were looked down upon by the property
owners in the 'high' village, until they too were overlooked by the
bungalows and villas which sprang up on the slopes of Corstorphine
Hill.

The early history of Corstorphine is undoubtedly centred on the
'low' village with its church, its castle and its ancient wells. Indeed
the 1777 estate plan shows very little development along the line of
what is now St John's Road. Mature trees lined both sides of the
road, but opposite the foot of Clermiston Road there was a brewery
and an inn. Further to the west between the Bank of Scotland
building and the Trustee Savings Bank there was a small group of
houses known as Laburnum Cottages. The smiddy was on the north
side of the road, the site of which is now occupied by a modern office
at the foot of St. Ninian's Drive. Ferrybank, to the west of the
smiddy, was famous for its bee-wall dating from the time when the
property was owned by John Johnston, a candlemaker in Edinburgh
in the early eighteenth century. Another of Corstorphine's famous
trees, the copper beech, stands on the pavement only a few feet from
where the smiddy used to be. This beech and an old elm in the garden
of 198 St. John's Road are probably the only remaining trees which
at one time lined both sides of the main road through the high village.

In the middle of the nineteenth century the area around St. John's
Road was still open farmland with Featherhall Farm occupying land
on both sides of the main road, a few hundred yards west of Manse
Road. The large detached house lying between Manse Road and
Featherhall Farm was named Fixby Cottage and was owned by
William Girdwood, a cloth merchant. It was later renamed 'The
Cedars', part of which now houses the headquarters of the
Corstorphine Trust, custodians of a most interesting collection of
material on the history of the area.

The High Village c.1900 looking east in St. John's Road, with gas lamps and telegraph poles but no tram rails.

In the opening years of the twentieth century the 'high' village entered a new phase of development. St. John's Road had been established as the main route west from Edinburgh for some years previously, and shops and tenements were being erected at intervals along both sides of the road. Transport was still rudimentary, most people being dependent on the horse-bus which operated at hourly intervals from the bus depot on the south side of St. John's Road, to Haymarket. The nearest railway station was Corstorphine, but this was on the Edinburgh to Glasgow line, which meant either a fairly long walk or an expensive journey by hackney coach. In 1902, however, the North British Railway Company opened a branch line direct to Corstorphine at Station Road. Unfortunately pedestrian access to the station from the east end of the High Street, near the Public Hall, was refused, as the intended route cut across the policies of Corstorphine House. Another competitor was the electric tramcar in 1923. Corstorphine was served by service numbers 1, 12, and 25. Service number one ran from Liberton to Corstorphine, route colours red over blue; service number twelve ran from King's Road, via Seafield and Leith, to Corstorphine, route colours yellow over blue; and service number twenty-five ran from Craigentinny Avenue

North via Leith Walk and York Place to Corstorphine, route colours blue over yellow. When the trams to Corstorphine were discontinued in 1954, they were replaced by bus services 1, 12, 25 and 26.

St John's Road has lost most of its original buildings, and of those which remain many have been drastically altered. The old hostelries of the Harp Hotel and the Oak Inn are still thriving businesses, but the bus depot has long since closed, and the police station has been moved to Meadow Place Road. Even the manse was moved further south after three hundred years in wooded grounds at the north-east end of Manse Road. The most dominant landmark is still, however, the Gothic spire of St. Ninian's Church, erected as a Free Church in 1870 on the site of an earlier Free Church dating from 1844. The first minister was Rev. George Burns D.D., who resigned his parochial charge at Tweedsmuir at the Disruption in 1843. In 1929, at the union of the United Free Church and the Established Church, the name St. Ninian's was adopted. At the back of St. Ninian's Church, with its entrance into St. Ninian's Road, is the Roman Catholic Church of St. John the Baptist, its clean modern lines creating an interesting contrast with the Gothic spire of St. Ninian's. St. John's was designed by Charles W. Gray with a seating capacity of four hundred, and was opened for worship in 1963 by Cardinal Gordon Gray. The church held its first services in 1935 in a small hut in Kaimes Road before transferring to the old police station building in 1938.

Corstorphine has a rich heritage of churches, unrivalled for antiquity and variety of architecture. St. Anne's, on the north-west corner of St. John's Road and Kaimes Road, is a magnificent example of Romanesque architecture designed by P. Macgregor Chalmers and opened in 1913. The rather plain exterior of rough-faced Hailes stone in regular courses, and the absence of the intended campanile or tower above the entrance doorway, belies an interior of much greater detail. The internal furnishings are also by the architect Chalmers, with later additions, in the north chapel, by W.G. Dey in 1953. The pipe organ by Arthur E. Ingram was dedicated in 1922 (by the Right Rev. J. Smith, D.D., Moderator of the General Assembly) and there are several stained glass windows by Gordon Webster and William Wilson. Those in the north aisle are based on the Psalms; those in the south aisle illustrate the Creation, the Fall of Man, the Annunciation and the Baptist; and the five windows of the Apse deal with the Life of Christ. There is a most informative guide, giving the

Corporation motor bus at Station Road, Corstorphine, 1922.
Courtesy of D.L.G. Hunter. Photograph by the late E.O. Catford.

history and description of St. Anne's, prepared by W.G. Dey in 1966.

If there ever was any rivalry between the 'high' village and the 'low' village, Corstorphine had its own halfway house at which all class prejudice took a back seat. It was the Astoria Picture House, in Manse Road, designed by T. Bowhill Gibson and opened for F.R. Graham-Yooll on January 1st 1930. The interior was particularly sumptuous, with rose velvet curtains braided in gold, and an auditorium capable of seating 1,228 people. A particularly attractive feature was the Ingram organ which could produce a wide range of special effects, including cathedral chimes, harp, xylophone and drums. Sadly the cinema closed in 1974 when it was owned by Kingsway Entertainments of Kirkcaldy. The last Saturday children's show was *Anything for Laughs* and *Zeppelin,* and the last full programme was on 29th June 1974, *Magnum Force* starring Clint Eastwood and *You Don't Know Why You Came Here.* The cinema was later demolished and the site occupied by a supermarket.

Village Life and Character

Corstorphine can trace its buildings and its institutions back to the twelfth century, and it is surprising how many identifiable links can

19

be found in the chain. Whilst the events of national importance have all been recorded by several writers, the history of its ordinary people has been given less attention, until comparatively recent years. Corstorphine is in the fortunate position that Miss A.S. Cowper has taken the time and trouble since 1968 to record some of the available material in an interesting series of papers.

A hundred years ago Corstorphine was greatly influenced by its economic dependence on the surrounding farms and market gardens. People went about their business on foot, or, if necessary, by horse-drawn transport. Motorised vehicles were non-existent. Whilst the local doctor went his rounds on an old tricycle with solid tyres, Pringle Taylor of Dunsmuir, immaculately dressed in pinstriped trousers, tail coat, top hat and monocle, was driven to Edinburgh each morning in his own private carriage. Much earlier in the day, regardless of the weather, the postman, with his red barrow, accompanied by two or three paper boys, made the journey down to Corstorphine Station to collect the day's mail and papers. At that time in the morning traffic was light, and well intentioned. A farm labourer might have the use of his master's dray for an early morning flitting, before working in the fields in the afternoon. All his worldly possessions would be arranged in ordered confusion, with a space at the front of the cart reserved for his wife and family. At the height of the rhubarb season other lighter two-wheeled carts converged on the fields near Dovecot Road where the early traders got the pick of the crop for resale in Edinburgh later in the day. Any stragglers, on foot, picked their way warily along the path taken by the cows going down to the Glebe after milking at Chisholm's Dairy near Featherhall. With the men out of the house to earn the week's wages, the women settled down to the day's housework. The shops were small and intimate, but what the goods lacked in variety was compensated by the character of the shopkeepers. There was Miss Scott at Laburnum Cottage who was summoned from the back shop by the faintest jingle of the bell; Mrs Nangle at Irish Corner who was not averse to a bit of humorous advertising — Mrs Nangle, Mangling Done Here; and old Hinny Ony whose nickname apparently developed from acute difficulties with supply — 'Sorry, A hinny ony'.

The weekend brought welcome relief from the week's work. On a Saturday night the Gorgie Band marched all the way out to Corstorphine where they stopped outside the Inn in the low village to wet their whistles and to play to the assembled audience. Their itinerary also included the Harp Hotel and the Oak Inn before leaving the 'high' village to the strains of one of their favourite marches, *The Rowan Tree*. A band which visited less frequently was Millar and Richards, who played at some of the annual events. Their favourite stance was Irish Corner, where the bandsmen 'danced with the prim, stiff and non-smiling village belles while the rest of the villagers stood around and criticised'. The home band was the Corstorphine Pipe Band, dressed in kilts and plaids of the Hunting Stewart tartan, green tunics, red and black hose, and Glengarry bonnets. No band ever marched with greater pride through the old village streets. One of their favourite tunes was *The Green Hills of Tyrol* arranged for the bagpipes by Pipe Major William Ross late of the 42nd Highlanders (Black Watch) at the time of the Crimean War, the melody being taken from a section of the William Tell overture.

Romance was neither dead, nor wasted on the young. With a twinkle in his eye, and relying heavily on his enviable financial position, an old retired potato merchant proposed to a widow as he sat by her fireside discussing church affairs. To any nation, save the Scots, his proposal would be judged perfunctory: 'What's the guid o' two roofs coverin' us baith when yin wad dae?'

Early village life in Corstorphine was characterised by the independent nature of the people who formed numerous societies and clubs for the development of welfare, leisure and recreation.

As early as 1789 the Corstorphine Friendly Society was established: 'Taking under our serious consideration the many evils and calamities to which mankind are liable through the course of this life, we do purpose, under the blessing of God, to establish a Fund in order to the relief of ourselves and Brethren in time of necessity under the following regulations'. To begin with, contributions were 2/6d (12½p) for the enrolment fee and 1/- (5p) quarterly thereafter, in return for benefits of 3/- (15p) per week for sickness or distress, and £1 towards funeral charges in event of the death of a member or a member's wife. Colours were purchased for the Society in 1808 and 1827, the Old Banner depicting the five elms of the Cross of Corstorphine. Each year on the first Wednesday in June the Society held its Annual Dinner, after which there was the rouping of the Colours. The highest bidder was given the honour of leading the procession of members round the village houses where they obtained further donations for the Society. Although the Society ceased to function in 1927, many of its books and records are still extant in the original oak box, now with the Corstorphine Trust.

In 1980 Corstorphine celebrated the centenary of its Literary

Corstorphine Church in its modern setting, 1960.
Courtesy of W.G. Dey.

Association, which met for the first time in the back room of a tailor's shop in the High Street near the school. After a fairly informal first session, proper Rules and By-Laws were formulated for 1881–82, one of which declared 'That the Association be open to Gentlemen only'. Although the reference to *Gentlemen* clearly deprived ladies of the opportunity to join, it may also have implied, perhaps unintentionally, that not *all* persons of the male gender were necessarily eligible. The Rule was in fact relaxed from time to time to admit female visitors, presumably for such debates as 'Should the Franchise be extended to Women?' When the Public Hall Company was incorporated, the Association organised a very successful bazaar

Looking east on St. John's Road, Corstorphine, 1985, with the steeple of St. Ninian's Church in the centre.
Photograph by Graham C. Cant.

which provided sufficient funds for them to purchase a substantial number of shares in the new Company, and to secure accommodation in the Hall for their weekly meetings. From modest beginnings the Association increased its membership to 318 in 1895 and then to a peak of 573 in 1921. At the fiftieth anniversary in 1930 a booklet was published giving the history of the Association, and following expansion of its activities in the 1950s it altered its name in 1957 to the Corstorphine Literary and Geographical Society. The centenary dinner was held on 15th December 1980, the guest speaker being the Hon. Lord Birsay of Harray, and weekly meetings still take place each Monday in Corstorphine Public Hall.

In 1890 James Pringle Taylor laid out a bowling green in the grounds of his house, Dunsmuir, at the west end of the High Street. To foster interest in the game generally he allowed the village people to have the use of the green on two evenings each week, as a result of which a club was formed on 27th July 1891. Early committee meetings took place at the Public Hall, and it was soon agreed that a piece of ground to the south of the Hall would be most suitable for a club bowling green. In 1895 Corstorphine Bowling Club secured the ground on a ninety-nine year lease and a green was constructed at a cost of £385. Unfortunately, due to a dispute with the contractor the green was not opened until 22nd August 1898. When the finances of the Club improved, a pavilion was built and opened on 3rd July 1907 by Sir Robert Cranston, former Lord Provost of Edinburgh. In the early days of the Club its moment of glory was undoubtedly in 1923 when W.H. Scouller won for the second year running the Scottish Singlehanded Championship. On the evening of his triumphant return, the Corstorphine villagers turned out in their hundreds to receive him. The Gorgie Band came out to lead the procession, while the bowling champion stood in an open cab, with the cup held aloft, high above the heads of the men and boys who volunteered to replace the horse for this special journey. The procession started at Station Road, went along St. John's Road, down Manse Road and returned by the old village High Street to the Bowling Green at the east end.

In addition to the bowling club there was great interest in quoiting and curling. The Quoiting Club had two pitches, one at Janefield on the opposite side of the road from Dunsmuir, and the other on ground now occupied by St. Ninian's Drive. The Corstorphine Curling Club was founded on 25th December 1829 and had two artificial rinks, one at Clermiston and one belonging to the Waverley Curling Club to the south of what was Pinkhill Station. David B. Smith's *Curling: an Illustrated History* contains photographs of two medals belonging to the club: one is a gold medal of the Corstorphine Curling Club dating from 1830 which was recovered in 1905 after a lapse of seventy-five years; the other is a silver medal in the shape of a shield dated 1850 and showing three figures on the ice.

Today the people of Corstorphine have lost none of their enthusiasm for local involvement in a wide variety of clubs and associations. The Corstorphine District Association formed in 1946 to protect the amenity of the district was incorporated in the Corstorphine Trust in 1970. The Trust Common Room at 199a St. John's Road is open to all interested in the history and character of Corstorphine. The Trust Newsletter includes a most impressive list of Office Bearers, Committee Members and Members of Council whose duties include not only the administration of the Trust itself, but also more than thirty affiliated organisations. Present and future generations, anxious to maintain the history and dignity of Corstorphine, need have no fear in putting their trust in the able hands of the Corstorphine Trust.

CHAPTER 2

Cramond

The picture postcard image of Cramond is in stark contrast to its ancient history. In the second century A.D. it was a Roman defence post; in the eighteenth century it created its own industrial revolution in the Almond valley; and in the early nineteenth century much of the oldest part of the village was demolished to enable Lady Torphichen to extend the policies of Cramond House.

Cramond, with its old Kirk dating from at least the seventeenth century, was at one time the biggest centre of population in the parish, which stretched from Granton to Turnhouse. The decline and eventual fall of the mills in the mid-nineteenth century, and the departure of the minister, kirk session and many of the congregation to Davidson's Mains at the Disruption in 1843, all contributed to a gradual decline in its relative importance. Cramond Kirk continued after the Disruption, but it no longer had an ecclesiastical monopoly, and matters such as the relief of the poor and education passed into secular hands. This gradual decline became progressively more obvious in the transport era of the early twentieth century on account of Cramond's geographical position.

Today Cramond lies peacefully at the northern edge of its suburban hinterland, conscious of its unique heritage, and poised to bring more of it to the attention of its many visitors.

The Romans at Cramond

The Romans came to Cramond about 142 A.D. by order of Emperor Antoninus Pius to establish a fort on the eastern flank of a frontier line across Scotland from the Forth to the Clyde. Cramond was ideally suited to their requirements. Local stone, cut from the valley of the Almond, was plentiful for building; the surrounding land was fertile and capable of further cultivation; and the mouth of the Almond provided sheltered mooring for their boats. A Roman garrison of almost five hundred men set about the task of building a harbour for communication, and an extensive fort covering almost six acres of ground.

Although the presence of the Romans at Cramond had been known about for many years, it was not until 1954 that the fort was discovered. Several years of patient excavation since then have pieced together a substantial part of early history, not hitherto recorded. The various finds have been deposited with Huntly House Museum in the Canongate, and part of the fort has been permanently excavated to the north of Cramond Church. Sadly, however, lack of financial backing has prevented the whole site being opened up permanently, and protected from the elements in such a way as to allow access by the public.

Recent archaeological research has established a fairly accurate description of the Roman buildings. The fort was rectangular in shape with its long walls or ramparts running north to south. These walls were built of clay or turf twenty-seven feet thick with a stone facing and probably fifteen feet high. Gates, flanked by towers, were set in each of the four sides, allowing constant surveillance in every direction. Internally a road running between the east and west gates divided the rectangle into a small section to the north, and a larger section to the south. Located to the north of the road were the workshops, the kiln and a latrine: to the south of the road lay the garrison headquarters in the centre, flanked by granaries and the commander's house.

Later excavations revealed substantial evidence of other buildings outside the protection of the fort. Work carried out in the back garden of the Manse (immediately south of Cramond Church) has revealed two defensive ditches running parallel to the east wall of the fort. The westernmost ditch continues north beyond the north-east corner of the fort, to form the east boundary of a military annexe lying between the fort and the sea. Within the annexe is one of the most important archaeological discoveries, the garrison bath-house situated about one hundred yards north of the north wall of the fort. The other important discovery, to the east, is the 'industrial estate' where open-ended sheds provided adequate working facilities for carpenters, ironworkers, tanners and shoemakers. Beyond the industrial area, a native settlement developed along the line of the road leading from the east gate.

The Romans' occupation of Cramond appears to have been rather sporadic. They came first in 142 A.D. in the time of Emperor Antoninus Pius, but the troops were withdrawn about fifteen years later, presumably to protect defences farther south. They returned a few years later when the Cramond defences were repaired. Their visit was again shortlived, however, in the face of a decision by Rome to pull back to the line of Hadrian's Wall between the Tyne and the Solway. Sometime between 208 A.D. and 211 A.D. the army of Emperor Septimius Severus is also recorded at Cramond repairing the fort and improving the roads and drainage, but there is no evidence that Severus was there in person.

Cramond Parish Church

Cramond Parish Church, in Cramond Glebe Road, stands on the site of previous ecclesiastical buildings dating almost from time immemorial. It is probable that the old Roman settlement was used by Christian communities in the sixth century before a more permanent building was erected. Very little is known about the early Christian community except that it came within the jurisdiction of the Bishop of Dunkeld, ecclesiastical superior of the parish, and feudal superior of Nether Cramond. It is known that a medieval church existed on the site but had become ruinous by 1656. The problem facing the Kirk Session was ably recorded in the Minutes:

> ....taking to consideratioun the ruinousnes of the kirk and that the tyme of yeir meit for the building of the same draweth nigh think fitt that the whole heritouris of the paroche be desyred to convene in the kirk the tenth of marche instand (1656) to consult about the building of the samyne.

This resolution appears to have been acted upon almost immediately. A new church was built in 1656 incorporating the fifteenth-century tower at the west end, and the Cramond vault at the east end, later set aside as the burial place of the Inglis of Cramond.

Several additions and alterations have been made to the church since 1656. In 1701 the north aisle was enlarged to the west, and the south aisle was enlarged to the south, to form the Barnton vault, which contains the body of John, Earl of Selkirk and Ruglen, one-time Master of the Mint in Scotland who died in 1744. A little more than a century after the 1701 additions, the stone masons were busy again, in 1811, under the direction of Robert Burn. They added the distinctive castellated parapet round the fifteenth-century tower, and created more space in the interior. A vestry was added to the east of the north aisle, and the south aisle was extended again, to the west.

Cramond Parish Church, showing the fifteenth-century tower. The distinctive castellated parapet was added in the early nineteenth century. From a drawing by Graham Forbes.

Less significant nineteenth-century alterations were made by William Burn in 1828, Robert Bell in 1843 and David Bryce in 1851 and 1868. It was not until 1911, however, that the church began to take on its present-day appearance. The north aisle was completely rebuilt and an organ chamber was constructed east of the south aisle. Internally almost all the fabric dates from 1911 with uniform galleries round each of four sides. The chief monument is on the east wall, a marble bust of Lord James Hope who died in 1661.

The final addition was the session house, constructed in 1955 at the north-east corner of the church.

Various contributions to *Cramond*, by the Cramond Association, provide an interesting insight into the social history of the parish as seen through the Minutes of the Kirk Session meetings. Parish accounts from 1639 have survived as well as Kirk Session minutes from 1651. The Sabbath was observed by everyone, with a substantial part of the day taken up by the main church service which lasted anything up to three or four hours. The local gentry and their families sat in comparative comfort in one of the small galleries or boxes around the walls of the church, whilst the ordinary folk sat either on the floor or on whatever small stool or seat they brought with them. The prospect of three hours' continuous worship tended to create an atmosphere of general informality, although there were limits which had to be enforced, as the occasion arose:

> The Session considering that divine service is disturbed by ye fighting of doges in ye Church on the Sabbath dayes therefore they appoint ye Beddell to beat yaim out of ye Church, and also to speake to the people, that they keep them at home behind yaim on the Sabbath days (3rd December 1691).

The sermon began with an hour-long reading from the scriptures by the precentor who was usually also the local schoolmaster and session clerk. When he had completed his chosen text, the minister continued the service with two hours of preaching, broken by occasional prayers. A significant part of the proceedings dealt with penitents who were required to sit on the cutty stool, set on a raised platform, to be publicly rebuked for their misdemeanours.

Presbyterian discipline was not confined within the four walls of the Kirk. Public decency and morality were kept under strict observation by the members of the Kirk Session who made regular visits in the neighbourhood to ensure that everything was in order. Noncompliance attracted the attention of the full Kirk Session who retained the power to pass miscreants to the civil courts for sentence. The commonest offences were adultery, drunkenness, breach of the peace, failure to attend church, and failure to produce a testimonial, this last offence arising from the inability to produce evidence of good standing in the parish. Absence of it precluded anyone from moving to another part of the country to escape the effect of previous punishment.

Although no case of witchcraft was ever recorded, slanderous allegations were frequently made in the heat of the moment, which were dealt with fairly strictly even in Episcopal days, as the following case illustrates:

> Margrat Corstoune, in Nether Cramond, gave in a bill of slander against Isbell Wallace in Nether Cramond quhairin was conteind that the said Isbell Wallace had said that the said Margrat was a witch or that shee had the carriage of a witch, and a runnagate, and blackned bitch. The said Isbell gave in a bill against Margrat Corstoune quhairin was conteind that the said Margrat had cald hir a drunken harlot and lowne. James Walker being admitted a witness proves nothing onlye he

deponed that he heard yaim in yair flyting speaking of witchcraft, but heard not Isbell Wallace call Margrat Corstoune a witch. The Session finding by yair awne confessions that they had unchristianlye slandered on another apoints yaim to be reconciled betwixt and this day eight days (5th August 1660).

The Kirk Session also had responsibility for maintaining church buildings in liaison with the heritors who were frequently opposed to the idea of making financial contributions until repairs were long overdue. Education and the provision of benefits for the poor and needy of the parish all made impossible demands on the meagre resources available to the church.

With such a long history it is not surprising that Cramond should also have attracted several ministers whose involvement with matters of national importance frequently vied with their parochial duties.

During part of the reign of James VI (1567–1625) Rev. Michael Cranstoun was minister of Cramond. The *Biographical History of the Scottish Nation* contains an interesting account of his opposition to state interference in church affairs. With other ministers, he was ordered to be apprehended for the treasonable and seditious uproar in Edinburgh on 17th December 1596, his involvement in the affair being that he read the history of Haman and Mordecai to the people assembled in St. Giles.

Cranstoun was succeeded by William Colvill, who had the honour of being elected Principal of the University of Edinburgh on two separate occasions. On the first occasion, in 1652, his appointment was revoked, apparently for political reasons, but he was elected again in 1662 in succession to Dr Leighton. He seems to have harboured episcopalian leanings at a time when it was dangerous to do so, which resulted in his being suspended by the General Assembly for proposing dialogue between the presbyterians and the episcopalians. The suspension was revoked in 1655.

In addition to Colvill, two other ministers at Cramond were also Principals of Edinburgh University. Perhaps the most famous was William Hamilton, born in 1675, minister of Cramond from 1694 until 1709 when he was appointed Professor of Divinity at Edinburgh. Several times Moderator of the General Assembly, he was, in the words of John Ramsay of Ochtertyre, 'supposed to be the chief leader of the General Assembly where his wisdom and moderation procured for him the esteem of contending parties'.

The third minister to be Principal of the University was James Smith, whose career showed a remarkable similarity with that of his predecessor William Hamilton. He held the Chair of Divinity at Edinburgh and came to Cramond at a time when there was considerable disagreement in the parish as to Hamilton's successor.

Cramond Churchyard

Cramond Church is surrounded by a most interesting churchyard with a variety of stones of different age and style, many depicting the symbols of death — skulls, bones and hourglasses, and others the symbols of immortality — the winged soul and the angel. Some of these stones are almost three hundred years old.

Set against the south wall of the church a large plain slab dated 1687 marks the burial place of George Sheiell, Fearmour in Grothill. A few yards to the east, a lengthy inscription marks the tomb of Lord James Hope of Hopetoun who died in 1670, and on the corresponding part of the south wall, at its east end, two huge stones to the Howison Craufurd family reflect the contrasting styles of different ages. The stone on the left is by far the older of the two, badly worn, but still showing a wealth of detail arranged around twin Corinthian columns. The other stone is of equal size, but less ornate, to Mrs. Elizabeth Howison Craufurd of Brachead, 1823.

On the north boundary wall of the churchyard an otherwise plain tablet has an unusual white oval inset for Sir John Gordon Bart. of Earlstone in Galloway, 1795. Further along the same wall a stone in polished granite with perpendicular 'church window' tracery provides a fitting tribute to: Rev. Walter Laidlaw Colvin D.D; thirty four years the minister at Cramond; born at Johnstone Manse 1812; died at Cramond Manse 1877; Until the Day Break.

The east boundary wall also tells its own story, though sometimes in rather faltering style: a very small stone, shunning even the most elementary rules of symmetrical presentation, commemorates ELEZABATH 1791. The same could not be said of the regular pedimented marble monument of the same period to William Davidson of Muirhouse, 1794. Its more elaborate presentation and lengthy inscriptions are, however, losing the battle for permanence, with the right-hand pilaster beginning to break away. Also on the east wall, the oldest stone in the churchyard is to John Stalker who died on

In a quiet corner of Cramond kirkyard, a wealth of detail arranged around the twin Corinthian columns of the Howison Craufurd tombstone.
Photograph by Graham C. Cant.

6th February 1608. It is a massive piece of masonry capped with three miniature obelisks, the central one of which bears a grinning skull, beneath which is the reason — MORS. The east wall also contains the graves of two of Cramond's early ministers: Rev. Archibald Bonor who died in 1816 after being minister at Cramond for thirty-one years; and Rev. George Muirhead D.D., minister at Dysart and Cramond, who died in 1847. The monument to Dr Muirhead recalls his heroic departure with the Kirk Session and part of the congregation in 1843 'being fully persuaded in his own mind he was steadfastly to the principles of the Disruption'. The stone to Cramond's Disruption minister provides an interesting contrast with the more ornate tracery on the north wall for Rev. Walter Laidlaw Colvin, who was the first minister at Cramond after the Disruption.

The south wall contains two interesting monuments, appropriately made of iron, commemorating members of the Cadell family who owned the iron mills in the Almond valley during the eighteenth and nineteenth centuries. One is to William Cadell who died in 1844 at the age of twenty-four. The other recalls the passing, in 1851, of Anne Wilson who, as a young woman, married one of the iron masters, Alexander Cadell. Also on the south wall a long low memorial in polished blue grey stone records the names of those whose ashes have been committed to Cramond Kirkyard.

The most prominent memorial in the central area is the iron obelisk for the Reoch family, the north face of which is to Andrew Reoch, 1854, engineer in Demerara, and the south face for Andrew Reoch, 1811, blacksmith at Blackhall. By contrast a comparatively modest stone marks the graves of William Robert Reid of Lauriston Castle, his wife Margaret Johnstone Barton and her brother William Davidson Barton. Nearby there is a fitting tribute to Cramond Willie:

> Erected by the Parish of Cramond and other friends in memory of Cramond Willie William Henderson who was for many years a faithful messenger between Cramond village and Edinburgh – in character and conduct he was an honest upright man.
> Born 4th March 1821
> Died 24th November 1878

Opposite the west wall a small three-foot stone ornately carved with a winged hourglass reminds everyone of the day, in 1707, when SPOTSWOOD, FERMER IN LENIE returned to the soil!

Cramond Old Schoolhouse

There was a time in Cramond, as with other parts of the country, when the church was closely involved in the provision of education in the parish. Before the days of local Education Authorities or even School Boards, the upkeep of school buildings and the appointment and remuneration of the schoolmaster came within the jurisdiction of the heritors. It was their duty, among other things, to consult with the minister to determine what expenses should be incurred, and how the necessary finance was to be raised. As the heritors were, themselves, the principal benefactors, there was a natural reluctance to agree anything more than was absolutely necessary.

On 16th November 1764 Ninian Paton was summoned before a meeting of the heritors at the manse, in connection with his application for the vacancy of schoolmaster. He had already met with Rev. Gilbert Hamilton who was able to inform the meeting 'that he had taken Tryall of the said Mr Paton as to his skill in the Latin language and in Arithmetick and was satisfied'. In addition to the academic qualifications, Ninian was required to submit a specimen of his handwriting, and a testimonial of his moral conduct from the minister at the West Kirk. He appears to have satisfied the heritors on all counts and was duly appointed.

His duties were quite onerous because the schoolmaster also acted as the session clerk and the precentor. This meant that at each church service he was required to read the lesson, and to lead the congregation in praise, whatever their vocal range and without the advantage of 'a sinfu' kist o' whistles'. Church organs were not introduced until at least a century later, and even then, amid great controversy. The schoolmaster also had to find time to record the minutes for the meetings of the heritors and the Kirk Session, as well as to collect money due from the heritors for authorised expenditure. Expenditure which was not authorised attracted cautionary words, as Ninian discovered at a fairly early stage in his career. Having been left a small sum of money by his predecessor for repairs to the church, he used 13/9d. to repair his garden wall, 6d. for a new key for the precentor's desk and 6/9d. for an exchange of the school bell. After considering the matter very seriously the heritors 'allowed the above articles to pass as they stood only it should not be deemed a precedent in the Time coming for the schoolmaster to give out any of their money without he is properly authorised to do'. Ninian's main task, of course, was to teach seventy or eighty children the three Rs, Latin and the singing of psalms, in a one-roomed building in the churchyard. In return for these onerous duties, which must have taken up many hours in the week, the schoolmaster could expect his various fees to total about £35 per annum plus the use of the school house.

In 1778 Raeburn's 'Skating Minister', Robert Walker, and the second Sir John Inglis had a series of meetings with the heritors to resolve the long outstanding matter of the school buildings which were 'so ruinous that it was more in the interest of the Heritours to rebuild them than to bestow money on the repair of them'. The heritors left the matter in the hands of the minister and Sir John Inglis, as a result of which a plan emerged to build a new school west of the churchyard. The opportunity was also taken to realign the public road so that it ran on the west side of the churchyard through the Glebe instead of between the churchyard and Sir John's residence at Cramond House. The effect of this plan was to provide excellent new facilities for the school, but no mention was made of the considerable improvement in amenity which the plan brought to Sir John's estate.

The school was built for the sum of £148:16:6 by James Robb the builder and provided a ground-floor schoolroom measuring twenty feet square. Also on the ground floor was a private room for the schoolmaster reached by a separate entrance, which also led to the upper floor containing four additional rooms. By any standards this was the height of luxury for a country schoolmaster in 1778, which may have had some bearing on the fact that Ninian Paton lived to be eighty years of age and died in 1816 after being schoolmaster for fifty-two years.

For some years now the old schoolhouse has been used as a private dwelling, later schools being built at the top of School Brae in 1875 and then in Cramond Crescent in 1976.

Cramond Tower

Cramond Tower, a tall medieval defensive tower of uncertain date, lies a few hundred yards north of Cramond Churchyard. One theory is that the Tower was part of the Palace of the Bishop of Dunkeld who held the lands of Cramond from King David I in the twelfth century. Documentary evidence supports the contention that Robert de Cardney, Bishop of Dunkeld, exchanged his lands of Cammo in 1409 for Cramond Tower, then owned by John de Nudre. In 1574 James Paton sold the Tower to Archibald Douglas of Kilspindie, who later sold to Alexander Douglas. It was Alexander Douglas who eventually sold the property to the first of the Inglis family in 1622.

Cramond Tower, a tall medieval defensive tower of uncertain date, now renovated as a private residence.
Photograph by S. Jamieson.

Whether the tower was ever the Palace of the Bishop of Dunkeld, as suggested by John Philp Wood, is a matter of conjecture. There is certainly evidence of some building structure adjacent to it, both on the east side and on the west side. According to Wood's account in 1794, the building to the east was the Bishop's Palace, and that to the west was the Chapel. An archaeological excavation carried out to the west of the Tower in 1977 failed to prove Wood's contention. It did however reveal the existence of another building, although not directly abutting onto the Tower itself. Later excavations on the east side revealed mortared wall foundations suggesting a late rectangular addition to the Tower. Although the mystery remains unsolved, perhaps the most tantalising evidence is the easily observed raggled stonework high up on the east and west walls. During the excavations several finds were made which, although interesting in themselves, did not assist in proving the existence of any other building. Among the finds were the remains of a seventeenth-century wine bottle marked 'Cramond' and a coin of the reign of Charles II (1660–1685).

Cramond Tower seems to have flourished under a long line of influential owners up to 1680 when the Inglis family moved to Cramond House, but it fared less well in the years that followed. A watercolour by James Skene in 1837 shows the Tower in ruins, and MacGibbon and Ross, in *The Castellated and Domestic Architecture of Scotland* (1889), say: 'it [the Tower] is in an unfortunate condition being entirely crowned with ivy which has got such a hold of it (the branches in some places going through the walls) as to greatly imperil its safety'. The Tower lay in that state until the 1960s, when Edinburgh Corporation began restoration work which they quickly abandoned shortly thereafter on discovering that they were not actually the owners. In 1978 Cramond Tower was acquired by George Jamieson the wildlife artist and taxidermist who set about a comprehensive programme of restoration with advice from Robert Hurd and Partners and the Historic Buildings Council. The result is a most interesting four-storey tower of rough stone finish with a projecting stairtower on the south-east corner, all capped with a slated roof but without the encumbrances of rhones and downpipes.

Internally each of the four floors has been extensively renovated. The ground floor, previously below ground level and reached by a short flight of stone steps, has been given a wooden floor and is used by Mr George Jamieson as a gallery for his paintings and taxidermy displays. On the floor above, the main hall has a restored arched fireplace with a canopy and chimney breast, and Georgian windows have been fitted in each wall except the north. The main features of the second floor are the window embrasure with stone seats, and the garderobe built into the thickness of the east wall. The top floor provides bedroom and bathroom accommodation.

Seen through the mature trees which now surround it on all sides, Cramond Tower presents an interesting example of a medieval stronghold sympathetically restored to twentieth-century living.

Cramond House

Cramond House, lying between Cramond Churchyard and
Cramond Tower, dates from about 1680. The history of its
development is most easily understood by studying its H-plan
formation, the parallel lines of which run north and south, and the
central part east and west. The central block is substantially the house
built by John Inglis of Cramond in 1680 shortly before his death. It is
three storeys in height, built of harled rubble, with exposed window
dressings. How and when the basic house developed first to T-
formation, and then H-formation, is a matter on which there are
different opinions. John Small, in *Castles and Mansions of the
Lothians* (1883), states that additions were made in 1772 by Sir Adam
Inglis and his brother Sir John Inglis, and that Sir John's daughter,
Lady Torphichen, added a new front elevation to the house. This
information is followed in part by the *Thirteenth Report* of the *Royal
Commission on the Ancient Monuments of Scotland* (1951), which
says that John and Adam Inglis refashioned the interior of the old
house in 1771 and that Sir Adam is credited with the west wing in
1772. The Report goes on to say that about twenty years after 1772 a
parallel wing was built to the east. On the other hand *The Buildings
of Scotland-Edinburgh* (1984) states that the east wing was built first,
about 1760, and the west wing was added in 1818 by Charles Black,
the builder.

Although there is doubt as to the order in which the house was
built, there is no doubt about the ordered appearance of its imposing
east facade, reached by a spreading flight of steps with square
balusters. The entire east wing is of two storeys only, of polished
ashlar, the main storey, over the basement, being identified by very
tall astragalled windows with semi-circular heads. The central part of
the frontage projects slightly and carries a pediment with the Inglis
crest carved in stone. From the raised position of the front entrance
there is a magnificent view down through a broad avenue of trees
taking as the focal point, in the distance, the summit of Berwick Law
in East Lothian.

It is believed that the square balusters of the steps and the screen
wall and belfry on the north side were added about 1850 by William
Burn.

Internally the most imposing features are in the east wing. The
spacious entrance hall has very high coved ceilings and leads to the

stone staircase, lit by a cupola. Two corresponding rooms lead off the entrance hall, namely the drawing room to the south, and the dining room to the north. The staircase leads to the old house beyond, an unusual feature of which is the long passage running east to west, to communicate with the west wing. Although a central passage is unusual in seventeenth-century houses, it may well be an original feature, possibly built in anticipation of the house being extended at a later date.

When the Inglis baronetcy came to an end in 1817 for want of a male heir, the estate passed to Lady Torphichen, daughter of Sir John Inglis. The involvement of the families Craigie and Halkett through marriage made the Craigie-Halketts the new lairds of Cramond, until some time after the First World War when the House was in the hands of the last of the line, Miss Craigie-Halkett, who lived latterly in very reduced circumstances.

In its heyday Cramond House was visited by royalty, notably in the summer of 1860 when the Duchess of Kent, mother of Queen Victoria, resided there for a few weeks. Queen Victoria, en route for Balmoral, visited the Duchess at Cramond House and made an unexpected return visit in September of the same year when she attended Cramond Kirk along with the Prince Consort. The report in *The Scotsman* for 17th September 1860 is as follows:

> After Divine service, Her Majesty and the royal party walked for some time in the grounds of Cramond House and along the margin of the firth....
> The Royal visitors lunched with the Duchess of Kent about two o'clock and shortly before four o'clock the carriages were brought up to the entrance and the royal party got in protecting themselves from the rain by umbrellas.

After the demise of the Craigie-Halkett family, Cramond House was acquired by Cramond Parish Church. It is now used as the beadle's residence, and as a meeting place for a variety of organisations connected with the church. Although access is by a driveway from Cramond Glebe Road, the original entrance is much farther to the south at the sharp dogleg bend in Cramond Road North. The massive pedimented archway supports one chimneybreast to serve each of the two single-roomed lodges on either side of the main carriageway.

Early reports of Cramond House and Cramond Tower make reference to an interesting sundial which stood in the driveway to the

House. It was approximately six feet in height and stood on a square baluster. It had a peculiarly faceted double head, the lower part of which had four circular upright dials with grotesque faces between the sloping dials. The name Sir Robert Dickson and the date 1732 could be read on one of the round dials, Sir Robert being a descendant of David Dickson, Professor of Divinity in Edinburgh University. On the other side of the dial the inscription read ARCH. HANDASYDE FECIT, which may suggest an earlier connection with Inveresk, as Sir Robert Dickson was laird of Inveresk until his death in 1760, and Handasyde is known to have been a mason in Musselburgh.

MacGibbon and Ross relate that around 1880 the sundial was found lying in a bad state of repair in an outhouse at Cramond and that an old gardener recalled that it had once stood in the grounds of Lauriston Castle nearby. The sundial was repaired and displayed at the International Exhibition of Industry, Science and Art in the Meadows in 1886, after which it was brought to Cramond and set up in front of Cramond House.

Industries on the River Almond

In the seventeenth century Cramond was ideally suited as a centre for agricultural produce. Good arable land was plentiful; the Almond valley produced adequate water to power the mill machinery; and the harbour gave clear lines of communication for the removal of bulky products. Around 1700, five separate mills were operating between Old Cramond Brig and the sea. The highest of these was Dowie's Mill on the east bank, then Peggie's Mill, also on the east bank, followed by Craigie's Mill on the west bank, all three being used as grain mills. Further downstream, on the east bank, Fairafar operated also as a waulkmill for weavers. Nearest to the sea, Cockle Mill, which took its name from the cockle weed which grows with corn crops, was first recorded in 1178 as a possession of the abbot of Inchcolm.

This apparent natural harmony between man and his environment had the tacit approval of the riparian gentry, namely Sir John Inglis of Cramond on the east side and Lord Rosebery on the west side. But progress was not long in coming to Cramond. Intended future development was revealed in a feu charter dated 23rd July 1752, drawn up between Sir John Inglis and the Smith and Wright Work

The ruins of Fairafar Mill on the banks of the River Almond, with the weir, on the right, almost intact.
Courtesy of Edinburgh City Libraries.

Company of Leith, which referred to 'the nethermost mill next to the sea upon the Water of Cramond, commonly called the Cockle Mill, and which was formerly used as a Corn Mill, but is now converted into an Iron slitting mill by the said Company'. Smith and Wright of Leith were founded in 1747, and although they took a lease of Cockle Mill and Fairafar Mill in 1752, they confined their operations to the former which was used for the manufacture of rod iron for nails, and for making spades, hoes, chains and anchors. In 1759 the business was bought by the Carron Company of Falkirk for £1,010. Although Cramond retained considerable expertise in the combined business, it was not long before its influence began to wane in the face of rising capacity from the new blast furnaces and forges at Carron. By 1770 Carron had sold out their interest in Cramond, to concentrate their production at the main works.

However, Cramond retained considerable potential which was recognised by William Cadell Jnr., when he bought the company in 1770, in exchange for his own share of the Carron Company in which he had been a director. Some idea of his business acumen can be obtained from his correspondence, in which he instructs Thomas Edington, the mill manager, 'never to keep any person an hour

41

longer than he's really useful', and, with an eye to increased production, 'when water is plentiful you might hire one or two more hands and go double shift'. It was against this background that Cadell and his partners planned considerable expansion of the iron industry in the Almond valley. Peggie's Mill was bought in 1781 and Dowie's Mill in 1782. Dowie's Mill was used by the spademakers and included a sawmill where the handles were made, and Peggie's Mill was later used for making hoops. The business probably reached its heyday around this time. The accounts show that three hundred tons of rod iron were made annually in 1778 at a time when the nail trade had reached the peak of refinement, advertising clasps, pounds, sharps, spriggs and brads, all for sale by weight per thousand. Rod iron in various sizes was sold to Edinburgh, Glasgow and London, 'best liked when the rods are long drawn, tough iron and carefully tyed'. Eighteen tons of hoops were produced every week for the use of coopers, with a significant part of the trade going for export to the winegrowing areas of Spain, Portugal and Madeira, as well as to the West Indies for rum and sugar barrels.

Cramond never smelted its own iron. It was imported from Russia, Sweden, Holland and other parts of Britain as bar iron, i.e. after the first stage of refinement. Consignments usually came in through Leith, as Cramond was not allowed to handle foreign imports without the services of a customs officer. The same difficulty did not apply to coal, which was also required in large quantities. The ratio of the weight of coal burned to the weight of finished products was obviously of paramount importance, yet this was an aspect of the business which was constantly in trouble. From March 1766 to March 1767 the company hoped to use about 250 tons of coal to produce 500 tons of finished products, but in practice the ratio appears to have come much nearer ton for ton at certain times. The higher ratio was caused in part by the need for frequent reheating and led to a further instruction to the manager that the furnaces should be filled up over the weekend with coal culm and ashes to prevent them cooling down completely. The problem was compounded by an insufficient fall of water on the Almond. Inadequate power meant that the iron took longer to go through the rollers and cutters so that the bars cooled down too quickly.

Despite these difficulties the Cadells prospered until about 1797, but by 1810 Cramond was no longer an important iron works. It had failed to keep pace with larger firms mainly on account of its restricted position in the valley, and the inadequate water supply. The Cadells tried to diversify by introducing paper-making at Peggie's Mill, but the water was found to be suitable only for the coarser qualities of paper. The first mention of the introduction of steam power was in 1852, but even this was insufficient to prevent the demise of the Cadells which came in 1860, through a combination of bad management and the inability to remain competitive.

After the Cadells left Cramond, the mills were put to a variety of uses. John Mackay used Peggie's Mill for his business as a manufacturing chemist, and Dowie's Mill was used as a sawmill. Later, furniture was made at Dowie's Mill and Peggie's Mill but no significant industrial revival ever took place. The mills became ruinous, the lades dried up, and a quiet riverside walk has replaced Cramond's contribution to the industrial revolution.

In and around Cramond

Much of Cramond's rich heritage remains, and is comparatively accessible to resident and visitor alike. A much deeper understanding of its historical background can be obtained by visiting the various places of interest.

Cramond is usually approached from Cramond Road North past the Dunfermline College of Physical Education designed by Robert Matthew, Johnson-Marshall & Partners in 1964 and extended in 1972. A few hundred yards north, Cramond Glebe Road leads down to the old village past the tearoom and market garden of George Laidlaw & Son. Traditional stone houses on the left contrast well with the modern dwellings of Cramond Glebe Gardens lying back from the main road on the right. Ahead, the four bulky stone pillars, set into the right of the pavement, lead to Cramond Manse, first built in 1745, and extended on numerous occasions since. On the left-hand side, a substantial white harled house announces on the timber gates its historical past — The Old Schoolhouse. To the north of Cramond Parish Church and its interesting graveyard, the entrance to Kirk Cramond is marked by old broken pillars and a small, lintelled iron gateway no longer in use. Kirk Cramond leads to open parkland where parts of the old Roman settlement have been excavated, beyond which is the private property of Cramond House and Cramond Tower.

Cramond Village, 1907 — a popular outing for all the family.
Courtesy of N.B. Traction Group Collection.

Lower down Cramond Glebe Road, the smart black and white paintwork of Cramond Inn, with the date 1670 above a window, matches exactly Cramond's remaining whitewashed cottages, arranged in layers down to the quayside. One of the more substantial buildings, the Old Maltings, is occupied as the Interpretation Centre for the Cramond Heritage Park where exhibitions are mounted in the summer months by the Cramond Heritage Trust, an offshoot of the local amenity association, the Cramond Association. Photographs, books and information sheets are on display, and guided tours of the district are arranged at 3.p.m. each Sunday from June to September starting at Cramond Kirk.

On the quayside 20p is the fare charged to ferry an adult across the short estuary of the Almond to Lord Rosebery's estate beyond. No bustling harbour remains, but pleasure boats abound – *Sequel, Amulet, Venture Forth* and many more, their moorings squeaking and rubbing, where the Almond meets the sea. Farther upstream Cramond Boat Club has large two-storey premises, beyond which is the boat park containing all manner of craft.

Beyond the boat park, the riverside walk enters the era of the grain mills and iron mills, long silent, but obstinately discernible, while on the opposite bank stone-lined cuttings are all that remain of the quarry wharves. The first settlement is Cockle Mill, renovated as a

Cramond Village, 1985. Vintage delivery vans from Charles Wilson, Scottish Brewers and MacGregors, delivering at the Cramond Inn. Courtesy of *The Scotsman*.

private house, at the foot of School Brae. Although the mill has not been operational for many years, remnants of the weir and lade remain. The dock, cut into the riverbank, measuring internally ninety-three feet long by twenty-one feet wide, gives some idea of the size of vessels berthing at Cockle Mill to deposit coal and to remove the completed products.

The next mill, on the same bank, is Fairafar, its arched masonry now completely ruinous, lying at the water's edge, beside a well-preserved weir about ten feet high. The square shell is all that remains of the west forge which contained two furnaces and a great tilt hammer. At one time the lade from the weir followed the line of the footpath and divided in two to power separate machinery.

Upstream from Fairafar the water runs deep and wide past a protruding cliff face which has been conveniently skirted by substantial timber steps carrying the path high above the river bank. This part of the walk was formed on ground from Inveralmond House gifted to Edinburgh Corporation by Captain H.K. Salvesen

The Twa Brigs. In the foreground Old Cramond Brig, believed to date from
about 1500, and in the background, barely discernible, one of the arches of
Rennie's new Cramond Bridge.
From Grant's *Old and New Edinburgh.*

who also contributed to the cost of the construction. At the highest
point there is a seat gifted by the Cramond Association to mark the
opening of that part of the walk on 14th May 1966.

Farther on again the last two mills lie close to one another. Peggie's
Mill, the last in operation, has very little remaining of its two large
buildings, but a few hundred yards on Dowie's Mill is marked by a
weir and lade, an interesting old house with a round-nosed gable and
a row of cottages with a wooden sign 'Dowie's Mill Cottages c.1690'.

Upstream from the lade a characteristically quiet section of water
curves round to the Twa Brigs. Fast-moving traffic on the new bridge
to Queensferry can be heard passing on the west side of Cramond
Brig Hotel but, on the east side, the Old Cramond Brig has long since
ceased to carry vehicular traffic. Its three heavy arches, protected by
massive cutwaters, carry the narrow road between low stone
parapets. Believed to date from about 1500, the bridge carries dates
on which it was 'repaired by both shires': 1687, 1761, 1776 and 1854.
On the outer side of the west parapet is another date, 1619, with the
tails of the 6 and the 9 elongated in a style described as 'absolutely

Postcards and bric-a-brac tempt visitors at Fairafar Cottages, 1909.

Cramond Village, 1905, looking west between the old cottages to the River Almond and Lord Rosebery's estate beyond.
Photograph by Phyllis Margaret Cant.

unique in Midlothian' by Dr. George A. Fothergill in *Stones and Curiosities of Edinburgh and Neighbourhood*. Old Cramond Brig's greatest claim to fame is, of course, its connection with Jock Howison. According to tradition, King James V was strolling, incognito, across Old Cramond Brig when he was suddenly set upon by a marauding gang. Without knowing the identity of the King, young Jock came to the rescue and took King James into his cottage where he dressed the wounds and sent him on his way. When the King got back to Holyrood he sent for Howison, to reveal his involvement in the fracas and to reward Jock with a grant of land in gratitude for his courageous act.

Turning east before crossing Old Cramond Brig leads one to Brae Park Road, part of the old road to Queensferry. About halfway along on the right-hand side a small plaque commemorates Pet Marjorie (1803–1811), with the following inscription:

> Marjory Fleming wandered here 'in rural felicity, festivity and pleasure' and praised it in her journal as 'a delightful place, Braehead by name, where there is ducks hens, bubblyjocks, two dogs, two cats, swine, and which is delightful'.

Marjory Fleming was born on 15th January 1803 the third child of James Fleming, an accountant in Kirkcaldy, and his wife Isabella. Marjory died before reaching her ninth birthday but left a fascinating collection of works, including three journals, some verses and a few letters, all written in the last three years of her life. *Pet Marjorie* was included with *Rab and his Friends* and other short stories in a volume of essays and sketches under the title *Leisure Hours* by Dr John Brown, physician and author.

At the top of Brae Park Road opposite its junction with Whitehouse Road, twin-arched gate piers, with curtain walls pierced by arrow slits, once led to Barnton House. Turning left into Whitehouse Road, both sides of the road are flanked by a variety of detached villas and bungalows, Whitehouse, Caeramon, Beverley and others. The only break is at Fairafar Cottages, now with front porches, hardwood doors, and high market values. The Infant Department of Cramond School is at the head of School Brae, and within welcoming sight there is a comfortable bench to the memory of Helen Rose Laidlaw of Almond Bank House, Cramond.

CHAPTER 3

Davidson's Mains

Davidson's Mains is not one of Edinburgh's oldest villages, but it does retain much of its original lay-out, and some of its earliest houses and cottages. The village, originally known as Muttonhole, undoubtedly owes its origin to the confluence of two important highways, namely the roads from Leith and from Edinburgh, to Queensferry and to Cramond. Subsequent development of the village, particularly after 1843, was in many respects greatly influenced by the relative decline of Cramond as the centre of population and activity in the parish. The other great influence of the late nineteenth century was, of course, the railway which crossed under Ferry Road and ran in a single track, north of Main Street, to Barnton Gate Station at Davidson's Mains. With the improvement of road transport in the early twentieth century, Davidson's Mains, in common with many other outlying communities, continued its gradual integration with the City of Edinburgh.

Muttonhole to Davidson's Mains

Davidson's Mains was known as Muttonhole until about 1850. The exact date of origin of the name Muttonhole is uncertain but it appears on Laurie's Map of 1763, and there are at least two references which confirm its existence before that date. Grant quotes an advertisement in the *Edinburgh Courant* for 5th October 1761:

> ... that there was this day lodged in the High Council House an old silver snuff box which was found upon the highway leading from *Muttonhole* to Cramond Bridge in the month of July last ...

About a century earlier the Records of the Old Tolbooth highlight the practical difficulties of maintaining law and order so far from the authority of the Justices. The date is 24th September 1669:

> These ar to command and requyre all constables within the shiradome of edr ore aney of them to tacke and apprehend William Ackfoord smyth in *Muttonholl* and being apprehendit to incarcerat him within ye tolbuth of edr and thair to remain till furder order be given to the justice of peace...

49

The derivation of the name Muttonhole is also shrouded in mystery, although there is no shortage of ingenious suggestions. The popular belief that Muttonhole is derived from *Mutton hole* — a hollow in which sheep were slaughtered — has the advantage of simplicity, but has very little proof. On the other hand, the more academic suggestions are equally tantalising in their absence of anything even approaching proof. Ian A. Fraser, a leading authority on Scottish place names, points out that variations of the name have existed in various parts of Scotland since at least 1601, and that the ending may be *hall* rather than *hole*, thus signifying *house* or *hill*. Another source postulates the theory that Muttonhole is derived from an Old English word meaning the confluence of two streams or two roads.

There is no doubt that Muttonhole developed around the junction of two important roads, west of Edinburgh. Laurie's Map shows the long straight approach of Ferry Road from Leith, passing the farms of East Pilton and West Pilton, to enter the village at the east end of what is now Main Street. The road from Edinburgh, through Dean Village and Blackhall, approached in a straight line from Blackhall, past House o' Hill farm, along the line of Corbiehill Road and into Main Street. Queensferry Road had not yet been realigned to skirt the village on its south side. The road to Queensferry past Barnton House left the west end of the village through what are now the stone pillars leading to the public park. In 1763 the village consisted of only a few houses at the west end of Main Street. On what is now Corbiehill Road a property known as Corbiehill stood close to the present school, and Marchfield was surrounded by extensive policies of its own. The larger estates were at Craigcrook Castle, Lauriston Castle, and Barnton House. To the north, the Muirhouse estate with its mansionhouse dating from 1670 was acquired by the Davidson family in 1776.

In 1823 Queensferry Road was realigned to the south of the village as part of a general road improvement scheme, incorporating the new Cramond Bridge. This realignment, which entailed cutting through the side of Corstorphine Hill and building the road high over the marsh near the Craigcrook marl pit, permitted the Barnton estate to be extended to the south. Had the main road continued to pass through the main street of Davidson's Mains it is likely that much of the old village would have been destroyed in subsequent road widening. This early bypass resulted in several properties, such as

Marchfield, being on the north side of the road to Queensferry instead of the south side as previously. It also provided the opportunity to develop Quality Street as one of the main approaches to the village. This challenge was convincingly met in 1827 by the architect James Gillespie Graham, who proposed a long line of symmetrical elevations for the east side of Quality Street. The plan envisaged a two-storey, slightly projecting, central block, flanked by single-storey terraces with elaborate porches over the front doors, and culminating at each end with two-storey blocks to match the central feature. The project was never implemented, but a few substantial houses with basement flats, designed by Gillespie Graham, were built at the south end of Quality Street.

Around the same time many of the surrounding estates were enclosed by their owners who encouraged estate workers and others to erect houses outside the perimeter walls. A fine new mansion by R. & R. Dickson was built at Muirhouse in 1830, and gradually the influence of the Davidson family was reflected in the community. Davidson's Mains began to oust the old name of Muttonhole, which had perhaps become unfashionable, and which even Grant described as 'grotesque'. At that time Muirhouse was owned by Henry Davidson and his wife Henrietta, who gave birth to a son on 7th April 1848 — Randall Thomas Davidson. He married Edith, the second daughter of Archibald Tait of Canterbury, and in 1903 he became Archbishop of Canterbury. Against such a pedigree, the name Muttonhole did not survive.

Another major influence of that period was in 1843 at the time of the Disruption when Dr. Muirhead of Cramond Kirk 'came out' with many of the congregation to set up Cramond Free Church in Davidson's Mains. From that date the growth in population tended to be at Davidson's Mains, as the geographical centre of the parish, rather than at Cramond which was experiencing an era of declining industry and population.

Churches in Davidson's Mains

For such a comparatively small community, Davidson's Mains is very well served by churches of various denominations. There are four active congregations which have grown up in the village at different times in its history, and which play a significant part in the community today.

In 1843, as we saw, Dr Muirhead and the entire Kirk Session from Cramond Kirk set up Cramond Free Church in Davidson's Mains. This was an act of considerable courage because it meant that Dr Muirhead was without a stipend, without a manse, and without even a church building in which to preach to those of his congregation who came with him. On 21st May 1843 the first congregational meeting of Cramond Free Church was held, the eastern section meeting in the old school house at the west end of Main Street and the western section meeting in the barn of Braehead. Two months later the first meeting of the Kirk Session was held at Cramond Brig, but there remained the problem of securing a permanent place for Sunday worship. Ground to the east of Quality Street was made available, plans were drawn up by David Cousin for a small church in the Gothic style, and in a remarkably short time the building was completed. The first Sunday service, on 17th December 1843, was taken by Dr Muirhead assisted by Rev. A.C. Fraser. The adjacent parish school was built in 1846, and in 1866 the church bellcote was added to complete Cousin's original plan. Cramond Free Church became a United Free Church in 1900 and was renamed Davidson's Mains Parish Church at the time of the historic Union with the Established Church in 1929. A church hall was built in 1933 and then replaced by a much grander hall costing £20,000 in 1964. A similar sum of money was spent in 1970 to provide further accommodation for the congregation by erecting an extension on the north side of the church. The church has served the community well under a comparatively small number of ministers since 1843. One of the best known was Rev. David Gibb Mitchell who came to Davidson's Mains in 1890 at the age of thirty-seven, having spent the early part of his life in the employment of the Caledonian Railway Company. A keen golfer, cricketer and poet, he is perhaps best remembered as the minister who delivered many sermons, prayers and readings in 'Braid Scots'.

Halfway along the south side of Quality Street Lane, a small private road, bounded by maturing Cypress trees, leads to a modern church building used by the Brethren who are simple believers in the Lord Jesus and whose ground of gathering is the second Epistle to Timothy, chapter 2, verse 19. Although the Brethren have been represented in the village for several years, it was only in September 1981 that their present meeting room was completed. This long, low, unassuming building, erected on the orchard ground of the adjacent dwelling, is the functional meeting place of all Brethren in the Edinburgh area. It forms an integral part of a universal fellowship which was begun in the 1820s by John Nelson Darby and reached Edinburgh about 1837. Each Sunday the Brethren assemble for the breaking of bread, followed by a reading of the Holy Scriptures, and preachings of the Word of God later in the day. The Brethren also assemble for a meeting every evening.

At the north end of Quality Street a woody corner of the old Barnton House estate creates an ideal setting for the simple Romanesque architecture of the Scottish Episcopal Church of the Holy Cross. Designed in 1912 by J.M. Dick Peddie, with natural-faced stone and large brown slates, it contains some interesting stained glass work in the east chancel by Christopher Webb. Like so many other churches, its early history was characterised by the enthusiasm of a handful of people determined to build a strong congregation. A short series of articles on the history of the church has been compiled by Miss Mary F. Harrison, Deaconess at Holy Cross (great-granddaughter of Sir George Harrison, Lord Provost of Edinburgh, 1882–1885), in which she traces all the milestones and relates many of the anecdotes. Alfred Griffiths was born at Norwood, Surrey on 20th March 1853 and was educated at St. John's College, Cambridge where he graduated B.A. in 1877 and M.A. in 1881. He was appointed Junior Chaplain at St. Mary's Episcopal Cathedral in Edinburgh in 1887. In addition to his duties at St. Mary's, Mr Griffiths started a fortnightly evensong in 1896 at Cramond Parish Church Hall, the site of which is now occupied by the offices of J. Smart & Co. (Contractors) Ltd. in Cramond Road South. Within two years the nucleus of a congregation had been formed, and an Iron Church (the Tin Tabernacle as it was called) was erected on the north-east corner of the church ground. In 1901 Holy Cross became an Independent Mission with its own Constitution, and two extensions were built onto the Iron Church to accommodate the growing congregation. It was not long, however, before even the extended Tin Tabernacle was found to be inadequate. In 1908 a decision was taken to build a stone church, to seat three hundred, at a cost of £2,500. Several sites were considered but rejected before the architect Mr Dick Peddie drew up definite plans and colour sketches of the proposed building. When work began in November 1912, it

Rev. Alfred Griffiths, first minister of the Scottish Episcopal Church of the
Holy Cross at Davidson's Mains. Also founder of St. Mary's Cathedral
Mission in Dean Village.
From *Edinburgh and the Lothians Contemporary Biographies.*

seems to have proceeded more quickly than anticipated, because in
May 1913 it was suddenly realised that no ceremony had been
arranged for the laying of the foundation stone. The apparent
dilemma was quickly resolved, the general view being 'that in view of
the advanced state of the building such a ceremony would be rather
pointless'. Unfortunately in 1912 ill health compelled Mr Griffiths to
resign just at a time when his congregation needed him most. When
he recovered later and took up an appointment at Prestonpans, the
old Iron Church was removed there 'as it was considered that no
more fitting use could be found for the church than as a mission
under the charge of Mr Griffiths'.

From around the mid-nineteenth century Davidson's Mains had a
significant Irish population, many of whom were members of the
Roman Catholic Church. Following the restoration of the Scottish
Hierarchy by Pope Leo XIII a decision was taken in 1882 to found

the parish of St. Margaret's at Davidson's Mains. The first priest was Father Michael James Turner who served Davidson's Mains as well as South Queensferry until 1889. Thereafter Davidson's Mains ceased to be an independent parish but was served by neighbouring parishes.

When the parish was founded, Father Turner held services at the Priest's House in Cramond and later at No. 1 Quality Street. As the population increased, the congregation moved to a new chapel built on the north side of Main Street about fifty yards west of the westernmost entrance to The Green. At that time, of course, The Green had not yet been built.

In 1952 St. Margaret's made another move, farther east on Main Street, to a site previously occupied by two old cottages, almost opposite the junction with Corbiehill Road. This tall triangular prism of modern church architecture was designed by Sir Peter Whiston, in a style substantially repeated in his later design for St. Mark's Roman Catholic Church in Oxgangs Avenue. The foundation stone was laid on 27th April 1952 by Archbishop Gordon J. Gray (later Cardinal Gray), and the opening service was on 26th April 1953. A stone plaque taken from the old chapel farther down Main Street was inserted in the wall of the new church commemorating an early benefactor:

> Erected by the Catholics of Davidson's Mains in Loving Memory of Matilda Justina Davidson of Tulloch Wife of Colonel Craigie Halkett of Cramond and Harthill the Founder and Pious Benefactor of this Mission on Whose Soul Sweet Jesus have Mercy.

Since 1959 St. Margaret's has been re-established as a parish covering Davidson's Mains, Silverknowes, Cramond, Barnton East, part of Blackhall, Craigcrook and Wester Drylaw.

Schools

In 1792 a parish school operated 'at Barnton' probably in or near Muttonhole with fifty to sixty pupils. By the middle of the nineteenth century the education of children in and around Davidson's Mains was under the control of the Cramond Free Church School which was built in 1845 to the south-east of Cramond Free Church. The small school and adjacent schoolmaster's house were designed by the architect Robert R. Raeburn, but unfortunately no record of the school's activities now exists.

William Bannerman, headmaster, and his wife Agnes outside the old Corbiehill Road school in 1909.
Courtesy of A.W. Bannerman.

The 1851 Ordnance Survey Map of the district also shows Lauriston School for Girls, at one time under the patronage of the Ramsays of Barnton, at the north-east corner of Main Street and Cramond Road South. It was a small cottage-type building of one storey with a projecting gable, heavy central chimneys, and interesting windows arranged in vertical groups of five small panes. The garden ground was planted with conifer trees and bounded by a low stone wall with rough copings. This school was later administered, almost single-handedly, by a Miss Fargie until she and her pupils transferred to the newly built school in Corbiehill Road.

Royal High School ceremony of leavetaking when pupils who have completed their schooling shake hands with the Rector and pass through the Memorial Doorway to be received by the President of the Royal High School Club. Photograph by Robin Gillanders.

The first Corbiehill Road school was built for the School Board in 1874. It was much bigger than the old Lauriston school, with classrooms in the single-storey section, and a schoolmaster's house of two storeys, nearest to the roadway. Some years elapsed before there was full integration of the classes under the control of Miss Fargie and those under the control of Mr Bannerman at Corbiehill. By 1907 the school roll had grown to almost two hundred, and again there was talk of further expansion. This time a much larger school was built on three storeys, with port-hole windows in the attic, and the 1874 school was refurbished and altered so that the two buildings were intercommunicating. The school continued in daily use until 1967 when it was demolished. The new Davidson's Mains Primary School, designed by the City Architect's Department, was opened on Tuesday 25th April 1967 by the Right Rev. R. Leonard Small, then Moderator of the General Assembly of the Church of Scotland.

In 1978 the Royal High School celebrated its 850th anniversary in fine modern accommodation at East Barnton Avenue on the fringe of the old village. Although the High School has been traditionally associated with numerous buildings in the centre of Edinburgh, the move to Barnton in the mid-1960s gave it the opportunity of greater space and better facilities. It is organised on the basis of a comprehensive co-educational school, maintaining its colours, motto and traditions which have been built up over a very long period. Its motto *Musis Respublica Floret* (a country flourishes by its culture) is as relevant today as in 1128 when the school first started, with the Abbots of Holyrood as the first Rectors.

Throughout history the school has produced a long line of able pupils who achieved great eminence in almost every discipline — Scott, Cockburn, Bell, Napier, and in much more recent years Norman MacCaig and a significant part of The Two Ronnies. The ceremony of leave-taking is an impressive and moving occasion. As the last act of the Commemoration and Prize-giving Day at the end of session, pupils who have completed their schooling shake hands with the Rector and, to the strains of the bagpipes on the terrace outside, pass through the Memorial Doorway to be received by the President of the Royal High School Club. It is a symbolic transition from the shelter and security of the school to the challenges and opportunities of the world outside.

The Village in the Twentieth Century

Davidson's Mains has a handful of residents whose memory of local events stretches back to around 1900. Their recollection of everyday life, in and around the village, is worth recording.

One of the village smiddies: John MacDonald, horseshoer and general blacksmith, at the east end of the village.
Courtesy of Mrs Sadie Fraser.

At the start of the twentieth century Davidson's Mains was a comparatively isolated village. The nearest communities were Blackhall, a mile or so south-east, and Cramond, two miles to the north. People lived and worked in the village most of their lives, requiring very little contact with Edinburgh. The community was self-supporting in shops, services and employment. Several people were employed in the seven or eight 'wet dairies' which sold milk locally and in Edinburgh, the cows being kept almost permanently in the byres. There were also piggeries in the field opposite Corbiehill School.

Public transport had been greatly improved a decade earlier on the introduction of the railway into Barnton Gate Station, en route for Barnton Station, farther west. Housing and street sanitation were primitive. Main Street was flanked by rows of single-storey cottages without electricity or gas, or running water. Dry closets were the order of the day, or the night. Water was carried from one of the metal standpipes, or from the village well at the west end of Main Street. Street furniture and road maintenance were rudimentary. The first street lighting consisted of a series of wooden posts about eight feet high at very long intervals on which were fixed metal brackets to hold oil-burning lamps. Later, gas lamps were introduced but not with automatic ignition. It was necessary for 'leerie' to walk round the streets to operate the balance lever, and to light the flow of gas, on each lamp. The road surface was rough and pitted, and consisted of mud or dry earth, depending on the prevailing weather. The very latest form of road mechanisation consisted of a horse-drawn mudscraper with a six-foot blade and roller brushes, set askew, so that the offending 'top soil' was deposited in long lines between the road and the pavement, to the great annoyance of pedestrians. By modern standards Davidson's Mains may have seemed very primitive but, in fact, it was no different to countless other villages or country areas, and infinitely preferable to many of the city slums of the same period. It was a close-knit community with a decidedly independent spirit, and to some extent a bilingual tongue, especially among the children. Spoken English was the means of communication with the headmaster, the doctor and the minister, but a more relaxed colloquialism was the only way to be understood in the street. Street games attracted a language of their own: tig, skin-the-cat, cuddy loups and henners, some of which were seasonal, though for reasons less obvious than the game of Scotch or Irish on St. Patrick's Day.

There were high days and holidays. The weekly routine was occasionally broken by the arrival of a balloon man or a hokey-pokey man, peddling his thirst-quenching wares in a specially designed barrow-cum-tricycle. Christmas was no less special than in any other age, although slate pencils were more common than computers. For the children of the Session Clerk at Cramond Church great excitement accompanied the distribution of gifts of coal or blankets to the needy of the parish. On the itinerary were a few people whose roots belonged to a different age. Sgt. Ross, a splendid old man with a great white beard, veteran of the Crimea and the Indian Mutiny, lived in a very small cottage, in the kitchen of which hung an old oleograph of Queen Victoria. One of the farthest calls was to Maggie Brash who retained a life tenancy of the West Lodge to the Barnton estate. The highlight of the visit was to be taken up the driveway to Barnton House, once the proud home of the Ramsays of Barnton. Maggie would unlock the front door and escort the group up the magnificent staircase, along the wood-panelled corridors and under elaborate cornices to one of the principal rooms of the house, in which a full-grown chestnut tree grew up through the middle of the floor.

The Christmas Treat was held in the Hall of the Parish Church in Cramond Road South, to which all the local children were invited, to see the latest Magic Lantern show. The practice of handing out a bag of buns to each person on entry was greatly enjoyed, but closely regulated, to ensure that only deserving cases were rewarded: the young reporter of the *Midlothian Advertiser*, anxious to cover the event, was dashed on hearing, as he passed in, 'Complimentary: nae bag'.

The modern village of Davidson's Mains contains numerous links with the past. If we start at the west end of the village, the old stone well bearing the date 1832 was at one time the main source of water supply. It was built at a time when the Barnton estate owners objected to villagers crossing their land to reach natural springs near Corstorphine Hill. Reservoirs were built along the line of Queensferry Road with supply pipes extending into the village. The scheme was administered locally by the Davidson's Mains Water Trust (1832) which continued until 1937 when responsibility was transferred to Edinburgh Corporation.

Near the village well two important landmarks have disappeared in comparatively recent years: the site of the present police box was occupied by a picturesque thatched cottage which once served as the East Lodge to Barnton House; and on the opposite side of the road the Royal Bank of Scotland occupies the site of Lauriston School for Girls. On Main Street many of the original cottages remain on the south side, but the north side has been extensively redeveloped. A tiny cottage has been sandwiched between the traditional construction of Ye Olde Inn and the modern building of the Clydesdale Bank. Near Cleland's Garage and McCracken's former cycle shop the Norhet pub faces directly into the gap between the cottages on the south side. It has not always been a pub. The building was erected in 1843 as Rosemount Cottage and was, for many years, the home of the Johnstone family. In 1957 Ron Johnstone decided to convert the old house into a pub and named it Norhet – a tantalising anagram of his own name spelt backwards, and his wife's name shortened from Hetta.

The west approach to The Green is the approximate location of the Hawkeree, an old building demolished many years ago, which is believed to have taken its name from where the falconers kept their birds in the days when Cramond Regis was a Royal Park. East of the two-storey building once known as Marshall Place, two adjacent cottages with very low ceilings have made way, ironically, for Low Freeze, and Mains Electrical Co. Ltd. occupy a refurbished building previously owned by Marshall the baker. On the angular corner of Main Street and Corbiehill Road the fish and chip shop was for many years the village police station from which P.C. Girvan made his rounds on foot.

The old Muirhouse Arms has recently been renamed MacKenzie's in tribute to a man who has spent the greater part of his working life as a publican in Davidson's Mains. James MacKenzie was born in 1901 in Tollcross and worked for a while in the Haymarket Bar before going abroad in 1921. On returning to Edinburgh he became a barman at the Muirhouse Arms in 1925, and bought the pub in 1932. He retired in 1965 but remembers well the days when Davidson's Mains was a farming community; when it was possible to see the Fife coast across open fields opposite the pub; when the iron grid of the hay weights occupied part of the roadway; and when Silverknowes Golf Club was inaugurated at a meeting of sixteen regulars at the Muirhouse Arms.

Past proprietors of the Muirhouse Arms, particularly Messrs. Twiss, McLaren and MacKenzie, have taken a keen interest in, and been elected President of the Maitland Bowling Club situated to the south of the road as it crosses the railway line. The club was formed in 1899 and took its name from the Maitland family, superiors of the ground, who leased it to the club for five shillings per annum. The club emblem is a ram's head linking the club with the old name of Mutton Hole. The first green was laid with turf from Silverknowes Quarry, a new club house was built in 1923, and the green was extended in 1928.

Not so long ago Davidson's Mains was fortunate to have a public park and sports ground (now built upon) in the centre of the village, which could be reached without the need to cross busy roadways. The ground lay to the south of Quality Street Lane and was for long the home ground of the local football team, Muirhouse Violet, who were never referred to as a bunch of pansies for a second time. The park was also the venue for 'The Games', an annual event at which there was a show of farm horses and a long train of caravans and show people on their summer sojourn. The Davidson's Mains Gala Day was also started here in 1932.

There is one other corner of Davidson's Mains which has undergone considerable redevelopment. The ground lying to the north-east of Cramond Road South is occupied by a large supermarket, car park and offices. Well within the memory of local

The Barnton Express at Davidson's Mains Station (formerly known as Barnton Gate Station), c. 1903-1907.
Courtesy of D.L.G. Hunter.

residents it was a marshalling yard and coal depot linked to the line to Barnton Gate Station (later Davidson's Mains), which was on a high banking on the west side of the roadway. Cramond Parish Church Hall also stood near the marshalling yards, and curling ponds were located on the north side of the railway.

Davidson's Mains Dramatic Club

Davidson's Mains Dramatic Club was formed in 1942 by the late H.M. Wylie and Albert Black, who is still an active member of the club. Prior to 1942 H.M. Wylie had produced several amateur dramatic productions with the local Women's Rural Institute who invited male players to join in their productions as the occasion demanded. Following a series of meetings between H.M. Wylie and Albert Black a decision was taken to form a separate dramatic club in Davidson's Mains. The first production was *Dear Octopus* in 1942 with a cast, some of whom had not had any previous experience of amateur dramatics. In these formative days considerable foresight and confidence was required to bring any production to fruition. H.M. Wylie's ability to select potential players for particular parts would have been much less successful but for the persuasive

Davidson's Mains Dramatic Club, suitably dressed by the Costume Society
of Scotland, portray life in the Georgian House, Charlotte Square for the
film produced by Scottish Gas to mark the tenth anniversary of the National
Trust for Scotland's Georgian House.
Courtesy of *The Scotsman*.

enthusiasm of Albert Black who undertook the job of recruiting
members from among the local population.

Early productions, including *Quiet Wedding* and *Robert's Wife*,
were given during the 1940s in Cramond Parish Church Hall, but by
the 1950s the Club had graduated to *Rebecca* at the Little Theatre in
the Pleasance. From there the Club went from strength to strength,
establishing a high reputation in the Scottish Community Drama
Association by winning the Full Length Play Festival on many
occasions. In 1970 it represented Scotland at the Dundalk Festival in
Ireland with *Every Other Evening* produced by Albert Black, in
which David Horne won the award for Best Supporting Actor. The
Club also continues to present an annual production at the
Edinburgh International Festival.

The Club's deservedly high reputation was given a further boost in
1985 when it was selected to appear in a short video film produced by
Scottish Gas to mark the tenth anniversary of the National Trust for
Scotland's Georgian House at 7 Charlotte Square, Edinburgh. The

film, with a script by Edinburgh author Bill Ritchie, portrays life in the Georgian House in 1815 when it was the house of John Lamont of Lamont. The film is on view to members of the public visiting the Georgian House.

Davidson's Mains Dramatic Club has a membership of approximately fifty people including three vice-presidents who were members of the original cast during the first performance of *Dear Octopus* in 1942 — Mildred E. Murray M.B.E., Allister Bryce and Albert Black.

Lauriston Castle

Lauriston Castle dates from the late sixteenth century. To the east, a much earlier structure existed until 1544 when it was partially destroyed by the Earl of Hertford, being finally demolished in the early nineteenth century. The present building, however, is a most interesting amalgam of sixteenth-century towerhouse and Jacobean-style additions by the architect William Burn. Gifted to the nation in 1926 by Margaret Johnstone Reid, Lauriston offers a unique opportunity to appreciate the interior of one of Edinburgh's grand houses, still furnished in the personal style of the Reid family.

Lauriston lies to the east of Cramond Road South in a garden of about thirty acres, commanding a fine view of the islands in the Firth of Forth. Its architectural development is at once evident, yet interestingly harmonised to create a unified exterior. The story of its development is in many respects the story of its many, and varied, owners.

As suggested in *Lauriston Castle* by Ann Martha Rowan, the architectural history of Lauriston can best be appreciated by walking round the castle in a clockwise direction, beginning on the south side near the original door of the towerhouse. The tall, five-storey towerhouse is immediately evident on the left, with twin corbelled turrets, ornamental window pediments, and a plethora of dates and inscriptions. To the right, the long two-storey extension was added by William Burn between 1824 and 1827 leading to the domestic offices and stables of the same period. The projecting front porch was added some time between 1844 and 1854 by Lord Rutherfurd.

The towerhouse was built in T-formation in the last quarter of the sixteenth century by Sir Archibald Napier and his second wife, Dame

Lauriston Castle, showing the sixteenth-century towerhouse on the left and on the right the Jacobean-style additions (1824–1827) by the architect William Burn.

Elizabeth Moubray. Following the traditions of the time, their initials were inscribed in the pediments above the windows, which project through the wallhead. The left-hand window with the initials S.A.N. was replaced in 1856, but the right-hand window displays the initials D.E.M. The south-facing wall also contains two interesting inscriptions which give some account of the different thinking of past owners. The stone to the left depicts the horoscope of Sir Archibald Napier's son Alexander, and was transferred to the south wall of the towerhouse from a cottage in the grounds. The stone to the right, above the old doorway, is by Robert Dalgleish who bought Lauriston in 1656. Its lengthy inscription tries hard to distance itself from its celestial neighbour. In translation it reads, 'I do not acknowledge the stars as either the rulers of life or the causes of my good fortune. The things which I possess I ascribe to the goodness of God. I commit their protection to His faith, their disposal to His will. From Him I hope and pray to use them all for Him'.

Very little alteration was made to the towerhouse by William Burn: the original front door was blocked up and made into a window; and the slated caps on the twin turrets were lengthened into true witches' hats. Burn's apparent deference to antiquity in saving the old towerhouse receives scant credence, however, from Sir Walter Scott in his Journal for 3rd December 1827:

... went with Thom Allan to see his building at Lauriston, where he has displayed good taste — supporting instead of tearing down or destroying the old chateau, which once belonged to the famous Mississippi Law. The additions are in very good taste and will make a most comfortable house. Mr Burn, architect, would fain have had the old house pulled down, which I wonder at in him, though it would have been the practice of most of his brethren.

Lauriston without its towerhouse would have deprived the estate of a significant part of its heritage, but fortunately it was saved. The limits of the original towerhouse, with its north-facing stair tower, are clearly visible from the west front, also designed by William Burn. The north facade, by Burn also, consists of a long two-storey elevation, incorporating two crowstepped sections, with broad bay windows linked by a stone balustrade. Slightly to the east of the bell-tower the original building consisted of one storey only. However, this was altered in 1872 by Thomas Macknight Crawfurd, who added a second storey to contain the library, and built a link between it and the coachman's cottage where the visitors' entrance is now located. The north wall of the library also contains two interesting inscriptions. The stone in the curtain wall is a carved panel of 1672 with the arms and motto of the Crawfurd family who brought it to Lauriston after the demolition of their former house at Cartsburn, near Greenock. The other plaque commemorates the gift of Lauriston Castle and its policies to the nation by Mr and Mrs Reid.

Lauriston Castle gives the impression of being a much bigger house than it is, but in fact the reception hall and the six principal rooms are all contained within the first-floor level. The main entrance leads immediately to a flight of stone steps giving access to the reception hall above. Just inside the front door there is a marble bust of Thomas Allan who commissioned the Burn extensions, and at the head of the stairs the double doors have stained glass panels depicting the coat-of-arms of Thomas Macknight Crawfurd. The reception hall is the focal point of the house, bringing together the original sixteenth-century towerhouse and the elegant extensions of 1827. Access to the towerhouse is on the left, the original principal room now greatly altered with a lowered ceiling, renamed the Oak Room, and used by William Robert Reid as a business room.

The bathroom is tucked in behind the sixteenth-century turnpike stair, the external corbels of which now project into the ceiling cornice. The bathroom fittings, consisting of a zinc bath with shower and mixer taps, Edwardian lavatory and heated towel-rail, were installed in 1903 by William Barton & Sons, the family business of Mrs Reid's father. Opposite the turnpike stair is the main bedroom containing mostly Sheraton and Hepplewhite-style furniture, a night commode disguised as a chest of drawers, and Mrs Reid's sit-down weighing machine.

Burn's principal achievement is, however, his north-facing billiard room (now a sitting room), and drawing room identified externally by the stone verandah which runs the whole length of the broad bay windows. The drawing room has had minor additions in the form of overdoors and fluted pilasters at each of the corners. In a recess on the south wall of the sitting room an elegant bookcase presently displays the larger part of the Lauriston collection of Derbyshire fluorspar, known as Blue John. This display, of almost one hundred pieces put together by Mr Reid, is one of the finest of its kind and includes urns, vases and various other ornaments. The drawing room, like the sitting room, is decorated in Edwardian taste in deep red, providing an excellent contrast alongside the white painted woodwork of the north-facing rooms. The furniture consists mainly of mid-eighteenth century Italian commodes with many Edwardian reproductions of the Louis XV style, and there is a Broadwood grand piano given to Mrs Reid by her brother at the time of her marriage in 1896.

The last apartment dating from 1827 is the dining room, now greatly altered from Burn's own design. The ceiling has been lowered, and oak-grained plaster panelling has been installed.

To the east of the dining room the library corridor leads to the 1872 additions built by Thomas Macknight Crawfurd. The principal feature is the library, which is also reached from the visitors' waiting room by a concealed door in one of the bookcases. Few of the existing books belonged to the Reids, however, as the bulk of their library was bequeathed after the death of Mrs Reid to the National Library of Scotland, where it now forms one of the special collections. The room contains several interesting pieces of eighteenth-century furniture, and a pair of reproduction tambour-fronted cabinets by Mr Reid's own firm, Morison & Co. of Edinburgh.

Lauriston, over the centuries, has been in the hands of several families, some of whom were important and influential people whilst others appear to have remained in relative obscurity. The Napier family ceased to have any involvement in Lauriston in 1622, after which it was owned by the families Cant and Rigg, and then in 1656 by the dexterous Robert Dalgleish, Solicitor in Scotland to Charles I, the Commonwealth and Charles II.

From 1683 Lauriston was owned by the famous Law family. Although they were in possession for one hundred and forty years, there is no direct evidence that any of them ever lived there. By far the most notable of them was John Law (1671–1729), son of the first owner, William Law, a successful goldsmith and financier. Having inherited his father's money and his brilliant but restless nature, John went to London in search of fame and fortune. He was obliged to flee to the Continent, however, on account of rising debt, and a misguided duel in which he stabbed and killed his opponent. In Paris his temerity knew no bounds. In 1716 he set up a very successful private bank, and in the following year his trading company was sufficiently respected to take over control of the collection of all tax revenues in France. He went from strength to strength and was eventually declared Comptroller General of the Finances of France, but when his company crashed in 1720 he left France in disgrace. He spent the last years of his life in relative poverty, and died in Venice in 1729.

Lauriston remained in the hands of the Law family until 1823, when it was acquired by Thomas Allan, banker and proprietor of the *Caledonian Mercury*. Allan is remembered as an amateur mineralogist who had the mineral Allanite named after him posthumously. Following the death of Thomas Allan, without heirs, in 1833, Lauriston had many owners up to the turn of the century, including William Ramsay of Barnton, M.P., and Lord Rutherfurd, Solicitor General for Scotland and Lord Advocate.

Lauriston's closing chapter, however, belongs unreservedly to the Reid family who acquired it in 1902. William Robert Reid, proprietor of Morison & Co., cabinetmakers in Edinburgh, and his wife Margaret, both lived at Lauriston with Mrs Reid's brother William Davidson Barton until the death of Mr Reid in 1919. Mrs Reid continued to live at Lauriston until her death in 1926 when the house, contents, and grounds were left by her to the nation 'for the use of the public in all time coming and the intelligent education of the public taste'.

Barnton House

Barnton House lay amid extensive woodland to the west of Davidson's Mains. According to Small's *Castles and Mansions of the Lothians*, the original house was built around 1640 by Sir John Smith of Grotthill, Lord Provost of Edinburgh in 1643. In 1788 Lady Glenorchy sold the joint estate of Barnton and Cramond Regis to William Ramsay, banker in Edinburgh, who demolished the old house near Davidson's Mains and built a much grander house nearer the west boundary of the estate. The new house was dominated by a large circular tower of three storeys at the entrance, with a castellated roofline to match a flanking tower of equal proportions. Iron balconies were a feature at second-floor level, particularly round the entrance tower. The Ramsays spent considerable time and effort improving the estate for their own use, and obtained the benefit of having Queensferry Road realigned to the south of its original position. In the days of William Ramsay's grandson, William Ramsay Ramsay, the estate became famous as a sporting park, the laird holding the position of Master of the Linlithgow and Stirlingshire Hunt. Despite the Ramsays' great wealth they were never far from tragedy. William Ramsay Ramsay died young, and his heir died in a carriage accident in 1865, not long after coming of age.

The estate was acquired by Sir Alexander Charles Gibson Maitland of Clifton Hall in 1865, and later passed to the Steel Maitland family who were responsible for selling part of the land to the railway company, and to the Royal Burgess Golfing Society and Bruntsfield Links Golfing Society.

Although new Barnton House was demolished many years ago, the west gate piers and curtain wall still stand at the junction of Barnton Avenue West and Whitehouse Road. The estate grounds remain almost intact, beautifully laid out as golf courses for the two golfing societies.

Marchfield

The house known as Marchfield in Corbiehill Park is of uncertain date: the *Edinburgh* volume of *The Buildings of Scotland* gives the date 1810–1813 'but looking fifty years earlier'; Laurie's Map of

1763 clearly shows a property known as Marchfield in the same location as it is now. Either the present structure *is* fifty years earlier than 1810, or the house shown in Laurie's Map is not the present house. There is no doubt, however, that the house has always been in private occupation, although the garden ground has been substantially reduced over the years by adjacent development.

Its most influential owner in the nineteenth century was John Donaldson, who was appointed Professor of Music at Edinburgh University, although he had previously qualified for the Scottish Bar. He found the Chair of Music to be inadequately paid, and that funds originally intended for its support had been diverted elsewhere. Matters came to a head in 1850 when a petition to the Court of Session was decided in his favour. During his lifetime Professor Donaldson gathered together a remarkable collection of instruments illustrating the history of music and acoustics, but it was generally considered that he was not a good practical musician. He died at Marchfield on 12th August 1865.

In more recent years Marchfield underwent refurbishment when it was owned by Sir Andrew Murray, Lord Provost of Edinburgh from 1947 to 1951. The house had fallen into a poor state of repair, but it was found that no serious structural repairs were necessary. Modernisation, installation of new fittings and re-designing the garden were all undertaken by Sir Andrew, much of the work being done by him personally. On the top floor he had a small self-contained flat — a home within a home — to which he could retreat when the pressures of public life demanded.

Much of the original garden of seven acres has been sold for the construction of elegant villas, and the nineteenth-century coach-house to the north forms a separate property, Marchfield Lodge.

Craigcrook Castle

To the south of Davidson's Mains the old castle of Craigcrook shelters on the lower slopes of Corstorphine Hill at a distance just sufficient to escape the continual roar of traffic on Queensferry Road. Elegant houses now rise around the dry bed of Craigcrook Loch, quite unperturbed by the old legend of the coach and horses. It is said that one dark night a drunken coachman lost control of his horses on a sharp bend, and ran off the road into the yawning quagmire below.

Ownership of the lands of Craigcrook can be traced back to the fourteenth century when they were in the hands of the Graham family who owned other large estates in and around Midlothian. A deed of 1362 transferred Craigcrook from the Grahams, firstly to John de Allyncrum, a burgess in Edinburgh, and then, by way of a pious gift, to a chaplain of St. Giles Cathedral. In 1542 Craigcrook was assigned, with the consent of the Collegiate Church of St. Giles, to William Adamson, burgess of Edinburgh, who died at the battle of Pinkie in 1547. William had already acquired considerable property at Clermiston, Craigleith and Cramond, and it was probably he who built Craigcrook Castle. The Adamson family relinquished control in 1659, and following a sequence of short-term ownership, the property was bequeathed in 1719 by John Strachan to the Craigcrook Mortification 'for charitable and pious uses', the benefits to be conferred on 'poor old men, women, and orphans'.

It was during the occupancy of the Strachans that Craigcrook became associated with a particularly horrific crime, which is sometimes recorded incorrectly as having occurred at the Castle itself. John Strachan was a man of considerable means who kept a town house in Edinburgh in addition to his country estate at Craigcrook. The Edinburgh house was looked after by a young servant, Helen Bell, who became acquainted with two young men, William Thomson, employed as a wright in Edinburgh, and John Robertson, a smith in the Pleasance. When she foolishly announced to them on the night of Hallowe'en 1707 her intention to go out to Craigcrook, the two men resolved to take advantage of the situation. A few days later when she set out to walk to Craigcrook, intending to go by Dean village, the two villains lay in wait for her, pretending to escort her on the journey. When the cheerful threesome reached the Three Steps near the foot of Edinburgh Castle rock, Thomson and Robertson attacked and killed the unsuspecting girl with blows from a hammer, and stole the key to Mr Strachan's house. The men returned to Strachan's town house to steal a large quantity of cash, and for several weeks their crime remained undetected. Contemporary accounts of the incident vary in their record of events from then on. Some say that Thomson made a voluntary confession, which resulted in both men being executed in the Grassmarket, whereas Grant, in *Old and New Edinburgh*, infers that Robertson escaped detection. The most interesting account, however, is that of Lady Strachan's dream, which, had it been authentic, might well have challenged

Sixteenth-century Craigcrook Castle, once the home of Lord Jeffrey, now beautifully restored by the architects Alison & Hutchison & Partners for their own use.
Courtesy of H.H. Macdonald.

either the evidence, or the identity of Thomson. Some months after the crime, Lady Strachan dreamt that she saw the criminal and recognised him as a former servant at Craigcrook Castle, and that enquiries made by her husband revealed the remainder of the stolen cash hidden in the servant's house.

In 1736 Craigcrook Castle and its policies were let on a lease of ninety-nine years, and in the opening years of the nineteenth century were held by Thomas Constable, the renowned Edinburgh publisher. The Constable family were followed by the Castle's most famous and influential resident, Lord Jeffrey.

Francis Jeffrey was born at 7 Charles Street near George Square in Edinburgh on 23rd October 1773, elder son of George Jeffrey, depute clerk of the Court of Session. His mother was Henrietta, daughter of John Louden, a farmer near Lanark. Jeffrey was educated at the Royal High School and later studied law at the universities of Glasgow and Oxford. He was called to the Scottish Bar in 1794 and soon became an accomplished advocate, renowned for his quick wit and ready sarcasm, qualities which, along with his political persuasions as a Whig, did not always endear him to his opponents. Upon entering Parliament in 1830, he became Lord Advocate, and in

1834 he was made a Lord of Session, taking his seat on the bench as Lord Jeffrey. Altogether it was a brilliant career in which his love of literature and debate were always to the fore. As early as 1792 he became a member of the Speculative Society, the most famous of the literary associations connected with Edinburgh University, which gave him the opportunity to meet Scott, Henry Brougham and other distinguished men of letters. His crowning glory in the world of literature was, however, his involvement in founding the *Edinburgh Review* in 1802 with Sydney Smith and Henry Brougham. Jeffrey became editor the following year, and for more than twenty-five years exercised considerable influence over public opinion, and literature in general, covering subjects as diverse as metaphysics, politics, morals and physical science.

Francis Jeffrey came to Craigcrook Castle in 1815. He described it then as 'an old manor-house eighteen feet wide and fifty feet long, with irregular projections of all sorts, three staircases, turrets, and a large round tower at one end with a multitude of windows of all sorts and sizes'. But he was not one to let the grass grow beneath his feet, nor for that matter in parts of the garden which he had earmarked for further development. On taking up residence he added the castellated drawing-room wing to the north of the original sixteenth-century main block, and in 1835 he employed William H. Playfair to carry out major reconstruction of the east extension. This involved the removal of the mezzanine floor with consequent rebuilding of the north and south walls and raising the wallheads and roofline. Craigcrook became a comfortable and spacious country house to which all the leading literary and legal talents of the day flocked in their hundreds to sharpen their wit and wisdom in the company of the great Lord Jeffrey. After occupying the castle for thirty-five years Lord Jeffrey died on 26th January 1850 and was buried in the 'judges' row' in Dean Cemetery. His biography was written by Lord Cockburn, and his statue, by Steell, is in Parliament House.

On the death of such a leading member of society it might be thought that Craigcrook would have subsided into relative obscurity. In many ways perhaps it did, but thanks to the recent research done by Helen Watt, a completely new chapter in the history of the castle has been written in her interesting *John Hunter: The Forgotten Tenant of Craigcrook*. John Hunter, eldest son of Dr. James Hunter, Professor of Logic at the University of St. Andrews, was Auditor of the Court of Session from 1849 to 1866. He was born in 1801 in the

North side of Main Street, 1985, showing Ye Olde Inn on the extreme left. The line of traditional houses is broken by the neo-vernacular Clydesdale Bank by the Waters Jamieson Partnership (1982).

manse of Dunino in Fife, and at the age of sixteen was apprenticed to an Edinburgh lawyer. Later in life he was a founder member of the Edinburgh and Leith Bank and acted as private agent to Lord Jeffrey, from whom he acquired the tenancy of Craigcrook on his death. His dedication to the Whig party and his interest in law and literature made him ideally suited to maintain the old traditions of Craigcrook. But there the similarity ended. Reserved and serious by nature, Hunter aspired to be a successful lawyer, but at heart he was a poet and a lover of music and natural beauty. His surviving diaries, from 1838 to 1842, carefully researched by Helen Watt, give a fascinating insight into the man, his politics, his descriptions of Edinburgh events, and above all his penetrating observation of his fellow men. He died at Craigcrook in 1869, his life temporarily overlooked by subsequent generations, but not, as it turned out, entirely forgotten.

Craigcrook was acquired in 1874 by Robert Croall, whose son R. Douglas Croall became a director of the famous Edinburgh firm of motor hirers John Croall & Sons Ltd. For almost a century Craigcrook was occupied by the Croall family until it was finally sold by the Craigcrook Mortification Trustees in 1968.

In that year Craigcrook entered a new phase of its history, under the able direction of Alison & Hutchison & Partners, who bought the Castle and its policies for their expanding business as Architects, Engineers and Planning Consultants. Their ambitious move from the traffic congestion of Drumsheugh Gardens was fraught with all the problems of creating a twentieth-century workspace in a sixteenth-century castle. That they succeeded in harmonising the old and the new, with only minimal alteration to the basic structure, was in no small way due to the dedication and skill of the senior partners of the firm at that time. The main problems were insufficient floor space for the drawing-office staff, poor heating and ventilation in the castle itself, and long-established deterioration of the fabric from the effects of dryrot and rising damp. The accommodation problem was solved by creating a new single-storey modern drawing-office communicating with the east side of the castle. The worst aspect of the fabric was dampness in the basement, caused by a long period of neglect. Field drains were inserted, and the outer walls, below ground level, were sealed with asphalt, in the same way as was the stone-flagged floor of the interior. A new electricity supply was brought from an adjacent sub-station to replace the obsolete private generator, and special electro-osmotic equipment was installed to repel rising damp. After complete refurbishment, the original castle provided accommodation for seven partners, secretaries, typing pool, conference room, a reference library and storage. The two vaulted cellars were converted into the partners' dining room and a small private bar. Externally the stonework was repointed, and the oldest parts of the castle, including the tower, were finished in ochre-coloured traditional roughcast to simulate the original.

Thus one of Edinburgh's most interesting ancient castles has been preserved and enhanced in a way which would not normally be attainable by a private individual. Much of the interior of the castle has been retained, and the literary associations with Jeffrey are still well established. From a small sixteenth-century fortified keep, Craigcrook Castle has been enlarged and developed over the centuries to meet changing social needs, and only in recent years has it lost its status as a private residence. Craigcrook is inextricably linked with a past which it cannot forget, and which it will not allow others to forget. Its ghost has been seen, and heard, and feared on several occasions in modern times and will, no doubt, continue to watch over Craigcrook for many years to come. Footsteps in the hall;

the white lady at the turret window; a poltergeist; and the phantom coach and horses — all suggest that the murder of Helen Bell and the legend of the drunken coachman may not yet be solved.

CHAPTER 4

Dean

Dean is one of Edinburgh's most ancient and picturesque villages, lying in comparative repose beneath the tall arches of Telford's Dean Bridge. Modern terminology has caused confusion between two separate communities. The present Dean village, below the bridge, was once known as Water of Leith Village, whereas Village of Dean was the name given to a separate, much smaller community, on the north side of the river, near the gates to Dean Cemetery. Despite the confusing names it is possible to trace the history of Dean, through its association with the Incorporation of Baxters or Bakers, back to the time of King David I who conferred the profits of the mills on the Abbot and Canons Regular of St. Augustine at Holyrood.

Bridges of Bell's Brae, Bell's Mills, Belford and Dean

There is probably no more commanding view of the Dean village than that from the parapet of Telford's magnificent Dean Bridge opened in 1832 as the main route out of Edinburgh to Queensferry and the north. Even today, with vastly improved communications and an unbelievable increase in the volume of traffic, Telford's masterpiece of engineering still carries the bulk of Edinburgh's traffic to and from the West End and the north-west suburbs of the city.

Before 1832 the route to the north was very much more arduous, requiring a steep descent by Bell's Brae to the old single-arch bridge in the centre of the village, and then, perhaps with the assistance of a trace horse, up the equally steep gradient of Dean Path, past Village of Dean and into the open countryside beyond. In 1784 some relief was brought to the village by a decision to choose Bell's Mills as the site of a new bridge to replace a much narrower one slightly upstream. Though perhaps convenient to the travelling population, the new bridge does not appear to have won universal acclaim:

> This bridge looks not like a work of the first county in Scotland. It is a tall, narrow, starved, consumptive object unable to support even its own feebleness without the awkward assistance of buttress-crutches, in

Dean Bridge, designed by Thomas Telford and opened in 1832.

addition to the original plan. It must stand (while it is able to stand) a spectacle of studied deformity.

Deformed or not, the new bridge carried most of the traffic from Edinburgh to South Queensferry and the north until it was superseded by Telford's Dean Bridge in 1832. With much of the heavy traffic diverted, the bridge at Bell's Mills became much less important until its state of repair demanded the construction of a replacement bridge on the same site. The replacement bridge known as Belford Bridge was opened on 22nd July 1887 by the Rt. Hon. Sir Thomas Clark Bart., Lord Provost of Edinburgh. On the castellated south parapet, overlooking the Dragonara Hotel, there is a plaque stating that the bridge was erected by the Magistrates and Town Council of the City of Edinburgh with the aid of local subscriptions obtained by the Belford Bridge Association. The engineers were Cunningham Blyth & Westland and the contractors were Henderson Matthew & Co.

Shortage of money and the need to rely on private subscriptions for the construction of bridges in Edinburgh was by no means uncommon in the early nineteenth century. Indeed had it not been for the vision and financial backing of one man, Edinburgh might never have benefited from the engineering skills of Scotland's foremost bridge builder of all time, Thomas Telford. By the first quarter of the nineteenth century much of Edinburgh's New Town had been built, but there were large tracts of land lying to the north-west of the city which had not been fully developed owing to the difficulty of access across the deep ravine of the Water of Leith. The old estate of the Nisbets of Dean House had been acquired by John Learmonth, Lord Provost of Edinburgh, who decided in consultation with the Cramond Road Trustees that a new bridge should be built giving access to his land, which he intended to feu for private building. The Cramond Road Trustees agreed to contribute to the cost on condition that there should be no toll on the bridge and that it should be designed by Telford. The work was commenced in October 1829 and, after significant alterations to the plans to increase the number of arches from three to four, the project was completed in December 1831. When it was opened in the following year, it was described as 'this stupendous structure which forms one of the most splendid monuments in the city'. As far as Telford was concerned, it was certainly a splendid monument which greatly enhanced his reputation, but for Learmonth it remained a monument for much longer than his financial predictions had allowed. For upwards of twenty years he waited before the tide of building work turned again towards further extensions of the New Town, with the first of the houses being built in Clarendon Crescent in the 1850s.

During the construction of the bridge, the old communities of Water of Leith Village and Village of Dean were rejuvenated in a manner which has probably never been repeated since. Many local men were employed in carting and hewing Craigleith stone used in the construction of the huge piers and arches, whilst other villagers benefited from the ancillary tasks of providing food, drink and shelter for the entire workforce. Each morning began with the ancient practice of 'beating the mett': at the appointed hour one of the millers gifted in the matter of early rising beat the large corn measure with the corn rolling pin to a particular time or rhythm. The man in charge of the bridge project was John Gibb, civil engineer from Aberdeen, who worked in close liaison with Telford, if not in close harmony with the workforce. He had built for himself an elevated perch from which he could survey the progress of the work and bellow criticism at his men if they did not execute each task with the precision demanded, and in the event of any of them seeming to take umbrage 'he would descend to exchange blows, banter and snuff'. It is said that Gibb completed the bridge before the contract date but refused to hand it over until the actual date on the contract, a decision which may well have been influenced by the fact that in the intervening period he charged sightseers 1d. each to walk across the completed structure.

After completion, the bridge stood for many years without the need for alterations or significant repairs, but there was one aspect of its gracious spans which had not occurred to Telford, or Gibb, or for that matter Learmonth, as he waited for his investment to bear fruit. Although the bridge had an excellent accident record during its construction, on completion it was not long in gaining notoriety as the place

> Where many a man
> Alas has ran
> There in an evil hour
> And cast away
> His life that day
> Beyond all human pow'r.

Robert McCandless wrote his poem in 1887, and in the following year the Burgh Engineer submitted a report to Edinburgh Corporation giving details of how the parapets could be protected without detracting from the appearance of the bridge itself. Several schemes were considered but rejected. It was thought that complete removal of the parapet and replacement with a high railing would be too costly and would, in any case, create a significant wind hazard for pedestrians. A system of bars and netting fitted on the outer side of the parapet was rejected on account of its being too suggestive, and it would, in any case, catch rather than deter. After much deliberation it was eventually resolved to heighten the existing stone parapet, a precaution which proved reasonably effective, although it removed, for those of shorter stature, one of the grandest views of the old village below.

In 1957 a plaque was erected on the east parapet by the Institution of Civil Engineers to commemorate the bicentenary of the birth of Thomas Telford, who was the first president of the Institution. Unfortunately the plaque was stolen and had to be replaced in 1982, when the new plaque was unveiled by Councillor Ian Cramond.

Sunbury and Bell's Mills

Slightly upstream from Dean village the community around old Sunbury House and the distilleries has almost completely succumbed to modern development. Sunbury now presents an interesting combination of residential flats in buff brick, and turreted mews properties of the late nineteenth century.

The most dominant building is Whytock & Reid's three-storey cabinet-works built for Robert and Hugh Reid in 1884. This old family business of Decorators and Furnishers, now in its fifth generation, are Royal Appointment Holders to Her Majesty the Queen. Richard Whytock established his business at 9/11 George Street, Edinburgh in 1807 and pioneered many new techniques in the weaving of carpets and damasks for which he received the Royal Warrant in 1838. Meantime John Reid completed his apprenticeship as an upholsterer in 1829 and began his own business in Ayr and later in Glasgow. His eldest son Robert came to Edinburgh in 1858 where he formed a partnership with Walter Davidson. After Davidson retired, Robert was joined by his brother Hugh, and in 1875 the Reids and the Whytocks came together to form Whytock Reid & Co. in George Street, Edinburgh. In 1934 the George Street showroom was moved to 7 Charlotte Square, and in 1975 when the National Trust for Scotland opened No. 7 as the Georgian House, Whytock & Reid took the opportunity to build new showrooms beside their cabinet-works at Sunbury. In a fitting tribute to old Sunbury House, the new complex, built partly on the site of the old house, was also named Sunbury House.

Bell's Mills is upstream from Sunbury on the west bank of the Water of Leith, near Belford Bridge. Originally two mills stood within about fifty yards of one another, but from about 1800 they operated as one unit, until 1972 when they were destroyed in a violent dust explosion. That tragedy brought to an end the Walker family's production at Bell's Mills which had been under their control since 1890. Prior to that Gideon Walker had been a miller at Greenlands Mill about sixty yards downstream from the Dean Bridge, where he produced large quantities of provender (animal foodstuffs) and wood flour (ground sawdust). The trade in animal foodstuffs was greatly affected in the early 1890s when Edinburgh began to abandon horse-drawn transport in favour of cable cars and later electric tramways. The production of wood flour used in the manufacture of paper and linoleum was continued by Gideon Walker when he transferred to Bell's Mills in 1890.

After Bell's Mills was destroyed in 1972 the site was developed for the Dragonara Hotel, the name of which was taken from a famous palace in Malta where Ladbrokes had commercial interests. In the design of the hotel the architects Crerar and Partners incorporated the old granary dated 1807, which is now tastefully restored as the Granary Bar.

The only other visual reminder of the old mill is Bell's Mills House immediately west of the hotel, built around 1780 and owned by a Trust for the Walker family, descendants of Gideon Walker who came to Greenlands in 1880.

Village of Dean; Dean House; Dean Cemetery

At one time there was a small community known as Village of Dean which was quite separate from the community now known as the Dean Village. Although the names have developed in a very confusing way, originally there was no cause for confusion at all: Village of Dean was at the top of the hill near the present-day Dean Cemetery gates, and Water of Leith Village was in the hollow below the Dean Bridge. Village of Dean, on the hill, disappeared about 1880, and Water of Leith Village, in the hollow, eventually became known as the Dean Village. It is interesting, however, to consider more closely the forgotten Village of Dean, associated as it was with the ancient Dean House, demolished to make way for the construction of Dean Cemetery in 1845.

Village of Dean consisted of one main street with two or three small lanes running off to the east. For the most part the houses were small and single-storeyed with thatched roofs, but there were other larger dwellings of two storeys, the upper floor being reached by an outside stair. The inhabitants were mostly carters and quarrymen at Craigleith Quarry or were employed as labourers at Dean Farm. As early as 1743 there was a population of almost four hundred, which was quite adequate to support the main aspects of village life. There was a shoemaker, a smithy and a cartwright, and above Mrs Burr's hostelry hung an old squeaking sign with the picture of a horse and cart and the words 'Lang may the wheel row'. Drinking water was obtained from an old draw well in the centre of the village close to the school, which for many years was under the direction of Thomas Shirref. Altogether it seemed a most unlikely place to find men whose political aspirations were aimed at parliamentary reform, but such seems to have been the case. Around 1790, as part of a much larger national organisation, the British Convention, there was an association in Edinburgh known as the Friends of the People, whose aim was to bring about parliamentary reform, by force if need be. One of their most ardent and useful sympathisers was Robert Orrock, blacksmith in Village of Dean. In association with others he spent much of his time in the village smithy making pikes in anticipation of the great uprising. It is said that when challenged on the nature of the work which kept him at the anvil so late at night, Orrock replied that he was busy making ornamentations for a gentleman's gate. A plan was formed by the Friends of the People by which it was expected that the city and the Castle would fall into their hands. A fire was to be started near the old Excise Office to draw out the Castle garrison, and thereby put them in a position where they could be more easily attacked. The Castle was to be taken by force, the judges and the magistrates were to be seized and all the public banks were to be taken over by the usurpers. The plot, however, was eventually discovered when some of Orrock's pikes were found in the village by two sheriff officers. As a result, several members of the Friends of the People were brought to trial and convicted, apparently on the strength of evidence given by Orrock himself.

The ancient turreted mansion of Dean House lay to the west of the village, amid extensive grounds. This handsome building displayed every conceivable example of Scottish vernacular architecture, with a variety of turrets, corbels and crowstepped gables. On its door lintels and within the circled pediments above the windows were carved a plethora of dates, initials, coats-of-arms and divers words of wisdom, all indicative of a long and eventful history. Internally there was a 'Great Hall' the ceiling of which was decorated by a series of wooden panels painted with oil and tempera. Seven of these panels are now in the custody of the National Museum of Antiquities of Scotland. Although the style of painting, and the costume of the figures represented, suggest an early seventeenth-century date, there is no actual date on any of the panels. Of the six panels on display, three are of biblical scenes: the Sacrifice of Isaac; King David playing his

Dean House, demolished 1845, the romantic setting for James Ballantine's novel *Miller of Deanhaugh*.
From Grant's *Old and New Edinburgh.*

harp; and Judith with the head of Holofernes. The other three panels are personifications of the senses of taste, hearing and sight; the personification of sight is shown looking in a mirror with Arthur's Seat and Edinburgh in the background.

James Ballantine of Westerhall, author of *Miller of Deanhaugh*, used Dean House as the centre of his novel set in and around Village of Dean towards the end of the eighteenth century. He depicted Dean House in the ownership of an old miserly recluse, who, as the elder son and in accordance with the law of primogeniture, had taken possession of the estate on the death of his father to the exclusion of his younger brother. The two brothers were the issue of the old laird's *second* marriage, the *first* marriage having produced one son, Oliver, who it was believed had never married and had been lost at sea. Ballantine weaves a wonderful web of mystery and intrigue before revealing, in the closing chapters, the identity of the real heir to the estate — the legitimate son of a clandestine marriage contracted many years before by Oliver, the only son of the *first* marriage.

The real Dean House was for many generations the seat of the Nisbet family, William Nisbet of Dean, Lord Provost of Edinburgh,

One of the seven painted ceiling panels saved from Dean House depicting the Sacrifice of Isaac, now in the possession of the National Museum of Antiquities of Scotland.
Courtesy of the National Museum of Antiquities of Scotland.

being knighted by James VI when he visited Edinburgh in 1617. Many of the initials and armorial bearings on Dean House related to the Nisbet family, and when it was demolished in 1845 some of the more interesting stones were preserved in the boundary wall of Dean Cemetery and 'Cabbie Stewart's' house at the top of Bell's Brae. A detailed study of the meaning of the Dean stones was made by John Geddie and was published in the first volume of the *Book of the Old Edinburgh Club* in 1908.

No sooner had the dust and rubble of Dean House been cleared away than the Doric porticos and obelisks of Dean Cemetery began to appear. One of the last occupants of Dean House was James David Forbes, the physicist, who watched the progress of demolition and the construction of the new cemetery. Commenting in December 1846 only months after the first burial, he observed that 'the gateway, bell and all, is as it was — the avenue and holly hedges are there, but instead of terminating in the tall pile of masonry it opens in a flat turf soon to be full of graves'. His prediction was not without an element of self-interest. In 1869 he was laid to rest in the shadow of the yew tree which had overhung his window when he lived at Dean House, and by the end of the century the elegant and fashionable Dean Cemetery had become a veritable 'Who's Where' of Edinburgh dignitaries from every walk of life. Along the west wall are buried several eminent judges of the Court of Session, including Lords Cowan, Handyside, Cockburn and Jeffrey. Also buried in the Dean are Sir Thomas Bouch, designer of the ill-fated Tay Bridge, and the architects W.H. Playfair and Robert Reid. Playfair (1790–1857) designed many of Edinburgh's classical buildings, including the National Gallery and Royal Scottish Academy at the Mound, Surgeons' Hall, and the National Monument and City Observatory on Calton Hill. His pre-eminence in the classical style did not, however, inhibit his versatility in the design of Donaldson's Hospital, St Stephen's Church and New College on the Mound. He once wrote that 'nothing good in Architecture can be effected without a monstrous expenditure of patience and Indian Rubber'.

Robert Reid (1774–1856) was King's Architect and Surveyor in Scotland, a post which was later combined with that of Master of Works to the Scottish Crown to form the new position of Master of Works and Architect to the King in Scotland which attracted a salary of £200 per year. His architectural style followed that of the Adam brothers although not equal to it in refinement of proportion. He designed St. George's Church in Charlotte Square (now West Register House), the Law Courts in Parliament Square, the exterior of the Signet and Advocates' Library, and the Custom House, Leith. One of his earliest commissions was the original building of the Bank of Scotland on the Mound, later extended and remodelled by David Bryce.

Dean Cemetery is, however, perhaps more than any other Edinburgh cemetery, a place of visual impact, with examples of some of the finest sculpture of its type. There is a Grecian temple for James Buchanan, founder of the Educational Institute of Glasgow, and nearby four white pelicans stand guard over James Leishman W.S. There is a thirty-foot granite obelisk to mark the grave of Alexander

Russel, editor of *The Scotsman*, and a huge pyramid of red polished granite for Lord Rutherfurd of Lauriston Castle.

Water of Leith Village (Dean Village)

Although Village of Dean earned itself a short but infamous reputation for making pikes, by contrast Water of Leith Village formed an enduring and respectable association with the ancient trades of the baxters (bakers) and the weavers. Even today, although the mill wheels no longer turn, several old buildings and inscriptions bear witness to this important era in the life of the village. The existence of mills and granaries at Dean can be traced back to the twelfth century, their importance to the community being jealously guarded by the Ancient Incorporation of Baxters or Bakers. Their influence in matters of employment, and the general economy, found expression in the annual Feeing of the Millers at which the hiring of labour and settling of wages took place. After the formal business was settled, the day was not without its moments of relaxation and indulgence, if the old accounts of expenditure are anything to go by:

'*Water of Leith, 17th March 1716*
Account spent with the Deacon and the Brod (Board) at the feeing of the Millers, —

Imprimis for beef	4: 12: 0
Item for veall	3: 16: 6
Item for eal (ale)	1: 16: 0
Item for brandie	2: 08: 0
Item for broth and other necessaries	1: 06: 0
Item for breid	1: 10: 0
Item for pypes and tobacko	0: 03: 4
Item more to the Millers for eal,	1: 12: 0
	17: 03:10
Item more for brandie and eal,	01: 03:00
	18: 06:10

[Scots money]'

Re-enactment of the Feeing of the Baxters outside Bell's Brae House, with Mr Basil Skinner, Director of the Extra-Mural Department of Edinburgh University, presiding.
Courtesy of *The Scotsman*.

In addition to the Baxters, there was the Incorporation of Weavers of the Water of Leith recorded as early as 1728, but probably of much earlier date. Although the last of the weavers disappeared around 1880, before that there was a thriving industry in the weaving shops at the Damside and at the back of West Mill. The older women would wind the pirns whilst the younger women and men worked on the looms making linen and damask, assisted by the draw boys whose job it was to draw through the long warp threads in the loom. The actual weaving was not, however, the exclusive domain of the female population, as is evident by the short conversation which took place one morning in Princes Street between Rev. Dr John Cormack and John McDermid, both of whom had spent their early days at the looms:

> 'Well John, what web have you on the now?'
> 'Bird's Eye.'
> 'Man, that's a dreich job!'

The long hours of monotonous preparation and the intricate work required on the cloth may well have been dreich, but the work established a lifestyle which contributed greatly to the feeling of independence in the locality.

As the influence of the millers and the weavers began to decline, the village diversified into other trades and occupations. In the early nineteenth century there were distilleries at Sunbury and Miller Row, a limited brewing industry and also a small chemical works and several tanneries. The most famous tannery was situated at the north-west end of the old pedestrian bridge over the Water of Leith near Well Court. It was here that the Legget family operated for more than a century, treating the skins which exuded a pungent odour throughout that part of the Dean. Sheepskins were brought in from the slaughterhouses of Aberdeen, Dundee and Edinburgh, the wool being plucked by hand and despatched to the hosiery trade, whilst the skins were later sold to manufacturers of various leather goods. As recently as the 1960s Robert Legget & Sons, skinners, tanners and wool merchants, maintained an interesting link with the original village by giving their address as Water of Leith in the Edinburgh & Leith Post Office Directory.

Although Dean Village has lost several interesting buildings, nevertheless much of its old architecture remains. Perhaps the most dominant single influence is that of the Baxters, whose numerous carved panels appear on various buildings. Because of the precipitous position of the village and the meandering nature of its streets, there is a tendency for the visitor to wander and to investigate at random, rather than to follow a predetermined route. That is perhaps excusable because 'here, thrown together in artistic negligence are the features of a forgotten time'.

At the head of Bell's Brae, at its junction with the south end of Dean Bridge, there is a curious old building, Kirkbrae House, obviously constructed at different times. The older part is believed to be from the seventeenth century, whilst the newer part was built in 1892. At one time it was occupied as Stewart's Cab Office and has been frequently confused with the Tollhouse which stood nearby opposite Lynedoch Place. Around the turn of the century the cab proprietor James Stewart was a rather quaint, bearded gentleman with a top hat and a ruddy complexion who spent much of the day attending to the business at a pace in keeping with his advancing

Baxters' Arms on Kirkbrae House at the south-west corner of Dean Bridge:
In the sweat of thy face shalt thou eat bread, Gen. 3 verse 19, Anno Dom.
1619.
From a sketch by Dr. G.A. Fothergill.

years. He lived there from 1860 to 1917, when he died at the age of
eighty-seven. The building displays several interesting features
including a sundial, and pieces of decorated sculpture believed to
have come from Dean House. There is also a sculptured panel taken
from the ruins of Jericho, a range of old mill buildings which stood in
Miller Row immediately below Stewart's house. The upper corners
of the panel are occupied by cherubs' heads between which is a
circular garland with the sun in glory at the top and scrolls on each
side. Below is the inscription: 'In the sweat of thy face shalt thou eat
bread, Gen. 3 verse 19'. Further down Bell's Brae is Stewart's Coach
House, designed in 1881 by Thomas Moncur and beautifully
restored by Robert Matthew, Johnson-Marshall & Partners for their
own offices.

Descending further into the village, but before crossing the old
single-arch bridge over the Water of Leith, there is further evidence
of the Baxters' ancient presence. On the right, set into the masonry, a
panel bears two crossed peels (used for extracting hot loaves or cakes
from the ovens), and the date 1643. Beside them is a window lintel

with the words 'Blesit be God for al his Giftis'. On the opposite pavement, facing down towards the bridge, is a very old building which belonged originally to the Baxters but which was used as a chapel and mission hall for St. Mary's Episcopal Cathedral before being restored as flats by F.R. Stevenson in 1974. The sculptured panel bears the crossed peels, other heraldic devices, and the legend 'God's Providence is our Inheritans'. On the door lintel are the words 'God bless the Baxters of Edinburgh who bult this Hous 1675'. Opposite this building is the entrance to Miller Row, giving access to the Water of Leith Walkway from Dean to Stockbridge. On the right is the shell of the warehouse occupied by the famous theatrical costumery business, William Mutrie & Son Ltd, until the building was destroyed by fire in 1957. Further down on the left the three mill stones are all that remain of Lindsay's Mill, and on the right the site named 'Jericho' (the origin of which is unknown) is being redeveloped by the architects Robert Matthew, Johnson-Marshall and Partners. The last building, sheltering beneath the spans of the Dean Bridge, is the castellated and turreted headquarters of Oxylitre (Edinburgh) Ltd., built originally as a squash court in 1912 on the site of Mar's Mill.

Returning to the bridge at the foot of Bell's Brae, there is one other property on the left, Bell's Brae House, which should not go unnoticed, particularly in view of the effort expended in saving it from demolition. Originally built in the mid-seventeenth century, its early use is unknown, but in more recent times parts of it were used as a school and as a laundry before it fell into a serious state of neglect in 1946. It was bought by the artist Alexander Zyw, restored by Sir Basil Spence, and used by Zyw as his private house with his studio in the old joiner's shop nearby.

On the far side of Bell's Brae Bridge, with the Water of Leith lapping against its bulky walls, is West Mill, constructed in 1805 and restored as flats by Philip Cocker & Partners in 1973. On the left beyond the school is Well Court. This intriguing building was the brainchild of John Ritchie Findlay, philanthropic owner of *The Scotsman*, who had it built in 1884 as an experiment in model housing for working people. The architect was Sydney Mitchell, who designed it to be seen from Mr Findlay's own house in Rothesay Terrace nearby. Well Court contained a range of flats built in a square with an inner courtyard, a hall used as a club room for men and for social functions, and a gracious clock tower, apparently

West Mill, built in 1805 on the banks of the Water of Leith, and restored as flats by Philip Cocker & Partners, 1973.
Courtesy of Philip Cocker & Partners. Photograph by A.L. Hunter.

modelled on the original steeple of the Tron Kirk in the High Street. Today Well Court is mainly residential, but the hall is occupied by a firm of architects. The south-facing garden overlooking the Water of Leith has recently acquired, as an ornament, the font from the old Belford Church which was also designed by Sydney Mitchell.

At this point it is possible to leave the centre of the village by climbing the steep slope of Dean Path, past Dean Path Buildings and Convening Court. An alternative route, however, is to recross the Water of Leith by the pedestrian bridge constructed in 1889 by Robert Peddie & Co. of Tynecastle Ironworks. This is the site of the

Hawthorn Buildings, with half-timbered upper floor, designed by Dunn & Findlay, 1895, restored by Philip Cocker & Partners, 1978.
Photograph by A.L. Hunter.

old ford across the water where the causey stones on each side can still be seen. To the west of Well Court is the site of Legget's Tannery, now being developed for new housing. From a half-derelict corner nearby, one of the Dean's ghosts from the past looks on with cautious optimism — the painted sign of Burnside the family grocer, the last shop to close in the Dean Village. Across the bridge the yellow-ochre half-timbered houses of Hawthorn Buildings (1895) stand perched above the Water, and immediately ahead the High Green patiently awaits the imaginative redevelopment plans by T.M. Gray Associates. At the top of the High Green a narrow cobbled street, with a line of house frontages only, leads onto Belford Road. One of the most interesting buildings in Belford Road is at the top end near the junction with Bell's Brae. Across the door lintel is the name Drumsheugh Toll. The building was designed by George Washington Browne in 1891 in a free Tudor style. Closer examination of the external render provides an interesting clue as to its history. Imprinted on the pink exterior are thistles, eagles and the letter H repeated at various intervals. The explanation is that the house was once owned by Charles Martin Hardie R.S.A., the artist, and his Polish wife. Today part of the building is owned by the Waddell School of Musicians, whilst the upper floor is used by the Edinburgh Society of Musicians. The 'Dean Studio' gatepiers next door are all that remain of the Free Church by David Cousin (1844), converted to a studio in 1890 and demolished around 1952.

The visual impact of Dean Village is undoubtedly enhanced by its picturesque setting in the valley of the Water of Leith, but it also has a most interesting skyline. On the high ground to the west of the village the twin towers of Dean Education Centre rise elegantly above the surrounding woodland. Originally built as the Orphan Hospital in 1833, it was designed by Thomas Hamilton and cost £16,000. The large central block with a portico of columns is flanked by two projecting wings supporting the square, arched towers.

Maintaining a slightly lower profile on the west side of Belford Road is the former John Watson's School. It was designed in 1828 by William Burn, but other than the projecting central Greek Doric portico, the facade is rather plain and lacking in detail. Like the Orphan Hospital it was established by charitable funds. The original bequest was made in 1759 by John Watson, Writer to the Signet, whose accumulated funds eventually reached almost £100,000. A special Act of Parliament was obtained authorising the fund to be used for the maintenance and education of destitute children. Following closure of John Watson's School, the building was refurbished as the new home of the Scottish National Gallery of Modern Art.

School, Baths and Churches

No study of the Dean Village would be complete without reference to the village school, the baths and the various churches, each striving to enrich mind, body and soul, respectively.

Prior to 1873 the education of Dean children was largely under the direction of the Dean Free Church School which operated for many years in rather humble surroundings in various parts of the village. Like any school of its day, Dean was beset with problems relating to inadequate facilities and staff shortages, which in turn contributed to lack of discipline and in some cases to a low level of academic achievement. Following the class examinations in June 1872 all the 'passes' were put together whilst all the 'failures' were formed into a single class to be drilled after regular school hours. If any further confirmation were needed of the spartan approach to education, it was surely provided by the single entry in the headmaster's log for Christmas Day 1872 — 'work as usual'. Shortly thereafter the Edinburgh School Board took over responsibility for Dean School, and on 8th December 1875 the new primary school was opened, designed by the Board's architect, Robert Wilson. Although the new school provided excellent facilities, the reasons for non-attendance were as varied as before: several boys absent herding at Old Hallow Fair; more children of coachmen leave for the country with their employers; attendance irregular for want of boots and sufficient clothing; twelve cases of body vermin sent home by Nurse Maxton; fever rages at Grove Cottage, Brown's Court, Convening Court and Dean Path. Even as late as 1911 the feeding of 'necessitous children' was undertaken by the School in liaison with the Salvation Army.

Despite these early difficulties which did not, of course, apply to all families, Dean School continued to provide very sound education through the period of both World Wars. In 1939 when the main building was requisitioned by the War Office, classes were held in St. Mary's Cathedral Mission Hall in Bell's Brae. By 1961, however, the roll had been reduced to only thirty-seven pupils and the school was closed on 20th January 1961. The remaining children were transferred to Flora Stevenson's School.

The rather squat profile of Drumsheugh Baths, as seen from Belford Road, gives little indication of the full extent of this interesting building. Designed by John J. Burnet in 1882 with a distinctly Moorish flavour, it exploits fully the steeply falling ground to incorporate three separate floors to Bell's Brae below. Following the opening ceremony of the baths on 20th December 1884, *The Scotsman* carried a comprehensive review of the building and the facilities offered. Entry from Belford Road was by a spacious vestibule with the shoe-room and clubmaster's office adjoining. A wide fireproof staircase led to the middle floor, containing the plunge and other baths, one of the novelties being a Russian steam bath. The main portion of the building consisted of a large hall divided into nave and aisles by a series of round-headed arches carried on iron pillars with Moorish capitals. The swimming pool measured seventy by thirty-five feet, and the depth increased gradually from three feet to eight feet. Special attention was given to the Turkish baths, which were divided into four chambers opening into one another, the cooling room, the tepidarium, the outer calidarium, and the inner calidarium. All the Turkish baths were heated by steam coils, and lighting was by antique Turkish lamps. Acquisition of the site and construction of the baths cost £11,000 financed by a limited liability company, whose subscribers were the members of the Baths Club.

By 1974 much of the internal fabric of the building had fallen into a poor state of repair, and only piecemeal maintenance had been done on the exterior. The Edinburgh architects, the Bamber, Gray Partnership, were commissioned to make a full study of the building with particular regard to its status as a B-listed building. It was found that Burnet's original design, though aesthetically pleasing, was not constructed in materials which would last indefinitely in such humid conditions. A long-term plan, divided into three time phases, was drawn up and implemented, giving priority to the essential work required to arrest major areas of deterioration. The opportunity was also taken to modernise the heating and electrical installations to bring Drumsheugh once more into line with its long reputation as a prestigious private baths club.

For a few minutes on the afternoon of 15th May 1836, Edinburgh was plunged into an eerie darkness by an annular eclipse of the sun. The apparent juxtaposition of heavenly bodies did not, however, distract Dr Thomas Chalmers from the day's main business. By an interesting coincidence it was also the day planned for the opening of the first Dean Church in Dean Path near Queensferry Road. With characteristic zest, and slight alteration to his usual timetable, Dr Chalmers was able to preach the opening sermon in the morning and follow it with a lecture to the congregation on the subject of astronomy. To mark the occasion his sermon was later published with an engraving of the church showing the sun in eclipse in the background. These deepening shadows were not however to remain in the background for long: in 1843, at the Disruption, part of the congregation broke away and formed the new Dean Free Church, opened in November 1844 near the east end of Belford Road. The Free Church congregation worshipped at the old Belford Road building until 1889 when a fine new building designed by Sydney

Mitchell (who was also the architect of Well Court) was built further along Belford Road on the corner with Douglas Gardens. At the Union of the Free Church and the United Presbyterian Church in 1900 the congregation took the name Dean United Free Church, and at the Union with the Established Church it became Belford Church. In 1970 Belford Church united with Palmerston Place Church.

The original Dean Free Church near the east end of Belford Road was sold after 1889 and was destroyed by fire around 1952. Before the Second World War the building was used by the Makars Theatrical Company. Dean Church in Dean Path was demolished and replaced by another church for the same denomination in 1903.

In the 1880s one of Dean's oldest buildings, the Tolbooth, was adapted as a church hall and caretaker's flat for St Mary's Cathedral Mission. Founded by Alfred Griffiths, formerly the Precentor at St. Mary's Cathedral, the Mission supported in its heyday a well-trained, surpliced choir, a thriving Sunday School and a Youth Club, and a large number of communicants before, in the words of Hubert Fenwick, 'the indigenous folk moved to dreich housing estates on the outskirts of the City'. Unfortunately by 1976 the congregation had dwindled to the point where it was no longer possible to maintain the Mission Hall and it was therefore closed. It will always be remembered, however, by the older generation of Dean Village as a popular meeting place of people of all ages, and of many denominations.

There must be few churches in Edinburgh which have fixed to their front doors a prominent sign warning visitors of the high voltage cables concealed within its solid walls. Yet such is the case with the former Holy Trinity Church built in 1838 for the Scottish Episcopal Church, at the north end of Telford's Dean Bridge, and surrounded by a nineteenth-century graveyard and prehistoric burial chambers. For upwards of a century Holy Trinity Church was the home of one of the city's largest Episcopal congregations, but by 1942 the congregation had dwindled to a mere handful. At the end of the Second World War the building was used for a while by the German Church, but in the mid-1950s it was put up for sale, subject to certain important provisos. The vestry, the vaults and the graveyard were to be kept in the possession of the Episcopal Church, and the new owners were held bound to preserve the external appearance of the building and its clock tower, which had become such a prominent Edinburgh landmark.

Dean Village from the High Green, 1985, with Well Court on the left, Hawthorn Buildings on the right, and the tower of the former Holy Trinity Church on the skyline.

The new owner was the South of Scotland Electricity Board, which took the unusual step of buying the church in 1957 for use as a district sub-station for consumers in the West End of Edinburgh. Thus one of Edinburgh's most interesting examples of church architecture has been preserved, albeit in a rather unusual way; perhaps not for ever, but in the meantime at least the power and the glory belong to the South of Scotland Electricity Board.

CHAPTER 5

Duddingston

Whilst no one would suggest that Duddingston has remained completely unchanged over the years, nevertheless it has been more successful than many villages in retaining so much of its quiet rural setting. Dating from at least the twelfth century, Duddingston remained, until 1901, a distinct entity surprisingly uninfluenced by the proximity of the city. It owes its existence to the early church built on the shore of Duddingston Loch by the monks of Kelso around the year 1143. The name Duddingston also dates from that period through a variety of spellings to its present-day usage. With such a long unbroken history it would indeed be surprising if Duddingston had not often featured in Scottish history and in the development of Edinburgh.

En route to Duddingston Village

Although Duddingston can now be reached without difficulty by car from the east or the west, many people still prefer to approach it by walking through Holyrood Park on the low road beneath Samson's Ribs, or by descending Jacob's Ladder from Dunsapie Loch. Whichever route is chosen, there is every likelihood that Duddingston will be reached without serious mishap. Indeed it is unlikely that much thought will be given to those poor mortals from the pages of history whose journey along similar paths ended some way short of the safety of the village. Unlike the modern-day assailant, who threw his young bride to her death from the top of Salisbury Crags in an ill-fated attempt to secure the benefits of life assurance, Muschat's crime in 1720 was simply the work of an evil mind, apparently without motive, or remorse.

Nicol Muschat of Boghall was sentenced to death by the High Court of Justiciary in Edinburgh on 5th December 1720 for the murder of his young wife to whom he had been married for only a few months. Although Muschat had benefited from a good home background, his natural obstinacy became more apparent in later

Duddingston village from the slopes of Arthur's Seat, with the church in the centre and Bawsinch Nature Reserve beyond the Loch.
Courtesy of W.G. Cruikshank.

life, particularly after the death of his father. In August 1719 Muschat met Margaret Hall, the daughter of Adam Hall, a merchant in Edinburgh. They were married on 5th September, but it was soon obvious that he had no intention of conducting himself in the manner expected of a young husband. In collusion with another arch-villain, James Campbell of Burnbank, several unsuccessful attempts were made to dispose of poor hapless Maggie. Exasperated by his inability to bring the matter to a successful conclusion, Muschat resolved to complete the foul deed at last on 17th October 1720. With sickening insincerity he invited his wife out for a walk, saying that he wanted to take her to Duddingston for the evening. They entered Holyrood Park near the Palace, but instead of taking the usual route to Duddingston by the south, he turned left along the Duke's Walk where he suddenly set upon Margaret and, ignoring her pleas for clemency, cut her throat to the bone.

Despite the barbaric nature of the crime, the story of Nicol Muschat could well have been lost forever had it not been for his *Last Speech and Confession* published on numerous occasions and commented upon in detail by Ross MacDonald in his book, *Famous Edinburgh Crimes.* Not only was the crime given ample publicity in

101

the printed word, but on the site of the gruesome murder a cairn was erected to mark the sense of public outrage felt at the time. Although the original cairn was removed in the early part of the nineteenth century, its place in history was assured when Sir Walter Scott, in *The Heart of Midlothian*, chose Muschat's Cairn as the clandestine meeting place of Jeanie Deans and the outlaw George Robertson. Some time after the publication of *The Heart of Midlothian*, the cairn was re-erected as near as possible to the original site and can be seen today opposite the East Lodge at the Meadowbank entrance to Holyrood Park.

There are, of course, other ways of reaching Duddingston without encountering the awful memory of Muschat's Cairn. The other popular route, past Samson's Ribs, is by the Hangman's Crag, so called from yet another of Duddingston's ghosts from the past. In Edinburgh, in the reign of Charles II, there were several notorious executioners. One such gentleman came to accept the position of public executioner at a time when, in the words of Robert Chambers, 'this wretched office must have been unusually obnoxious to popular odium, on account of the frequent executions of innocent and religious men'. Little is known of the reluctant executioner, save that he found himself compelled to accept this degrading position, in preference to walking the streets as a penniless beggar. His early life had been an utter disaster, spent in profligacy, squandering the fortune which had come to him as the last surviving member of a reputable family, landowners near Melrose. There are two accounts of how he eventually came to grief. Motivated by the desire to live the life that might have been, or perhaps just to rid himself of the guilt which pervaded his conscience, this unfortunate man took it upon himself to be seen in the company of more respectable citizens. In the evening he would don the garb of a gentleman, and renewing the wit and manners that were his birthright, proceeded to Bruntsfield Links where he mingled with those who took pleasure at the golf. Unfortunately his guise was insufficient to mask his reputation, and on being identified by the crowd, he fled to Holyrood Park, hoping to find comfort in the solitude of its surroundings. Overcome by the folly of his ways and the loathing of his fellow men, he committed his future to the law of gravity, and was found the next day, quite dead, at the foot of a precipice, which to this day is known as the Hangman's Crag. The second account varies only as to the motive for ending this tragic life. It is said that the Hangman reached a point of utter despair and suicide, when his refusal to hang a fellow profligate was not accepted by the authorities. On completion of the execution in the Grassmarket, he came to Duddingston and concluded that his own life should also be forfeited.

Lest it be thought that the way to Duddingston is fraught with danger, consider first the reassuring tale of Half-Hangit Maggie, whose antics chilled the bones of her closest contemporaries. Margaret Dickson, a fishwife from Musselburgh, was condemned to death in 1724 for the murder of her illegitimate child. After the execution, when the coffin containing her body was being taken back to Musselburgh by her friends, they stopped at an Inn, near Duddingston, in order to take some refreshment. It is not recorded how long they had been at the Inn when they were suddenly startled to see the coffin lid open and Maggie sit bolt upright, apparently beginning to take notice of her surroundings. No doubt reeling from the effects of their spirituous encounter, the terrified men fled from the scene, but with curiosity getting the better of them, they returned to the tavern, to find that Maggie was alive and well. According to legend, she walked back to Musselburgh the following day, and having survived the sentence of the court, was left in peace to live out her 'second' life as Half-Hangit Maggie.

The Innocent Railway

The mishaps of Muschat, the Hangman and Half-Hangit Maggie en route to Duddingston were, however, in sharp contrast to the experience of those citizens of Edinburgh who entrusted the success of their annual vacation to the staff and rolling stock of the Innocent Railway. Built and designed by one of Edinburgh's most famous civil engineers, James Jardine, it was opened in July 1831 primarily to carry coal from the pits around Dalkeith to the goods yard at St. Leonard's in the Pleasance. As it was the first railway ever built in Edinburgh, technology was in its infancy, so much so that the Edinburgh & Dalkeith Railway Company, incorporated in 1826 to run the service, did not actually possess any trains. The motive power was the humble horse. Despite this inauspicious start, the Innocent Railway became a very successful commercial enterprise, particularly after a decision was taken to encourage passenger services as well as freight haulage. The main terminus was at St. Leonard's, where the Company boasted station buildings, a few score open waggons and a team of horses specially trained for the arduous task of hauling the fully laden waggons all the way to Newton, near Dalkeith. As the Company prospered, branch lines were extended into Dalkeith and to Fisherrow and Leith, until by 1840 the annual volume of traffic was 300,000 passengers and 120,000 tons of freight. Riding the Innocent Railway had become a popular attraction for the citizens of Edinburgh, who flocked in their hundreds to board one of the long, flat, open-topped waggons for a day in the country. The scene at the St. Leonard's terminus must have been one of great excitement, packed with all manner of passengers, each with their own predetermined level of expectation. Each waggon was capable of holding thirty to forty people, but as the rolling stock was of a fairly crude design, it was frequently necessary for the driver, before embarking on the journey, to re-arrange his consignment of passengers. Children had to be made safe; obese ladies needed maximum comfort; cantankerous old men scowled and sulked for most of the journey if asked to surrender their favourite seat; and Newhaven fishwives, for reasons which became more apparent in the confines of the tunnels, were banished to a waggon of their own. After the initial exertion of getting the rolling stock to move, the horses had a fairly easy section of about 200 yards to the head of the tunnel, where the waggons were coupled together before entering the down section. As the gradient was very steep, an ingenious system was adopted of counter-balancing a down train with an up train, linked to the two twenty-five horsepower static steam engines which did the hauling from the top of the tunnel. Once out of the tunnel, the train was safely on the meandering track to Duddingston and all stations east. It was this idyllic setting which inspired Dr Robert Chambers to refer to the innocence of the railway, an expression which eventually gave rise to its being known as the Innocent Railway. That concept of innocence was not, however, so readily apparent when it came to such practicalities as paying the full fare for the journey undertaken:

'How mony hae ye the day, Willie?'
'Thirty-nine and a half'
'How mony came off?'
'Six-twa Leith, and four Da'keith.'

A pause ensued whilst the wee man wi' the cap brought his full concentration to bear on the matter in hand:

> 'There's forty, Willie. How could ye say there's only thirty-nine and a half?'
> 'Ye're blind, man. D'ye no see the callant sitting ahint?'
> 'That a callant! He's as muckle a man as ever he'll be.'
> 'Nae matter. I only got twopence frae him. Canna ye mak haste man?'
> 'Weel, Weel — ca' him a half. Thirty-nine and a half. A' richt noo.'
> 'Gi'e me the book then.'

It was not, however, possible to maintain the innocence of the railway indefinitely, in a world of fast-changing technology. By 1844 the North British Railway Company had been formed, and in the following year it acquired the Edinburgh & Dalkeith. The old gauge of 4'6" was replaced by the new standard gauge, paving the way for more than a century of service using steam power. After closure of the line in 1968, little use was made of it until 1981 (150 years after its official opening), when work was commenced on the construction of the Innocent Cycleway/Footpath, opened on 16th August, 1982 by Mrs Lynda Chalker M.P., Parliamentary Under-Secretary of State for Transport.

Duddingston Village

The village of Duddingston, or Wester Duddingston, as it was once called, lies relatively undisturbed at the south-eastern entrance to Holyrood Park. Although Old Church Lane suffers intermittently from the unwelcome noise of commuter traffic, the old village street, known as The Causeway, retains its quiet seclusion. Indeed, the whole village exudes old-world charm, with high stone walls and country gardens. Its houses, though varied in size and style, cannot match in antiquity the old Kirk on the high ground beside the loch. In recent years a great deal of conservation work has been done on the Kirk by the congregation, and in the village by the Society for the Preservation of Duddingston Village, but the present-day appearance of the village — of ordered prosperity — obscures a history of less affluent times.

In the early part of the eighteenth century Duddingston was a large and populous village of five hundred inhabitants, many of whom earned a scant living by carrying coal from the pits nearby to stoke the lums of Auld Reekie a mile or so to the west. The journey, even by horseback, was slow and arduous, the only direct route being along a rough and twisting path which entered the village by the narrow lane at the side of what is now the Lodge to Holyrood Park. Whilst the men laboured at the coal, the women worked at the looms, weaving a coarse flax known as Duddingston hardings for which they were paid 4d a yard. Those wives and widows who were not skilled in weaving were employed in washing linen and carrying milk. The farmland around the village, although potentially fertile, suffered severely from lack of efficient husbandry and proper understanding of crop cultivation. In the year 1746, ploughmen at Duddingston earned £3 a year and maidservants half that sum. Many would live in conditions of near squalor in badly designed, damp and ruinous cottages with the most basic forms of hygiene and sanitation.

By 1800 Duddingston was beginning to see a considerable reduction in its indigenous population. The decline in the coal trade and in the number of active looms meant that there was less work available, and as the farm buildings were improved, many of the workers moved away from the village to be nearer to the land. Wages had doubled from the previous low of 1746, and the village was beginning to develop in other ways. There was a school with about forty pupils, and in 1821 a library with over two thousand volumes was opened for a subscription of 6d per quarter. A post office was opened around 1840 and a Friendly Society established in 1842. For an entry fee of 5/- (25p) and a quarterly contribution of 1/6d (7½p), members were entitled to receive 5/- per week for the first five weeks of indisposition and thereafter, whilst still unable to work, the sum of 1/- (5p) per week for life. With the enhanced social order came a prohibition on public begging, the poor, of whom there were still too many, being supported from Parochial Funds derived from church collections, charity, burying-ground charges and mortcloth dues. The minister, Rev. James MacFarlane, though openly tolerating no fewer than four alehouses, insisted in his contribution to the Statistical Account of Scotland of 1845 that the presence of so many hostelries was justified only on account of the visiting clientèle from Edinburgh. Perhaps the most famous hostelry was the Sheep Heid Inn, to which 'many opulent citizens resorted in the summer months to solace themselves on one of the ancient homely dishes of Scotland', i.e. sheep heads boiled or baked! It is said that James VI frequented the Sheep Heid and in 1580 presented an embellished ram's head and

On the right, the house in which Bonnie Prince Charlie resided before his victory against Sir John Cope at the Battle of Prestonpans, 1745. From Grant's *Old and New Edinburgh.*

horns which for many years adorned the bar area. The original silver-mounted ram's head had a small recess to hold snuff, but unfortunately it was lost some years ago, and has not been recovered. Although sheep's heads have not been boiled or baked or made into broth for many years, other interesting traditions survive at the Inn. The old skittle alley is still the popular venue of the Trotters' Club, originally composed of Edinburgh journalists, and the Burns Club still holds regular meetings on the premises.

Duddingston's greatest claim to royal patronage must, however, be its short but memorable association with Prince Charles Edward Stuart during his occupation of Edinburgh at the time of the ill-fated '45 Rebellion. Whilst his troops camped on the flat ground to the east of Duddingston, Bonnie Prince Charlie took up residence in the village on the night before his victory at the Battle of Prestonpans. The house in The Causeway from which the Prince planned the defeat of General Cope still stands, immortalised in the words of the famous Scottish song:

Cope sent a challenge frae Dunbar
Charlie meet me an' ye daur
And I'll learn you the art o' war
If you'll meet wi' me in the morning.

Duddingston Kirk, dating from the twelfth century, showing the original chancel and nave, and the square tower added slightly later.
From Grant's *Old and New Edinburgh*.

Although Prince Charlie's house lay derelict in recent years, it has now been tastefully restored under the guidance of the Society for the Preservation of Duddingston Village, and is again in residential use. The Society was formed on 23rd July 1959 at a meeting in the Kirk Hall under the Chairmanship of the Hon. Lord Cameron. Since then it has become increasingly involved in the wellbeing of the village in general. In fulfilling its prime object of preserving Duddingston, it has been successful in arresting the insidious progress of speculative building, and it has done much to provide street furniture in sympathy with the special character of the area.

Duddingston Kirk

Duddingston Kirk, built originally in the twelfth century on a wooded promontory overlooking the Loch, can claim to be one of the oldest churches in Scotland still in everyday use. The church was built by the monks of Kelso on land gifted by David I to the Abbot of Kelso, and the feu charters remained in favour of the Abbot until the Reformation, when the interest reverted to the Crown.

The church is basically of Norman architecture, although its structure and individual detail have suffered considerably over the years from a variety of causes, not all of which were unavoidable. Fortunately, in recent years, the building has been extensively renovated in keeping with its great antiquity. It is believed that the church originally consisted of the nave and chancel only, the square tower, with the distinctive parapet of pointed stones, having been added slightly later. It is generally considered, however, that the basic Norman plan was spoiled by the addition, in 1631, of the north transept, built to accommodate the family and tenants of Sir James Hamilton of Priestfield. The south wall is supported by a series of buttresses surmounted by conical finials (this feature also being repeated on the gables), but the original entrance, also on the south wall and near the tower, has been filled in. The small Norman windows between the buttresses have also been filled in, the interior of the church now being lit by two large stained glass windows. The most significant external feature, dating from Norman times, is the arch over the original doorway, carved in chevron orders. On the left-hand pillar there is a figure of Christ on the cross and also a figure, in less detail, believed to be of St. Peter about to cut off the ear of Malchus but more likely to be St. Paul holding high the Sword of the Spirit.

Internally, the only remaining Norman feature is the chancel arch, the outer order of which repeats the chevron design, while the inner order has an angle roll between V-shaped channelling. The position of the pulpit has varied from time to time over the years, sometimes in response to the liturgical requirements of the day. At the time of the Reformation, when the high altar and wrought iron work were removed, a wooden pulpit was erected on the south wall between the two stained glass windows. About 1800 a stone pulpit was built in the corner, on the right-hand side of the chancel arch, and remained in use until 1968 when a new oak pulpit was again built on the south wall. Although the Church is surrounded by a most interesting graveyard, several parishioners have been laid to rest within. Just within the chancel on the left there is the tomb of Alexander Thomson, who died on the 6th December, 1603. The place of burial is marked by a square slab set into the wall, bearing a shield with the arms of the Preston and Thomson families, the initials MATMP and the Latin motto 'Dies mortis, aeternae vitae natalis est fidelibus', translated 'the day of death is for believers the birthday of eternal

The Norman arch on the south-facing entrance now blocked up; on the left-hand column a figure of Christ on the cross.
From *The Book of the Trotters Club*, Volume 1.

life'. There is also a small marble plaque on the wall near the left-hand pillar of the Norman arch with the following inscription:

> In memory of St. John William Keith only son of the Lt. Col. W.H. Dick Cunnyngham V.C., commanding 2nd Batt. Gordon Highlanders, aged 10 years 10 months who was drowned in the sea at Philorth 1897 whilst heroically rescuing his friend the Master of Saltoun 'Greater love hath no man than this that a man lay down his life for his friends.' St. John XV 13

The tragedy experienced by the Dick Cunnyngham family is told with great feeling by W.G. Cruikshank in *Duddingston Kirk and Village.* Apparently the Dick Cunnyngham family and the Saltoun family were on holiday in Aberdeenshire. The two young boys were playing in the sea when Master Saltoun got into difficulties and was rescued by William Keith, though at the expense of his own life. Cruikshank relates that in comparatively recent years a very old gentleman called at Duddingston Manse and asked if he could spend a short time alone in the church. When he was about to leave he told the Minister that he had felt compelled to revisit Duddingston to give thanks to God for a long and useful life. 'You see,' he said, 'I am the Master of Saltoun.'

The history of Duddingston Kirk is not, however, confined to the church building alone. The manse, gardens, policies, and graveyard all have their own story to tell, and each their own place in history. At the entrance to the churchyard there are several typical features whose original function has long since fallen into disuse but which undoubtedly have been instrumental in moulding the character of the Scottish nation — alive or dead! To the left of the main entrance gate is a curious hexagonal-shaped building of two storeys, with lattice windows and a castellated roofline, now known as the Session House. In the early nineteenth century it did, however, have a much more sinister use: it was built to combat the lucrative trade in freshly buried corpses. The practice of body snatching, which grew up in response to the almost complete absence of suitable subjects for anatomical research, had created such apprehension in Edinburgh that even the grave held the promise of something less than eternal rest. At a time when dwindling numbers were not a problem affecting the living members of the congregation, the elders of the Kirk were required, in rotation, to mount guard from the upper storey of the watch tower, to ensure that some poor mortal just newly buried was not dug up and carried off by a gang of rapacious villains from the Auld Toon.

On the other side of the entrance gate are two equally interesting relics of the past, the loupin-on stane and the jougs collar. The first of these, a short flight of rough stone steps leading onto a small square platform is, by no coincidence, about the height of a horse's belly. Built at a time when parishioners arrived on horseback, this simple pile of stones was a source of comfort for old or obese gentlemen, and of modesty for the ladies, as they struggled to mount their horses for the journey back home.

The jougs collar was quite another matter: it brought neither comfort nor modesty to any man or woman, parishioner or otherwise. The iron collar and chain were designed to provide, in one simple session, the time-honoured elements of punishment — retribution, deterrence and reformation. The success of the collar was obviously a matter of conjecture, but the ignominy experienced by the culprit was not a matter about which there was any doubt. It was resorted to for a wide variety of moral offences including blasphemy, drunkenness, adultery, and failure to attend Sunday worship. The number of appearances varied with the severity of the offence, and the previous record of the culprit. Frequently the victim would be chained to the collar for a while, released and made to stand in sackcloth at the entrance to the church and then taken in, to sit on the stool of repentance to ask God's forgiveness. Those guilty of the pleasures of the flesh were dealt with most severely, as witnessed by the following account in the old records:

> 14. OCTOBER 1660 The which day, Susan Douglas adulteress with David Howeyson, adulterer, being cited before the Session, confessed upon their knees and besought the Lord to pardon them of that great sin. The Session ordained them to begin their public repentance at the next Lord's Day and to stand at the Church door in sackcloth frae the second bell to the last, after being released from the Joug Collar and thence enter the Church in sackcloth.

The picture of Susan and David, together on seventeen consecutive Sundays, dressed in sackcloth, and left alone in one another's company whilst the congregation was at prayer in the church, might have conveyed the impression to some that the Kirk Session had either a curious degree of naivety or an unshakable belief in the deterrent value of punishment!

The manse at Duddingston lies in very extensive grounds with a southerly aspect, overlooking the Loch and sheltered from the north wind, and prying eyes, by a high stone wall running the whole length of Church Lane. The manse garden is beautifully wooded and leads on, through a small wooden door near the Session House, to a second garden, which runs down to the water's edge. Until comparatively recently this piece of land was completely derelict, but in the 1960s its botanical potential was realised by Dr Andrew Neil and his wife Dr Nancy Neil, who have, since then, spent a great deal of time and effort bringing the garden to maturity. In the biting wind of a late December afternoon, when the icy waters of the Loch barely reflect the dying sun, there is yet an awareness of its great potential and its natural beauty; but it is not until the fullness of the summer months that the true significance of the garden can be realised, and its serenity appreciated.

In the year 1678, however, that serenity may well have been shattered by the sound of headstones being heaved over the churchyard wall, because at that time the Kirk Session, in an unprecedented quest for economy, 'ordaint that nae headstane shall be set up in the Kirkyard without libertie given, asked and granted, and to pay into the box for such headstane fyve merks, Scots; and such as have already set up stanes, and have not as yet satisfied or obtained the session's libertie therefor, is ordainet to be removed and turned over the kirkyard dyke'. Despite the seventeenth-century purge of the stones and the nineteenth-century snatching of the bodies, the present-day appearance of the churchyard, with its ancient stones and epitaphs, suggests that at least those which survive now enjoy security of tenure. Among those buried in the churchyard are many eminent citizens: Archibald Bennet, Secretary of the Bank of Scotland; John Thomson, Minister at Duddingston, 1805–1840; and Patrick Haldane of Gleneagles. The obelisks, the urns and the slabs of polished marble convey, without emotion, in stone, cold and carved, the demise of national figures and the passage of national events, but tucked away in a grassy corner there is one simple little Celtic cross which speaks with a silent voice: WEE JIM — nothing more, no date, no age, no family name — but whoever he was and whenever he died, he would, no doubt, be missed just the same by those who loved him.

Ministers at Duddingston

Duddingston Kirk has an accurate record of all its ministers from the time of the Reformation to the present day except for the years 1691–1693 when no permanent minister was appointed. Among these stalwart men of the cloth were a few whose personal achievements extended well beyond the normal demands of a small rural parish. Unfortunately these achievements were not, in every case, viewed with favour by the church hierarchy.

Robert Montoith was the youngest son of Alexander Monteith, a fisherman who spent his days quietly tending his nets on the Forth, near Stirling. Robert, however, graduated M.A. at Edinburgh

University in 1621, and after an unsuccessful nomination as Professor of Divinity he succeeded in obtaining orders from Archbishop Spottiswood which enabled him to be presented to Duddingston in 1630. Shortly after his appointment, however, he seems to have developed an illicit association with the wife of an influential landowner nearby. In *Walks near Edinburgh*, Margaret Warrender describes the scene: 'in an hour of idleness the flame of an absorbing passion was lit in his breast by the beautiful eyes of Lady Hamilton of Priestfield, and, in the soft summer twilight, Monteith would unmoor the boat which lay hidden in the deep shadows below the church, and steal noiselessly across the loch to where his love was waiting'. Silent he may have been: unnoticed he was not. Despite the advantage of the prevailing wind on the return journey, Monteith seemed to row with less vigour, increasing greatly the time taken and the chances of being observed by one of his nocturnal parishioners. His future ebbed as the gossip flowed. Denied by his status the option of seventeen Sundays in the jougs collar, Monteith was deposed by the Privy Council, and fled the country, attributing his hasty retreat 'to the action of the extreme presbyterian party on account of his own episcopal leanings'. Monteith was, however, a brilliant and resourceful man with a modicum of guile and an inborn capacity for survival. He went to Paris and joined the Catholic Church, obtaining favour with Cardinal Richelieu by claiming pedigree through the old Scottish family of Monteith. On being asked which branch of the family he came from, it is said that the bold Monteith, recalling his father's occupation as a fisherman, replied 'the Monteiths of Salmonnet', whereupon the Cardinal, though not recognising the branch of the family, announced that he was prepared to accept the reference. Whether or not the story is true, the *Biographical History of the Scottish Nation* does maintain that Monteith was the son of an old and respectable family and that there was once a place in Stirlingshire named Salmonet. During Monteith's stay in France he made considerable progress in the church and was appointed one of the canons of Notre Dame in Paris by Cardinal de Retz. He also devoted much of his life to historical research and wrote a number of works of which the most famous was probably his *Histoire des Troubles de la Grande Bretagne,* but he was never pardoned for his early indiscretion and never returned to Duddingston. His exact date of death is not known but is believed to have been some time between 1652 and 1660.

Early in the eighteenth century Duddingston was visited by another man of letters, the Rev. David Malcolm, who served the church from 1705 to 1743. Although Malcolm's early years at Duddingston were characterised by 'learning, honesty, moderation, good nature and a benevolent disposition', his later years became progressively dominated by his all-consuming passion for philology. Gaelic dictionaries and tracing languages to their fountainhead were no doubt laudable pursuits in the rarefied atmosphere of the universities, but in 1740 a poor Scottish parish like Duddingston required someone with his feet more firmly on the ground. Matters came to a head when he decided to go off to London for two years to continue his studies, without making any provision for fulfilling his pastoral duties. On his ignoring the Presbytery's decision to call him home, he was deposed on 24th March 1742 and left to continue his literary career for the remainder of his days. These days were, however, numbered, because on 7th February 1748 he received another call home — which proved to be his last.

If Duddingston was dogged by the writer's pen, at least it did not bristle at the artist's brush, or at any rate not whilst in the able hand of the Rev. John Thomson, who took up the incumbency in 1805, exactly one hundred years after Rev. David Malcolm. One of his early successes was to persuade several up-and-coming young men to become elders in the church, one of whom, Walter Scott, Advocate, was already well on his way to becoming Scotland's leading poet and novelist.

John Thomson was a son of the manse, his father being the Rev. Thomas Thomson of Dailly in Ayrshire, who decided at a very early stage in John's life that he should follow in his father's footsteps and become a preacher. John, however, had other ideas, which he persisted in demonstrating with the aid of a pencil, an odd scrap of paper and a pawky sense of humour. Despite lengthy and impassioned pleas to allow his son to become an artist, Rev. Thomas Thomson would not be moved. Temporarily submitting to the premise that fathers 'have flinty hearts, no tears can move them', young John prepared himself for entry to the ministry. During his studies at Edinburgh University, however, he had ample opportunity to further his knowledge of the arts, including a short period of instruction under one of the foremost artists of the day, Alexander Nasmyth. In 1800 Rev. Thomas Thomson died, and at the very early age of twenty-one John was appointed minister at Dailly, in

Rev. John Thomson, distinguished landscape painter and minister at Duddingston, 1805 — 1840.
From *Biographical History of the Scottish Nation.*

succession to his father. The appointment may well have fulfilled his father's dying wish, but for John it was something less than the fulfilment of his own ambitions. A country parish in Ayrshire in 1800 was neither spiritually, nor intellectually, ready to accept an artist as a minister. Still less was it able to accept a minister with a sense of humour, particularly when so engagingly in rapport with his artistic ability. To enter the nineteenth century led, in matters spiritual, by a cartoonist was considered ungodly. His incumbency at Dailly was a short one, and in 1805 he transferred to Duddingston. Despite his strong predilection for the arts, he did not at any time neglect his parish either at Dailly or at Duddingston, but it was at Duddingston that he was able to combine his two great interests in life. Surrounded by the magnificent natural beauty of the Loch and Holyrood Park, he settled into building up the parish whilst enjoying the manse as a centre of cultural conviviality. The demands upon his time were, of course, considerable, and would frequently pose the question whether to canvass the needs of his flock, or flock to the needs of his canvas! He was well equipped to chart a path between these rival claims. That path ran down to the bottom of the manse garden, where he had adapted the upper storey of the stone tower into a comfortable studio overlooking the water. With a weather eye on the Loch, and conscious of the need to obey all the Commandments, he named his studio 'Edinburgh' which enabled him, with a clear conscience, to leave a note with his housekeeper explaining that if any parishioners called, they were to be told that the Minister was not available as he had gone to 'Edinburgh'. As the years went by, Rev. John Thomson became a celebrated painter of landscapes and Scottish castles, the sale of his pictures producing for him an income far in excess of his stipend. As well as having a reputation as an artist, he was an accomplished musician and, with the assistance of his wife and family, was able to maintain a high standard of entertainment for the numerous guests at the manse. After an eventful and rewarding life he died in 1840 at the manse, with his bed drawn up to the window to enable him to watch, for the last time, the sun setting across his beloved Duddingston.

In addition to its celebrities, of course, Duddingston, like any other church, has been served by a long line of able clergymen whose quiet lives of dedication and prayer have not earned them a page in history. To them, without exception, Duddingston owes its very existence.

Duddingston Loch and Bawsinch

It is many years since William Baird the historian overheard a lady visitor assert that if Duddingston Loch were only a little more modest, it would not call itself a loch at all but merely a pond. Whether it was that her level of expectation was too high, or that the level of the water was unexpectedly low, will never really be known, but at least the position was better than might have been the case had a civic plan of 1824 been put into effect. The idea then was to drain the Loch completely and pipe the springs to increase the supply of fresh water needed for Edinburgh. Fortunately for succeeding generations of curlers, skaters and wildlife enthusiasts the plan was never implemented.

David B. Smith, in his recent book entitled *Curling: an Illustrated History*, traces in fascinating detail the history of curling throughout the world, and devotes several pages of his impressive work to the early days of the game at Duddingston. Although curling existed at Duddingston before 1795, it was not until that year that a proper club was formed, the Duddingston Curling Society, with rules and regulations to govern its affairs. To begin with, the Society consisted mainly of local men, but by 1800 it had begun to attract several members from Edinburgh, one of whom, James Millar, Advocate, assisted in establishing the early rules of the game, and was also responsible for the Latin motto adopted by the Society: *Sic Scoti: alii non aeque felices* — This is the way the Scots play: the rest of the world isn't half so lucky. In the ensuing years the Society grew in strength and influence, special badges being struck in 1802 bearing the motto, and depicting curlers on the ice at Duddingston with Duddingston Kirk in the background, and on the reverse side the inscription 'Duddingston Curling Society Instituted 17th January 1795'. A code of curling laws devised and approved by the Society on 6th January 1804 was incorporated in the Lochmaben Curling Society rules in 1829, and contributed substantially to the first rules of the Grand Caledonian Curling Club. This scholarly interest in the game was given further weight when Rev. John Ramsay was admitted in 1808; he produced, in 1811, the first book on curling, entitled *An Account of the Game of Curling*. It is likely, however, that around this time some of the local members may have thought that the Society had changed out of all recognition from its original concept. Among its fifty-two members were two baronets, a marquis, a university principal, a professor and, later, Alexander Boswell, son of James Boswell the biographer, Sir George Clerk of Penicuik, James Hogg the Ettrick Shepherd, and Lord Cockburn, Solicitor General for Scotland. By 1823 the old curling house was in no condition to welcome such an august section of the community, and therefore a decision was taken to commission a new stone structure designed by the eminent architect W.H. Playfair. From then the membership increased to more than 200, but in the middle of the

Curlers at Duddingston Loch, c.1906, on a shallow water pond constructed on the south bank of the Loch.
Courtesy of David B. Smith.

Curling Medal, 1809, given to the victor by the Duddingston Curling Society, founded 1795.
Courtesy of David B. Smith.

nineteenth century the Society experienced a dramatic loss of prestige. Many of the Edinburgh members had transferred to Coates Curling Club, much nearer to their New Town residences; the Society declined rapidly, and the last Minute was recorded on 2nd March 1853.

In 1796, the year following the founding of the Duddingston Curling Society, the Old Statistical Account of Scotland drew attention to the fact that an interesting find of Roman spears and javelins had been made at Duddingston Loch a few years previously. The discovery was actually made in 1778 by workmen dredging for marl in the Loch, and although the weapons were, for long, believed to be of Roman origin, advances in archaeological expertise since then have shown beyond doubt that the artefacts date from the late Bronze Age (8th century B.C.). At the time of the find, the Loch was owned by Sir Alexander Dick, who appears to have been sufficiently public-spirited to make a gift in 1781 of most of the items to the embryonic Museum of the Society of Antiquaries of Scotland (now the National Museum of Antiquities of Scotland). These were in fact the first objects to be given to the Society, which was founded in 1780 by David, 11th Earl of Buchan. The Duddingston find was of considerable importance, consisting of a ring from a cauldron, thirty-two fragments of swords, the point of a rapier, part of a small dagger or knife, and fragments of fourteen spearheads, all of bronze. Unfortunately not all the items were deposited in the Museum, with the result that some have since been lost, or at any rate remain untraced.

The reedy waters of Duddingston Loch are the natural habitat of a wide variety of fish, wildfowl and other birds. It was not until 1925, however, that the area was officially designated Duddingston Bird Sanctuary after the Loch and its environs had been gifted to the nation by William Haggerston Askey of Ladykirk. Today, the Loch and Sanctuary come under the administration of the Scottish Development Department, who work in close liaison with the Scottish Wildlife Trust in matters of everyday management of this important reserve.

Since its inception in 1925 a great many species of birds have been recorded including the bittern in 1955, the peregrine falcon in 1956, and the golden oriole in 1978, and in the last few years herons have

Duddingston Village, 1985, from Old Church Lane, looking down The Causeway to the Sheep Heid Inn.
Photograph by Phyllis Margaret Cant.

started to nest. By far the most spectacular visitors are, however, the large flock of pochard which frequent the Loch during the winter months before flying off to the Scandinavian countries and Russia during the summer months. Their habit of roosting on the Loch at Duddingston by day and feeding on the Forth by night continued for several years until the City built the Seafield Sewage Works and deprived the birds of the nutrients of a rich feeding ground. This unfortunately had the effect of reducing the size of the flock. On the Loch there is also a resident flock of greylag geese, started in 1961 with only thirteen birds. There have, of course, been problems and disappointments from time to time, notably in maintaining an adequate volume of algae-free water. The Loch is fed by spring water only, but there is an artificial channel linking it to the Braid Burn near the old bridge of the Innocent Railway at Duddingston Station. This channel normally acts as an outflow from the Loch, but when the Braid Burn is in spate the direction of flow in the channel is automatically reversed and the excess water passes into the Loch. From time to time the Loch has been subject to an algal bloom, and in 1967 it reached catastrophic proportions. When the bloom

A village view. Springtime at Duddingston in the shelter of Arthur's Seat. Photograph by Phyllis Margaret Cant.

suddenly decayed, oxygen was taken up from the water in the decaying process, with the result that all the fish died of oxygen starvation. On that occasion re-stocking was done with roach and tench, and steps were taken to prevent a recurrence of the problem.

Shortly after the algal bloom problem had been solved, the Sanctuary came under threat from yet another source. To the south of the Loch, the triangular piece of ground known as Bawsinch had lain waste for many years, but in 1969 a proposal was put forward to use it for housing development. Following an enquiry, the plan was abandoned, and on 11th November 1971 Bawsinch was bought by the Scottish Wildlife Trust for £10,000 to create the Bawsinch Nature Reserve. Although the primary object of acquiring the ground was to provide a buffer zone for Duddingston Bird Sanctuary, it was soon obvious that Bawsinch had great potential of its own in providing additional habitat for a wide variety of wildlife. The land was in very poor condition, littered with abandoned property and the remains of derelict buildings, but with the assistance of Lothian Conservation Corps the area was cleared and planting began in 1973. Planting was done in natural groups to include trees and shrubs native to Scotland and other parts of Britain, as well as a few naturalised species. To extend the variety of habitat, artificial ponds were dug and later named Matthew, Mark, Luke and John. Following the death in 1982 of Peter Gunn, a lifelong member of the Edinburgh Natural History Society, a bequest was made to fund the building of a much larger pond, now known as the Gunn Loch. Its construction is still in its infancy, but already it shows great potential with two small islands varying in size and layout to create different habitats.

Additional grazing for water fowl has also been created by clearing land in the centre of Bawsinch and having it sown with grass seed. The resulting Meadow, now known as Goose Green, provides ideal grazing for greylag geese, mallard, grey partridges and a pair of pheasants. The Connell Hide was also constructed in recent years to provide shelter and a focal point for ornithologists to study the wildlife on the Loch and in the reed beds nearby. It is skilfully camouflaged and yet roomy enough to take visiting groups of at least twenty people.

CHAPTER 6

Newcraighall

The Edinburgh International Festival has taken the name of Edinburgh to almost every corner of the globe, but it falls to Newcraighall to carry the story of one of Edinburgh's villages to the Berlin Film Festival. It is no less ironical that this tiny mining community on the city's eastern boundary should be so little known by many of Edinburgh's literary and historical associations. In *Film Review 1973/74* Bill Douglas is described as 'the first autobiographer in celluloid', a description which takes on a special significance in his film trilogy based on his early traumatic life at Newcraighall. The opening film is *My Childhood,* made in 1972, followed by *My Ain Folk* in 1973, and completed with *My Way Home* in 1978. The trilogy is essentially personal, and by Douglas's own admission can in no way reflect the thoughts and experiences of the hard-working and good-hearted folk who live there. Nevertheless, the films, shot on location at Newcraighall, represent a very significant contribution to the history of the village.

Even in fairly recent times Newcraighall has remained quite detached from the city on account of both its geographical position and its independent mining traditions. On the other hand, closure of the pit in 1968, and the complete rebuilding of most of its houses, has meant that these traditions are very much less obvious than they were.

Coalmining and its Traditions

It is impossible to say exactly when coal was first mined in Scotland, but there are several early records which show that it was an important commodity as far back as the thirteenth century. The monks of Holyrood Abbey were granted a charter to work coal in the year 1200, and the monks at Newbattle Abbey had similar powers in 1210. During a visit to the Lothians around 1435, Aeneas Sylvius Piccolomini (later Pope Pius II) recorded that 'a sulphurous stone dug from the earth is used by the people as fuel'. The coal was dug

Aerial view of Newcraighall from the north-east with Wanton Walls farm steadings in the foreground and the rows of miners' houses in the centre. Courtesy of Newcraighall Primary School.

out in the most elementary manner, usually from the sides of a valley where the coal strata emerged naturally. Later, bell-pits were introduced, the vertical shaft being dug down to the nearest seam and opened out at the bottom to give a wider area from which to cut the coal. All these schemes, however, relied for their success on a large labour force, the men cutting the coal at the face while the women and children transported it in baskets on their backs. Not only was the work arduous, but the social status of the miner was reduced to that of a mere slave. By an Act of 1606, passed by the Scottish Parliament, a system of serfdom was introduced which gave the owner of a mine the right to the services of the miners and their families during their entire working life. Although the Act was repealed by subsequent legislation in 1775 and 1799, it was not until 1842 that an Act was passed prohibiting the employment in mines of all females and boys under ten. Even as late as 1842 the Commission of Enquiry into the Employment and Condition of Children in the Mines was able to

Water-Gin: a machine formerly used for raising coal from shallow shafts. Courtesy of the National Coal Board, Scottish Division.

record some very disturbing evidence in and around the Lothian coalmines:

> Alexander Gray (10 years) pump boy at Newcraighall 'I pump out water in the bottom of the pit to keep the men's rooms dry. I am obliged to pump fast or the water would cover me. I ran away a few weeks ago as the water came up so fast that I could not pump fast enough. I have no meal during the day.'

The 'rooms' which young Alexander struggled all day to keep dry were not, of course, rooms in the normal sense. One of the earliest systems of coalmining, which still existed in the early twentieth century, was the 'stoop and room' method. The 'stoops' were pillars of coal left uncut, at intervals of a few feet to support the roof, and the 'rooms' were the divisions into which the coal face was divided by the presence of the stoops. The dangers of coalmining, and the need to work in very close physical contact with one another, ensured that rooms were worked by the same family, or at least with a fellow miner with whom there was a bond of tolerance if not friendship. The room system also had significant financial implications for the miners: to be allocated a room with poor coal was bad enough, but if it was also very far from the main shaft, a disproportionate amount of time was used by the putters in taking away the full hutches and bringing back the empty ones. Each hutch was marked with a pin or token to denote the room from which the coal was cut, so that the check weighmen at the top of the shaft could keep a tally on the weight of coal cut by each room. The pins or tokens were essentially practical, such as a bent nail attached to the hutch, and immediately identifiable by the weighmen, one of whom was appointed by the Union and the other by the pit management. A further consequence of the pin system was of course that the empties came round in strict rotation, and if a man was not ready or willing to fill his hutch, he had to wait for the full cycle to come round again. To miss the 'ben' had an immediate effect on a man's weekly wage.

People who have spent all their working lives on the earth's surface cannot fully appreciate the dangers associated with mining, particularly in the early days when mine owners did not regard safety as a serious responsibility. Even now, with the advent of fully mechanised pits, vigilance is still required to combat the three basic dangers: the constant threat of roof falls; the pervasive presence of water; and the build up of noxious and explosive gases. The way these dangers have been tackled over the years is the story of coalmining itself.

It is difficult to imagine anything more frightening than working at the coal face when a roof fall occurs between the place of work and the bottom of the pit shaft. The idea of being entombed in the bowels of the earth, miles from the shaft, operates as a constant reminder that safety measures must be continually reviewed. When the stoop and room method was in its infancy, support of the upper strata was very haphazard, but as the mines became deeper and the roads longer, the use of wooden props, and later hydraulic props, became much more important. The constant danger was from soft roof strata, such as blaes.

Whilst a rock fall is usually sudden and unexpected, by contrast flooding is often slow and insidious. In the early days of mining, failure to keep mines free of water was one of the main reasons for closure before all the coal had been worked. At the beginning of the eighteenth century considerable progress was made in pumping water in the larger pits which could afford to instal and maintain one of Thomas Newcomen's famous atmospheric steam engines. These operated on the principle of creating a vacuum by condensing steam on one side of the piston and allowing normal atmospheric pressure to force the other end of the piston to drive the rods. The Newcomen engine was later replaced by a more efficient engine perfected by James Watt.

Falls of rock and floods of water, although dangerous, can at least be seen and heard and understood, but methane gas is quite another problem: it cannot be seen, and for many years it could not be understood either. In Scotland in the Middle Ages the popular belief was that it was the Deil himself who sent this noxious gas to repel anyone minded to have a wee keek at the life of eternal damnation! The idea is perhaps less flippant than might at first be thought. While coal mines remained in the upper strata, the biggest problem was black damp, a non-poisonous, non-inflammable gas produced by oxidation. It had the effect of starving the mine of oxygen but could be dispersed by installing furnaces in mines with two shafts — one to draw fresh air in and the other to drive the foul air out. But as the miners dug deeper in search of new seams, a new and potentially more dangerous gas was found — methane, or fire damp as it was commonly known. Methane gas evolves from the decay of buried vegetation and is found in dangerous quantities in most Scottish pits. It is colourless, usually odourless and, being lighter than air, tends to be suspended in pockets near roof level. Its danger pattern is also unusual. At a 5% mixture with air there is a danger of explosion, and this increases rapidly until the mixture is 9% methane. The danger then reduces as the mixture increases until, at 15%, the risk of explosion disappears altogether. The explanation for this is that under 5% there is insufficient gas to cause an explosion and over 15% there is insufficient oxygen to support ignition. While the early scientists struggled to understand the nature of methane gas, the miners displayed remarkable courage in respecting its reputation. Each working day was started with 'firing the damp': a miner would soak his clothing in water and enter the working areas with a lighted candle to burn off the explosive gas which had collected since the last shift. Twin shaft pits, made compulsory in 1862 following the Hartley

Newcraighall Mine Rescue Team, winners of the First Cup, National Coal Board Area Competition, 1950.
Courtesy of J. McFarlane.

Disaster in Northumberland, improved ventilation, but the furnaces themselves were a source of possible ignition unless they were correctly sealed to prevent contact with the gas. The last but by no means least dangerous gas is white damp or carbon monoxide, frequently found in mines after an explosion, or during a heating caused by rock pressure. Odourless, colourless and deadly poisonous, it would have claimed the lives of many more miners but for the uncanny, but timely, agitations of the resident canaries and mice.

One of the main sources of accidental ignition was, of course, the miner's own light. The problem was to create a sufficiently strong flame to give the necessary illumination without allowing the flame to escape and ignite the mine gases. This problem was studied in the latter half of the eighteenth century by eminent scientists of the day, Dr Clancy, George Stephenson, and Sir Humphrey Davy. Although the idea behind the safety lamp was well understood by Clancy and Stephenson, it was Davy who, in 1815, came up with a simple but effective method of protecting the naked light with wire gauze, thus enabling the flame to breathe without escaping and causing an explosion.

The introduction of steam power and later electric power into the mines transformed the early work methods in a way which would have seemed impossible in the days when women and children toiled at lifting the coal manually from the labyrinth of rooms. Although four-wheeled hutches, drawn by ponies, were introduced in the middle of the eighteenth century, human power was still in existence after 1842. Another early innovation was dependent for its success on the physical gradient of the coal seam. It operated by gravity in rise workings as distinct from dip workings. Provided the seam ran uphill from the main shaft, the loaded hutches would run by gravity. The momentum of the down run was sufficient to pull the empty hutches up on the other track. At the beginning of the nineteenth century the introduction of steam power more than doubled the hauling and winding capacity of most mines, and the twentieth century saw the use of electric power applied to automatic coal cutting equipment, hauling, winding and ventilation.

The technical aspects of coalmining are described in *A Short History of the Scottish Coalmining Industry,* published in 1958 by the Scottish Division of the National Coal Board. Other books, rich in anecdote, like *Blawearie,* first published in 1887, provide authentic descriptions of the social background of early mining life in the Lothians. The author of *Blawearie,* Peter McNeill, himself a miner, provides a wealth of detail in his documentary novel, as he follows the everyday life of miners at work. His account of a miner's widow striving to raise a family of four boys, all employed in the pits, is a masterpiece of social realism. Early morning rising was a daily struggle with few compensations:

'Tammie, Jamie, Sandie, Willie; will ye
ryse, an' be hanged t' ye?'
Another brief lull in the story, and then —
'Tammie, are ye snorin' aye yet, efter a'
my cryin' t' ye?'
'Ay, mother, ay.'
'Jamie, are ye lyin' mochin? My sang but ye
can act the auld man fine — '
'Haud yer tongue, wuman, and no bother folk.'
'Sandie, I'm share ye've no been sleepin' a' this time.'
'Another five minutes, mother, another five minutes.'
'Willie, my chick, what's the matter wi' you this morning?'
'I canna get my een tae open; I'm aye sleepin' yet I think.'

On a freezing cold morning the almost inevitable conflict arose about whose pit claes were at the warmest side of the fire. Once that was decided on a first come first served basis there was a further argument about who should claim the best pair of hoggars and fit-clouts. Hoggars were cut from old stockings and worn round the ankles to prevent wet and muddy trousers flapping against the bare leg and causing an irritation. Fit-clouts, on the other hand, were on the feet. They were made from small pieces of cloth about eight inches square and wrapped round the toes to give some protection against movement in the rigid pit boots, but they were not always popular owing to the need for frequent adjustment during the working day. A fit-clout, warm and dry at the start of the day, could become rumpled and sweaty long before dinner time.

The bosses were a natural target for derisory comment:

'What think ye o' 'im?'
'Awfu' smell o' snuff and whisky.'
'He looks gey stupid but he may
be clever fur a' that.'

Maintaining discipline and keeping control over such a robust group of men was no easy matter, particularly as most disputes were settled by lights out and a fight with oily caps! At one such mêlée, concluded by the inevitable intervention of the overseer, the explanation and remedy ran as follows:

'We had been sleepin', gude kens hoo
long, and were awoke, deil kens hoo,
and have made our way here and are
quite transmogrified to find everything
so outrageously transformed, but wi'
a' deference to you, sir; as there are
nae banes broken, I think if ye wad jist
flee up the shaft again, as lichtly as ye
seemed to flee doon, we'll soon put
everything in order.'

As the overseer returned to the main shaft, he would be more than relieved to observe 'the wisp' — a piece of twisted straw dropped down from the pithead to signify the end of the day's work.

Although *Blawearie* is a fascinating novel, it dealt primarily with mining practices up to the year 1850 and cannot, therefore, be considered accurate in relation to work practices since that date. The known dangers of roof collapse, water and gas constantly occupy the minds of responsible people engaged in the industry, and Parliament has passed an abundance of Acts and Regulations designed to ensure that, as far as is humanly possible, a mine is made safe for those who work in it.

The Klondyke Pit at Newcraighall

The history of coalmining at Newcraighall is accurately recorded from 1897, when an incline shaft was opened by the Niddrie and Benhar Colliery Company Ltd. The pit was named 'The Klondyke' after the great gold rush of 1896, a name which has been perpetuated in the street names of the new village. It is clear, however, that there was a coalmining industry in the neighbourhood long before 1897. The records show that land at Newcraighall was acquired by Niddrie Colliery Company in 1874 and by Benhar Colliery Company in 1876. In addition to this, in the National Coal Board's *Short History of the Scottish Coalmining Industry* a copy of an old engraving is reproduced showing the great steam pumping-engine built by Claud Girdwood & Co., Glasgow, and erected at Newcraighall Colliery in 1828. The Board acknowledge that nothing now remains of the pumping-engine, but from the engraving it would appear to have been the largest of its type in Scotland.

In 1910 Niddrie and Benhar sunk a vertical shaft sixteen feet in diameter and almost a thousand feet in depth which increased enormously the amount of coal extracted. Winding equipment was supplied by a steam-powered engine of two 25-inch bore cylinders driving a 14-foot diameter cable drum made in 1903 by Grant Ritchie of Kilmarnock. It was built originally for Niddrie and Benhar who ordered it for their hopeful new pit, Olive Bank Colliery, sunk in 1897 but closed in 1907 after being plagued by water and geological problems. At Newcraighall, extraction was originally by the stoop and room method, but this was later replaced by the long wall method. Around 1900 a large quantity of high-grade coal was being extracted for use in the manufacture of gas, but when incandescent mantles were introduced, more common types of coal could be used for that purpose. In the 1920s production ran at over 250,000 tons a year, with more than a thousand men employed producing coal for domestic and industrial use, and for export. From the vertical shaft, roads were pushed further and further out. Those driven towards Fisherrow Harbour were known as the sea dooks and went under the

Forth for a distance of over two miles from the Newcraighall shaft. The long wall method of extraction later allowed the effective use of electrically driven coal-cutting machinery on a face exceeding three hundred feet in length. The coal was then stripped from the face onto the automatic face conveyor, which in turn delivered it to the road conveyor, and then to the bottom of the shaft. When the industry was nationalised in 1947, the Niddrie and Benhar pit became known as Newcraighall, but in 1968 it was closed due partly to geological problems. When the pit eventually came to the end of its useful life, the miners had long since become used to mechanisation on quite a large scale, but several of the older miners still have clear recollections of the days when coal was moved either manually or with the use of pit ponies. Although the animals were properly cared for, they seldom, if ever, saw the light of day, and were fed and stabled several hundred feet below ground. Despite many difficulties Newcraighall pit had a remarkably good safety record, the worst incident being on 12th September 1955 when thirty-two men were injured in a hauling accident.

Today very little remains of the pithead, and within a short time the area will be completely redeveloped. All the pithead buildings on the north side of the A6095 have been swept away, leaving only a solid plug of concrete over the shaft which gave access to a labyrinth of roads and faces. A modern detached villa with a pantile roof has been built on the site, and the vast bing has been almost completely removed to build the base of the new Musselburgh bypass. On the south side of the A6095, within a hundred yards of the concrete flyover, the shell of the old pit baths serves as the only visual reminder at Newcraighall of the old Klondyke pit. In 1971, when the winding gear was moved from Newcraighall with the assistance of Territorial Army engineers, Anthony Troon of *The Scotsman* observed: 'the pipes are blackened and lifeless and they tangle like dead serpents among the dead buildings — they have had their last taste of steam'. It is true that the winding gear has never again been operational, but it has found a useful home at Prestongrange Mining Museum, where it forms one of the major exhibits.

Agriculture

Although no one would dispute that Newcraighall was predominantly a mining community, there has also been considerable involvement in agriculture. Wanton Walls at the Musselburgh end of Newcraighall is a very old farm under the control of the Denholm family since 1931. Although the farm is now fully mechanised for the production of grain and barley, George Denholm recalls clearly the days when his father was first at Wanton Walls. The pace of life was slower, the day's work was harder, and there was much greater involvement with the local people, in and around Newcraighall. On the farm, the livestock included breeding sows, a herd of dairy cattle, hens, and working horses. After early morning milking, the distribution to the village and outlying houses was done from large pitchers, carried on a low flat barrow.

With no mechanisation in the fields, the basic tasks of ploughing and harrowing were done with the use of horses. Bringing in the hay or the harvest was a lengthy process requiring long hours of work as soon as the weather and the crop were compatible. After the hay was cut, it was left to dry in the fields before being drawn together by 'Tumbling Maggie' and then built into rucks. Tumbling Maggie was a rudimentary but effective piece of equipment rather like a gigantic rake, drawn by one horse. It consisted of a pair of strong curved handles fixed to a series of wooden prongs which lay flat on the ground and became very polished on their underside through constant use across stubble fields. When a sufficient load had been collected, the horse was brought to a stop momentarily while the operator lifted the handles up and over in a tumbling motion, releasing the hay in long lines across the field. The next task was to build the rucks, the youngest and ablest workers taking up a position on top of the ruck, and the boys and girls 'puin' the butt', that is, removing the excess hay at ground level to shed the rainwater and keep the base dry. Bringing in a crop of barley or oats was equally labour-intensive, and there was the additional problem of assessing the right time to cut and dry. Provided this was judged correctly, the revolving steel drum used for threshing would separate the wheat from the chaff without difficulty. The wheat straw was used for thatching, and most of the barley crop, in the early days, went to the brewers, who frequently made an inspection of the standing crop before negotiating purchase. Potatoes were also an important cash crop. Planting was done by the women, who became very skilled at judging the exact spacing in each row. They would walk the drills with an old potato bag worn as an apron, with the mouth of it opened and wrapped round their forearm to support the weight of the potatoes. When the crop was ready the miners' wives and children would help at the 'tattie howking', and the farm workers would dig the potato pits at the edge of the field. These consisted of long shallow trenches about two feet deep, six feet across and perhaps two hundred feet in length. The potatoes were stored in these pits with a light covering of straw for five or six weeks, after which soil was drawn up over them to keep the pit free of frost over the winter months.

Leisure and Recreation

Long hours in the fields, or at the coal face, did not prevent the people of Newcraighall setting up numerous clubs for their leisure and recreation. Bowls, football, pigeon racing and dog racing have for many years formed an integral part of the social life of the village, much of which was centred on the Miners' Welfare Institute.

The first volume of the Institute minutes in 1907 records the existence of fairly modest premises in Whitehill Street, with a reading room, a library and a billiard room. In 1913 the Patron of the Institute, Sir Charles Dalrymple of Newhailes, suggested a site in the village for new recreational premises. It was agreed to hold a public meeting of residents of Newcraighall to consider these proposals, but it was not until 1925 that they were put into effect. On 24th October 1925 the Lord Provost of Edinburgh, Sir William Sleigh, opened the new building, consisting of a large assembly hall and gallery to hold four hundred people, and a new billiard room, reading room and library. Those in attendance included Robert Ramsay, General Manager of the Niddrie and Benhar Colliery Co. Ltd., Dr. Moore, the Chairman of the Board of Directors, Wm. Adamson M.P., G.A. Clark Hutchison M.P., and James Calder, the Scottish manager of the London and North-Eastern Railway. The Chairman in his opening speech said, 'These welfare schemes are not an endeavour to bolster up the capitalist system but rather an attempt to improve the relationship between masters and men, which is unfortunately at present too much embittered'. In the years that followed, the Institute premises were used for a wide variety of recreational and charitable purposes: there was the Poosie Nancy Club for followers of our national bard; there were sales of work, bazaars and whist drives for the Thistle Football Club, the Salvation Army and the Co-operative

Messrs. MacMillan and Brogan provide tap dancing in the streets of
Newcraighall during the General Strike, 1926.
Courtesy of Councillor David Brown.

Women's Guild; and various concerts the proceeds of which went to
the *Edinburgh Evening News* Shilling Fund for the Royal Infirmary
Extension.

Newcraighall has always had a long association with the game of
bowls. There are two greens at the east end of the village beside what
was Newhailes Railway Station. Originally the green farther from the
roadway belonged to Niddrie Bowling Club and the green nearer to
the roadway belonged to the Newcraighall Miners' Welfare Institute,
but for many years now the two greens have been run under the
auspices of the Institute. The Institute club is the younger of the two,
the first available records appearing around 1904 when Dr Andrew
Balfour was the President. The Niddrie Bowling Club, however,
started in 1889 on a small green nearer to the village but transferred

in 1897 to its present site which was gifted by the Dalrymples of Newhailes. At the Jubilee celebrations in June 1947 a full fixture was arranged with local clubs including the Jewel, Portobello, Musselburgh and Inveresk. Sir Mark Dalrymple, a grandson of Sir Charles Dalrymple, hoisted the club flag, threw the first jack and wished the club prosperity in the next fifty years. The President then made a special presentation to each of five men present who had been members in 1897. Also present that day was David Spence, the manager of the Newcraighall pit.

Mining communities have for long been closely involved in greyhound racing. The official Greyhound Racing Association meetings are held at Powderhall but the training, feeding and rearing of dogs is done in much less formal surroundings. Tucked away in a sheltered railway cutting at Newcraighall, John Douglas and other enthusiasts escape to a world geared to being first past the post. Breeding and training to championship standard requires careful planning, especially when values at peak performance can be more than £2,000. From a litter of perhaps twelve pups, eight are usually selected for competitive running. Schooling and training begins in earnest at eight months, but dogs cannot run at official meetings until they are at least fifteen months old. The time is not, however, wasted. Between eight and fifteen months the young animals are taken to race meetings where they soon absorb the atmosphere of the surroundings and get used to other dogs and handlers. Training dogs to enter the traps without fear of injury requires great patience. To begin with, a dog is set down on the open track to chase the mechanical rabbit and later will be introduced gradually to the starting traps. The dog is coaxed into the trap which is left open front and back so that it can become accustomed to its surroundings. After confidence is built up, the handler will then lead the animal into the trap with the front closed to allow it to get used to the enclosed space. The final hurdle is, of course, to get the dog to remain composed in a closed trap, but ready and willing to go as soon as it is sprung. Frequently a bitch is easier to train than a dog, and will also run faster.

If a dog is to do well at race meetings, it must be regularly exercised and kept on a proper diet. At the Newcraighall kennels breakfast is at 8 a.m. consisting of cornflakes, brown rolls, milk, glucose and eggs, followed later in the day by exercise of at least five miles each day. The evening feed consists of brown bread, vegetables and ox cheek with the addition of a proprietary dog food to maintain a balanced diet. A vitamin C tablet is given each day with a higher intake before race meetings. Regular visits to a veterinary surgeon are also essential, and the dogs are all ringed for identification to prevent any other dog being entered in its place.

At Newcraighall, racing champions are not the exclusive prerogative of the canine species. James Aitchison, one of the founder members of the Newcraighall Pigeon Club in 1928, has raced hundreds of birds and won many honours over the years, along with other members of the club.

The club is based at Newcraighall Bowling Club, but most of the lofts are on a small piece of ground on the opposite side of the road leading to Musselburgh. The club is part of the Midlothian Federation and arranges races each Saturday during the season between mid-April and mid-September. On the Friday evening before a race the competitors take their pigeons and clock along to the Bowling Club. Cocks and hens are placed in different baskets, and each competitor's timing device is set by one of the elected clock committee. Each competing bird also carries a ring identification which provides details of the Federation, the bird's own number and the appropriate year. Thereafter the birds are taken by transporter along with birds from other clubs to the liberation point which may be Longtown in Cumbria, Dorchester or even the north of France. It is the responsibility of the convoyer to look after the birds during the journey and to ensure that they reach the liberation point in safety. On the Saturday morning he telephones the Race Controller at Loanhead whose decision it is to tell the convoyer to release the birds if conditions are favourable. The convoyer's final duty is then to inform the Controller of the time of release and the direction and speed of the wind. Thereafter, the birds must rely on their natural homing instinct to find their way back to their own loft at Newcraighall and other clubs. With a good following wind birds have been known to fly back from the Borders at an average speed of 60 m.p.h., but if the wind freshens to the north-east the journey becomes more arduous and losses are not uncommon. Once home to the loft, the ring is taken off the bird and placed in a small brass thimble which is then inserted in the clocking device to record the exact time of arrival. At this stage a competitor does not, of course, know if he has won the race. The record must be taken along to the Bowling Club within one hour of arrival and compared with the other results, before the winner is announced.

For the younger generation, football was the natural choice. Shortly after the First World War the young men of Newcraighall and surrounding districts formed the Niddrie Thistle Football Club. Their first home ground was on agricultural land to the north of Whitehill Street, but in the 1920s they transferred to a new pitch in the public park to the south of the village. In these early years the club enjoyed considerable success in the Scottish Juvenile League under their trainer George Wood. During the season 1927–28 the red and white strip of Niddrie Thistle was cheered to victory in all four championships, the King Cup, the Swanfield Cup, the Avon-Clyde Cup and the Avon-Clyde League Shield. Later, several of their players went on to play full-time for Scottish clubs, including St Bernard's.

The School, the Churches, and Dr Balfour

Newcraighall, like any other village, is closely associated with the school, the church and other areas of social and educational involvement.

The first village school was very small and stood until recently at the rear of the single-storey cottages in Whitehill Street. With the opening of the new pit in 1897 and the consequent increase in the number of families with school-age children, Inveresk School Board found it necessary to build much bigger premises. The new school, still in use today, was built on the principle of a large central hall with adjacent classrooms for three hundred children. The site was an acre of ground on the south side of Whitehill Street gifted by Sir Charles Dalrymple; the architect was A. Murray Hardie of Edinburgh; the red facing stone came from Closeburn Quarry; and the total cost was £3,743. At the opening ceremony on 8th June 1906 James Gemmell, Chairman of the Inveresk School Board, was presented with an inscribed silver key by the architect who had also made a special feature of the Board's initials I.S.B. in the ventilation panels on the ceilings. As befitted the occasion, and the School Board's purse, songs were sung by Miss Janet Braid and Miss Helen Lettice, accompanied on the piano by Miss Martin, while 'the cup that cheers but not inebriates' was passed round the assembled company. The children were not admitted for classes until 4th September 1906, when the daily task of compiling the school log began. On re-reading school logs, there is a tendency to pay too much attention to isolated but interesting incidents to the exclusion of the everyday school work. Nevertheless some entries are worth recording: 1911, the habit of promiscuous answering should be eradicated or repressed; 1913, reading considerably marred by high-pitched tone and unnatural expression; 1921, feeding necessitous children — half a pint of milk, and bread and butter *or* jam; 1934, the first headmaster retires after twenty-eight years; 1947, eight staff go to the Usher Hall to hear Professor Schonell's lecture on backward children; 1953, Coronation. In more recent years the school has coped with a changing population and has done much to encourage and record, in written and audio-visual material, the early life and traditions of the coalmining community around it.

Newcraighall Parish Church, to the east of the school, was opened on 20th February 1878. It is of brick construction with supporting buttresses, designed by Henry Hardy, and built with the financial assistance of the Dalrymple and Wauchope families. The first minister was Rev. Archibald Prentice. Although the church served the community well for many years, in the 1970s the main church building became too large for the existing congregation. A decision was therefore taken to hold services in the small chapel adjacent to the main building, which then became a Community Centre in 1979. Since February 1980, services in the small church have been conducted by Rev. Mary Spowart, who holds the distinction of having been the first female parish minister with a full charge in Edinburgh.

It is many years, however, since services have been held at Newcraighall's other church. In 1876 the Methodist Church in Edinburgh noted that 'several persons having been found at Newcraighall who were members of our church removed thither from other Circuits'. Arrangements were therefore made to supply Newcraighall with local preachers on circuit from Musselburgh, Portobello and Eskbank. It may be assumed that the first premises were rather modest, because in 1885 it was recommended that the work of the church be recommenced if it was possible 'to re-open the room'. Major progress was, however, made in 1896 when a brick-built church was erected on a small corner of ground near the old Newcraighall pit shaft. Small memorial stones, now badly weathered, along one side of the building commemorate the names of those who were presumably instrumental in setting up the new church: Mrs. J.E. Cargill, Edinburgh; Mrs J. Dennis, Brixworth; Mrs Wauchope, Niddrie House; The Misses Taylor, Edinburgh; Dr Andrew Balfour, Portobello. Matters went reasonably well for a small church of a minor denomination in Scotland. A membership of thirty-two in 1911 rose to fifty-seven in 1913, dropping back to around forty during and immediately after the First World War. For much of its later life, Newcraighall shared a minister with Abbeyhill. There were two services on a Sunday, and an evening service each Wednesday. In the early 1950s the church was threatened with closure but was saved by the enthusiasm of the congregation led by the Rev. Kenneth G. Bloxham. Following careful examination of the membership and the work being done locally, it was decided to refurbish the church rather than allow it to close. Its proximity to the old Newcraighall pit shaft also ensured an added refinement to the completed building. Immediately adjacent to the church, the National Coal Board wanted to bring up an exhaust outlet from the workings of the pit below, but it was found that the outlet would encroach slightly on church property. Permission was, of course, given, but with one proviso — that the waste heat be carried in pipes round the church before being expelled into the air. Thus, for many years, a friendly disposition and a unique central heating system ensured that a warm welcome was extended to all who visited Newcraighall Methodist Church. The gradual depopulation of the older parts of the village in the 1950s and 1960s led to a greater proportion of the Methodist people living away from the village. The direct cause of closure in 1966 was not that interest had been extinguished, but rather that, of the twenty-nine members remaining, only one or two families still lived in Newcraighall, and no-one was willing to accept office. The decision to close was taken with great reluctance by the Circuit Meeting, the last minister being the late Rev. Frank Corp. After the church closed, the premises were used for a variety of commercial enterprises, before becoming a joiner's workshop.

On the south side of Whitehill Street there is a brightly painted drinking fountain which has recently been re-sited from its original position near the school. It bears the following inscription commemorating a man who spent his whole life in the service of those around him. At his premature death at the age of fifty-seven he held no fewer than thirty official appointments:

Balfour Fountain erected in 1907 to the memory of Dr Andrew Balfour who for thirty years took a great interest in the welfare of Newcraighall. Photograph by A.C. Robson.

Erected by
the
people
of this district
to show their high esteem
for the memory
of
Dr Andrew Balfour
who
for thirty years took a great interest
in the welfare of this village

Died 26th December 1906 Erected June 1907

Dr Balfour was born in Hong Kong, where his father had medical charge of the Seamen's Hospital. He was brought at the age of two to Portobello, where his father settled and developed a large family practice. Andrew Balfour took the degrees of M.B. and C.M. in 1873 at the University of Edinburgh, and immediately after graduation he joined his father in practice. Until Portobello became part of Edinburgh he was medical officer for that burgh, and he was also the local police casualty surgeon. His interests were not, however, exclusively medical: in 1877 he was chief founder of the Portobello Working Men's Institute; for many years he was Superintendent of the Sunday School at Newcraighall; in 1888 he founded the local company of the Boys' Brigade and later became President; and throughout his life he involved himself in the pastimes of the miners and their families. The fountain in memory of Dr Balfour was unveiled on 6th July 1907 by the Right Hon. Sir Charles Dalrymple, Bart., P.C. After the death of Dr Andrew Balfour his brother and partner, Dr John Balfour, continued the practice from Portobello, and is still remembered by the older residents of Newcraighall. In the days when motor cars were only beginning to appear on the streets of Edinburgh, Dr John Balfour went his rounds in a chauffeur-driven car, but instead of sitting comfortably in the back he stood on the nearside running board so that he could jump off and on as the occasion demanded.

The Old and the New Village

Despite the fact that coal has been mined in the Lothians for many centuries, Newcraighall, as the name might suggest, is one of Edinburgh's youngest villages. Indeed there is no evidence of any substantial community before about 1800. The oldest remaining part of the village is the long line of mainly single-storey cottages on the north side of Whitehill Street. These were built, probably in the early nineteenth century, in the typically Scottish style of the time, roofed with pantiles, and containing two rooms, back kitchen, and outside toilets. They were originally occupied by farm labourers, but by the mid-nineteenth century, when the village still consisted of one main street, most of the houses were occupied by miners.

Against a background of strong local traditions and a commitment to an established way of life it is indeed surprising that Newcraighall should have come almost to the brink of destruction, yet such was its fate in the mid-1950s. The housing stock was in a deplorable condition, and there was little sign of any official recognition of the problem. The village had been built in three fairly distinctive phases, and each phase presented different problems. The oldest section was the line of mainly single-storey cottages on the north side of Whitehill Street dating from about 1800. The second oldest phase was the rows of brick-built miners' houses on the south side of Whitehill Street forming First Avenue, Second Avenue, Third Avenue and the north side of Main Avenue, built towards the end of the nineteenth century. The newest phase was the additional miners' houses built in the late 1920s nearest to the public park. Interest in the renewal and renovation of the old village was led by Councillor David Brown.

In 1975 the Department of Architecture of Edinburgh District Council studied the cottages situated on the north side of Whitehill Street. There were twenty-nine houses built in five sections, all of which were inhabited except for a few at the east end of the village. None of the houses had bathrooms, and most of them had inadequate kitchen facilities. A strong case was put forward for renovation and refurbishment rather than complete demolition. Fortunately a decision was made to modernise the cottages, retaining much of their traditional appearance. They were rewired, new bathrooms and kitchens were built at the rear, and a solid-fuel heating system was installed based on an open coal fire.

On the south side of Whitehill Street the houses built at the end of last century presented an equally difficult problem. Those on Whitehill Street were one storey only, but in the rows to the south two-storey houses had been built in an unusual way. The houses on the upper floor faced First Avenue, but the houses on the ground floor faced Second Avenue. Similarly the upper storey of the next block faced Third Avenue and the ground floor faced Main Avenue. When they were built around 1890 they had no running water and no internal toilet facilities. Cold water was obtained from stand pipe wells placed at various intervals in the street, and dry toilets were built in a long row to the south of Main Avenue. Wash day in a mining family was an arduous process. Water was carried in from the street and heated in a big black pot on an open fire. The clothes were then washed and rinsed in succession and the dirty water carried out to the sheugh or drain in the street. Toilets and sculleries were not added onto the basic houses until 1910. In the 1950s the Tenants'

Association began its fight to have the houses improved, but progress was slow even after Edinburgh Corporation acquired the houses from the National Coal Board. In 1975, however, a scheme costing £1½m was approved for the demolition and rebuilding of 110 houses and the renovation of 48 more. At the present day the new houses with white harling are in pleasing contrast to the old brick terraces, which housed so many mining families. The most modern houses, built in the 1920s nearest to the park, were found to be still basically sound in construction and were renovated to complete the transformation of the village.

In addition to the houses on the south side of Whitehill Street there was a two-storey building at the west end immediately adjacent to the railway bridge. It was here that the old miners went in each day to buy sufficient shot to blast new sections of the coal face. The building belonged originally to the Niddrie Society, but early in 1904 it went into liquidation and was taken over by the Musselburgh & Fisherrow Co-operative Society Ltd. The premises were, however, only on lease for five years and were quite unsuitable for the expected increase in trade. In 1907 Musselburgh and Fisherrow acquired from Sir Charles Dalrymple a feu of ground at the east end of the village and proceeded to build new premises comprising Grocery, Drapery, Boots and Butchery Shops, with three houses above for Manager and Assistants, at a cost of £3,800. There is a plaque dated 1908 on the side of the building, but in recent years the Society has ceased to trade from these premises. Immediately opposite this plaque there is another sign now almost indecipherable — NEWCRAIGHALL POLICE STATION, from which Sgt. Wilson and his colleagues kept regular watch over the inhabitants of Newcraighall.

Newhailes

A short distance to the east of Newcraighall is Newhailes (formerly Whitehill), one of East Lothian's most interesting old houses, surrounded by an estate of greater antiquity. The house is occupied by Lady Antonia Dalrymple, widow of Sir Mark Dalrymple, whose ancestor Sir David Dalrymple took the title Lord Hailes on his appointment as a Lord of Session in 1766.

The house is reached by a short driveway leading from the main gates and lodge house on the road from Newcraighall to

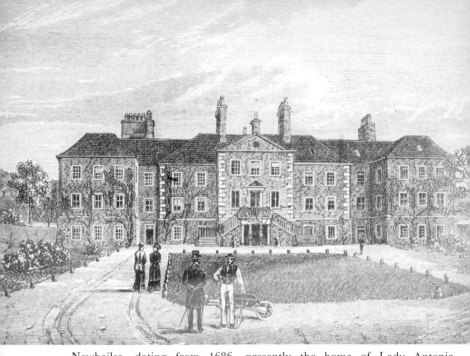

Newhailes, dating from 1686, presently the home of Lady Antonia Dalrymple.
From Grant's *Old and New Edinburgh*.

Musselburgh. It is in a very sheltered position, with curved ramparts on each side of the inner gateway, forming a large enclosed courtyard, the north side of which is completed by the house itself. Only the 'gun-hole' ventilators on the left betray the secrets of early domestic life: beneath the grass-covered rampart runs a long narrow tunnel giving speedy, but unobtrusive, access to the kitchen quarters of the house. Throughout the centuries, a succession of improvements has created a mansionhouse of considerable elegance, though greatly altered from its original design. The early part of the house is credited to James Smith, the architect, who is said to have had it built in 1686 for his own use. It is clear, however, that prior to the involvement of Smith other influential families owned the estate, probably when the house was much smaller. An early document records the interest of the Prestons of Craigmillar in the fifteenth century, after which the estate was known as Whitehill, and some time prior to 1707 it was owned by Lord Bellenden of Broughton.

James Smith had a considerable reputation as an architect in Scotland at the end of the seventeenth century. He was the son of a master mason from Tarbat in Ross-shire and is believed to have

146

studied for the ministry before turning to architecture. He married Janet, the eldest daughter of Robert Mylne, Master Mason of the Scottish Crown, and was later appointed Surveyor of the Royal Works. His first marriage produced eighteen children before Janet 'died of twins at age 37 in 1699', and his second marriage added a further fourteen children. Smith's obvious belief in strength in numbers was tinged with more than a hint of humour when he announced that one of his sons would be christened Climacterick Smith on account of his having been born in his father's seventieth year! Financial involvement in 'a drowned colliery near Musselburgh' compelled Smith to sell Whitehill in 1707, but he lived to be eighty-six and died on 6th November 1731.

Smith's sale of Whitehill opened another chapter in the history of the estate, which was bought in 1707 by Sir David Dalrymple of Hailes, son of the First Viscount Stair. It was Sir David who adopted the name Newhailes from the old family seat of Hailes Castle near East Linton. The second stage of building at Newhailes was undertaken by William Adam around 1720 and was followed by the much more ambitious plan to add the flanking wings to Smith's original frontage. The completed building of two storeys and basement has Smith's original work as the centrepiece, projecting and lightly pedimented. A double stairway is carried over the Roman Doric porch at the basement entrance, and leads to the main doorway flanked by tapered pilasters. Above the main doorway is a pediment containing a Janus with the double head of an old and a young man, and the inscription LAUDO MANENTEM — I HONOUR HE WHO STAYS — lightheartedly translated by subsequent generations of the Dalrymple family to read 'I honour he who stays *put*'. Internally the hall and staircase were designed by William Adam and executed by Samuel Calderwood, his plasterwork incorporating real shells in the angles of the cornice. The wing to the left contains the dining room, its magnificent chimneypiece having a lion's mask and paws on the lintel. The Ionic screen, built when the dining room was enlarged, leads to the sitting room beyond, containing several portraits of the family. The corresponding wing to the right of the hallway incorporates the beautifully symmetrical Chinese drawing room and the library, which fills the whole of one flanking block. The windows are positioned to the back of the house away from the direct rays of the sun, dummy windows being built on the front of the house to preserve its symmetry. The library is

Lord Hailes (1726 — 1792), judge and writer, creator of the Hailes library now in the possession of the National Library of Scotland.
From Kay's *Original Portraits.*

probably the finest room in the house, used by Sir David Dalrymple, lawyer and historian, who became Lord Hailes on his elevation to the Bench in 1766. His unique collection of books and papers, many by his own hand, graced the walls, ten shelves high, for many generations until 1976 when the whole collection was acquired by the National Library of Scotland. The Newhailes library still contains the paintings of Tantallon Castle and Hailes Castle by John Thomson of Duddingston, and the empty shelves have been used to exhibit the portrait photographs of Lady Dalrymple's family.

Details of the Hailes collection and its acquisition for the nation are given in the Annual Report of the National Library of Scotland for 1978-79 in which it is described as 'the greatest surviving contemporary collection of books of the period of the Scottish

Enlightenment and... a cohesive and comprehensive record of the work of Sir David Dalrymple, Lord Hailes (1726-1792)'. Almost the entire collection of seven thousand volumes and other papers of Lord Hailes' library (with post-1792 additions) has been preserved, with the exception of some books sold at Sotheby's in 1937. The existing collection includes many important works in literature and most branches of knowledge. Among the geographical works is Sanson's *Géographie* of 1691 and the four-volume Blaeu *Nouveau théâtre d'Italie* of 1704. Under architecture are the 1616 Venice edition of Palladio in Italian and Perrault's *Les dix livres d'architecture de Vitruve* (Paris, 1684). There is also Lord Hailes' manuscript of his *Annals of Scotland,* annotated by Johnson, and several examples of fine eighteenth-century Scottish bindings. The National Library Report also acknowledges that whilst there was general satisfaction that the Hailes library had been acquired for the nation, there was less agreement on the decision to remove the books from Newhailes. Several interested bodies expressed the view that the books formed an integral part of Newhailes and that they should remain there. The National Library, on the other hand, whilst recognising the relevance of that argument, pointed out that the additional factors of security, preservation and accessibility could not be met at Newhailes, without incurring disproportionate costs. For the time being, therefore, the library is in the safe custody of the National Library of Scotland until the day comes when circumstances justify its return to Newhailes.

The estate grounds at Newhailes also contain a number of interesting features in addition to the service tunnel already mentioned. At the back of the house were the lead sphinxes brought by Sir James Dalrymple in 1740, but stolen in 1947, and further into the wooded area is the stone obelisk erected in 1746 in memory of John, the Second Earl of Stair. There is also the Shell Grotto or Gazebo, built of shells by French prisoners of war. The most substantial building, however, is the Stable Block built in 1790 by John Craig, two storeys in height with a facade of coupled columns supporting a heavy pediment.

The *Ordnance Gazetteer of Scotland* relates that Newhailes was built by Sir David Dalrymple the eminent lawyer, antiquary and historian. That statement is inaccurate, but is perhaps excusable on the grounds that Sir David (later Lord Hailes) was undoubtedly its most influential owner. He was born in Edinburgh in 1726, the eldest of sixteen children of Sir James Dalrymple Bart. of New Hailes, and

Whitehill Street, Newcraighall, 1985, showing Councillor David Brown's house among the renovated cottages on the left, the former Parish Church in the centre (a Community Centre since 1979), and the new houses of Klondyke Street on the right.

of Lady Christian Hamilton. Both parents, being supporters of the Union and the Hanoverian dynasty, decided that David should be educated at Eton and Utrecht. On returning to Scotland, he was admitted to the Faculty of Advocates in 1748, where he practised for almost twenty years before reaching the Bench. Although considered to be a poor pleader, his unquestionable knowledge of the law made him a feared adversary: feared, that is, by all save him who feared no man — Lord Braxfield, the 'Hanging Judge'. It was Braxfield who, in reply to a remark that Hailes was a good judge, declared: 'Him — he knows nothing but the nook of the cause', meaning of course that Hailes was more concerned with trivial points than with the central issues. It is said that Hailes once dismissed an action because a document had the word 'justice' spelt without the final 'E', an incident which did not escape the able pen of James Boswell:

> To judge of this matter I cannot pretend,
> For justice my Lord wants an E at the end.

It is probably true that Hailes was of a rather aloof disposition and had a preference for English culture, a combination which did little to endear him to the robust Scottish judiciary of the time. In the words of W. Forbes Gray, 'he set himself to redeem the Scottish Bench from the stigma of being the home of buffoons, cranks, roisterers, rabid politicians and men of odd and clownish manners'. Hailes was, however, a prodigious writer, and his judgments were a study in unbiased lucidity. Of his many books, journals and reviews, his most outstanding work was his *Annals of Scotland,* produced in two parts between 1776 and 1779. Quiet and reserved by nature, he spent most of his leisure hours in the library at Newhailes. His first marriage was to the daughter of the judge Lord Coalston, and his second marriage was to the daughter of another judge, Lord Kilkerran. He died of apoplexy in 1792.

At the present day, almost two hundred years after the death of Lord Hailes, the estate of Newhailes is at a crossroads, caught between the desire to maintain a noble heritage and the need to eradicate the pernicious effects of dry rot. Fortunately the Trustees, with the assistance of the Historic Buildings Council for Scotland, have made substantial progress in preserving the fabric of the building and its irreplaceable craftsmanship — empty bookshelves and all!

CHAPTER 7

Newhaven

There are few communities within the city boundary which have been more independent in thought and in deed than the Newhaven fisherfolk of old. Destined to house the Royal Dockyards and the Chapel of St. Mary and St. James, the New Haven came to prominence in the early sixteenth century in opposition to the old haven of Blackness on the Forth. Known at one time as Our Lady's Port of Grace, Newhaven saw the construction and launching of the *Great Michael*, the largest warship of its time and the envy of every seafaring nation in the world. So great was the influence of Newhaven that Edinburgh took fright and bought the village and harbour in 1510 to protect its own port at Leith from unwelcome competition. Having lost the opportunity to build the royal docks and capitalise on the natural deepwater channels around the old harbour, Newhaven was usurped firstly by Leith and later by Granton. Newhaven established itself as a close-knit fishing community in which social convention dictated that young men and women should not marry outside the village. The confusion caused by the recurrence of the same surnames was avoided by introducing nicknames or by referring to a man by his own surname and his wife's maiden name. Thus Sandy Rutherford was known as Sandy Whitestar, the nickname being taken from the name of his father's fishing boat.

At the present day the fishing industry has all but gone; the fishwives no longer carry their creels in the streets of Edinburgh; and many of the old houses have been demolished and rebuilt. The cycle has been broken. As newcomers establish their own way of life, the old order remains only in the minds of the older inhabitants.

Sir Andrew Wood and the *Great Michael*

Andrew Wood was born in the middle of the fifteenth century in Largo, Fife and spent the early part of his life as a merchant and skipper operating out of the port of Leith. He was the proud owner of two ships, the *Flower* and the *Yellow Carvel*, each of 300 tons burden, which he used to build up significant trade routes with the Low Countries. His resilience, and skill in navigation, did not go unnoticed. James III granted him a lease of the lands of Largo on condition that he kept the *Yellow Carvel* in constant repair for the use of the King whenever required. In 1483 he obtained a grant of ownership of the land, and shortly thereafter he was knighted. Rapid rise to fame on account of naval ability was of great interest to other monarchs. Henry VII was clearly unhappy at the growing supremacy of Sir Andrew's fleet and issued a challenge to any of his subjects who would engage and defeat the impertinent Scot. Stephen Bull took up the challenge in 1489 and lay in wait for Sir Andrew in the shelter of the Isle of May. As Sir Andrew rounded St. Abb's Head and saw the English vessels blocking his route home, he made hurried preparation for battle, and addressed his men with characteristic confidence: 'Be stout against these your enemies who have sworn and avowed to make you prisoners to the King of England – – – set yourselves in order every man at his own station – – – for my part, with God to help I shall show you a good example'. There followed a bitter and determined fight to the finish, with unparalleled courage and determination shown on both sides. As darkness fell and hostilities subsided, neither side had any obvious advantage, but on the following day the superior skill of Sir Andrew began to win through. The ships, locked together with grappling irons, had drifted into the mouth of the Tay, where the local inhabitants shouted encouragement from the beaches. The three English vessels eventually succumbed and were brought into the port of Dundee, while Stephen Bull was taken as a prisoner before James IV. Bull was later pardoned and sent home with the clear message that Sir Andrew was master of Scottish waters.

The name of Sir Andrew Wood is inextricably linked with Newhaven's finest hour in 1511 when the *Great Michael* was launched as the largest ship then afloat. Designed by the famous naval architect Jacques Tarette, and costing £30,000, it required for its construction all the oak in Fife save that at Falkland Palace. The proportions were enormous, and the number of guns, officers, operating crew and fighting men more than in any other man-of-war then afloat. It was two hundred and forty feet long, thirty-six feet wide, and had sides ten feet thick and carried three hundred sailors, one hundred and twenty gunners and one thousand troops. Its fighting ability, however, never matched that of the much lighter and smaller *Yellow Carvel*. Indeed it was so big and cumbersome that it never successfully led the Scottish navy into any major conflict. With the death of James IV at Flodden in 1513, hopes of a successful navy evaporated, and the *Great Michael* was sold to France, allegedly for 40,000 livres.

Sir Andrew eventually retired to Largo, but he never lost his love for ships. With part of his vast fortune he had a canal built between his castle and the kirk in Upper Largo along which he was rowed to church every Sunday morning. He died in 1540 and was buried in Largo kirk.

Newhaven Harbour

Almost five hundred years have elapsed since Newhaven reached the peak of achievement in launching the *Great Michael*. Equal fame never returned, but in the half millennium which followed, Newhaven clung to a way of life utterly dominated by ships and the sea. Grant records several references to harbour-work in the sixteenth century at a time when building techniques were understandably modest by modern standards. In the early nineteenth century improved methods of construction, and the involvement of civil engineers, paved the way for much more ambitious schemes.

One such scheme was that of James Anderson, civil engineer, whose *Report on the Present State of Leith Harbour* was published by Adam and Charles Black of Edinburgh in 1834. Anderson began serious observation of the coastline, tides, currents and winds as early as 1816. He quickly came to the conclusion that Leith would never be anything other than a tidal harbour, hampered by shifting sandbanks at its entrance, and continually fouled by alluvial deposits from the Water of Leith. He acknowledged that steam power in ships was 'pre-eminently superior to every other mode of transit', but pointed out that most of the larger vessels could not get into Leith except at high tide. The practice of casting anchor in the Forth, and using smaller craft to convey passengers and freight ashore, was both costly and inconvenient. Anderson's remedy was simple. Leith had better facilities on land, and Newhaven had the advantage of a natural deepwater channel out into the Forth estuary. He proposed to form a new entrance at Newhaven about three hundred yards west of the pier, and to construct a ship canal running east to the docks at Leith.

The canal was to be two hundred feet wide with a stone quay along its entire length, protected at the Newhaven end by flood gates and substantial sea defences. At the height of the spring tides a depth of thirty feet was intended, even at low tide, by closing the flood gates and keeping the water level high. It was a most ambitious and far-reaching plan intended to provide adequate docking facilities for the biggest merchant ships as well as the Royal Navy. Anderson costed his scheme at £124,695 11/- and added the cautionary warning that if it was not taken up by those who had commissioned him, an alternative scheme would be adopted by their competitors. His worst fears were confirmed. Anderson's plan was rejected, and within ten years a second pier had been opened at Granton. Having lost the chance to be, in Anderson's own words, 'among the first commercial ports of the Empire', Newhaven made improvements to the sea walls in 1837, and added a breakwater by Robert Stevenson in 1864. When the harbour was completely reconstructed between 1876 and 1881, a lighthouse was erected on the east pier.

During these days of gradual if not revolutionary change, Newhaven built up significant trade routes for freight and passenger service. The steamer *Tourist* plied between Newhaven and Aberdeen, and there was also regular passage to and from Kirkcaldy, Burntisland and Pettycur. Long before the Forth Railway Bridge was constructed, all the mail from Aberdeen and the east coast was brought through Fife to the Pettycur boat for Newhaven and then by road to the General Post Office in Edinburgh. One of the longer sea routes was from London to Newhaven, which took about three days depending upon the weather and the time of year. On 7th July 1832 the steamship *James Watt* left London for the journey north, with Sir Walter Scott on board, returning from Italy. Although the captain John Jamieson had made available his own cabin, it is doubtful if Sir Walter was ever really aware of this kind gesture. He was desperately ill and remained unconscious even after the vessel berthed at Newhaven on 9th July. Still unaware of his surroundings, he was driven to the Douglas Hotel in St. Andrew Square, Edinburgh, where he rested for the following two days. He then made his last journey to Abbotsford, where he died on 21st September 1832, worn out by his prodigious efforts to clear his earlier debts.

Although the harbour was dependent for prosperity on handling as much freight and as many passengers as possible, certain cargoes were unpopular. At a time when regulations on the movement of

Yawls moored in Newhaven Harbour showing in the background the village and St. Andrew's Free Church before the spire was built in 1883.
From Grant's *Old and New Edinburgh.*

dangerous chemicals appear to have been non-existent, Newhaven was the main point of discharge for gunpowder! The powder, contained in wooden barrels and carried by road in open carts, came all the way from Rosslyn Gunpowder Company to be loaded at Newhaven on to ships belonging to Mr Davidson, a merchant from Leith. The cargo was then taken out to Government ships lying at anchor in the deep water of the Forth. Each consignment could take anything up to three days to load, during which time the barrels lay around the quayside and the carts waited in line outside the Free Church in Pier Place. Precautions were considered to be unnecessary. After strong representation by the local community, a ban on smoking by those handling the powder was reluctantly enforced. Unfortunately the rule had little effect on the community itself. Its elder statesmen still liked a daunder after their tea, and stood, ever-ready with gratuitous advice, watching the unloading, and all the while smoking their clay pipes. Following more local objection, a public meeting was held at Madras School on 13th February 1873, and a public enquiry was held on 22nd March 1873, as a result of which it was decided that gunpowder should be taken by rail to Leith. Newhaven handled its last shipment on 15th August 1874.

The uses to which the harbour has been put in recent years have been less controversial. On 29th August 1966 Rev. William Birrell, minister of St. Andrew's Church, Newhaven, dedicated the reconstructed boat, *Fearless*, gifted by the Admiralty to the Trinity Sea Cadets whose headquarters are at H.M.S. *Claverhouse*, Granton. Something of the flavour of the old port also returned on 23rd June 1984 when Newhaven celebrated its gala day. The Gala Queen, Kirsty Downie, of Victoria School, set sail in a fishing boat from Granton Harbour and arrived at Newhaven accompanied by a flotilla of craft from the Port o' Leith Motor Boat Club.

The Fishing Industry

Newhaven harbour was for many years the centre of a busy fishing industry until its gradual decline in the 1950s. Like any other fishing village in Scotland, there was hardly a single family in Newhaven which did not have some connection with the industry. Fathers and sons went to sea; mothers and daughters helped with the nets and lines; and intermarriage in the village ensured that young wives had, at least, a basic training in the harsh realities of a fisherman's family. Many of the womenfolk also worked as fishwives selling fish direct to housewives in most districts of Edinburgh.

The date 1793 is traditionally given as the year in which herring were discovered in the Firth of Forth. James Colston, author of *The Town and Port of Leith*, writing in 1892, relates the story of how 'this fertile source of revenue' was discovered accidentally by Thomas Brown of Donibristle when he was fishing one day with hook and line. The herrings were so plentiful then that they could be gathered in bucketfuls:

> Wha'll buy my caller herrin'?
> They're bonny fish and halesome farin';
> Wha'll buy caller herrin'?
> New drawn frae the Forth.

There was, of course, a darker side to the business of catching fish, when men and boys risked their lives to land a catch in atrocious weather conditions:

> Wha'll buy my caller herrin'?
> They're no brought here without brave darin',
> Buy my caller herrin',
> Ye little ken their worth.

'Wha'll buy my caller herrin?' Newhaven fisherwomen, in working costume, carrying their creels of fish round the streets of Edinburgh.
Courtesy of Edinburgh City Libraries.

> Wha'll buy my caller herrin'?
> O ye may ca' them vulgar farin';
> Wives and mithers, maist despairin',
> Ca' them lives o' men.

Much less risk was involved on a still moonlit night at the ring-net fishing across the Forth estuary. A boat with a crew of four men and a boy would set off at six or seven knots towards Cramond Island. The skill was to locate a shoal as quickly as possible and get the nets into position. The zinc buoy 'winkie' was lit and made ready to go overboard, while the practised ear of the fishermen listened for the 'flop, flop' of herring on the surface of the water. As soon as they thought that a shoal was nearby, the winkie was put overboard with a sweepline and net attached to it. The skipper signalled to his pairing boat, which came in and attached a second line and net. The two boats then steamed away from one another in the arc of a circle, playing out the net as they went, and coming together again to complete the ring and encircle the fish. As the winch began to draw the net in, excitement mounted, and herring began to appear on the surface of the water. The fish were unloaded and the nets made ready for another sweep — perhaps four or five times before morning.

The other great source of revenue was the oyster beds, harvested amidst almost constant controversy from the sixteenth century. Edinburgh always maintained that it owned what was generally known as the City Scalps, yet the men of Newhaven depended upon them for a decent living. Many attempts were made during the seventeenth and eighteenth centuries to regulate their conflicting interests so that the industry could survive and the owners derive a reasonable profit. Little was achieved, and matters were made much worse by the intervention of boats from Cockenzie and Prestonpans which came in to gather oysters on beds traditionally fished by Newhaven men. Amid great acrimony and even pitched battles, the case was heard by the High Court of Admiralty from 1791 to 1793. For the Newhaven men the Court's decision in their favour was something of a Pyrrhic victory. Whilst the Court affirmed that the men from Prestonpans and Cockenzie had no right to the oysters, it re-established Edinburgh's claim to ownership, with the important rider that it could be exercised only through the Society of Free Fishermen of Newhaven. The industry survived to meet equally difficult times caused by erratic variations in supply and demand. In the 1830s oysters were so plentiful that women travelled well outside Edinburgh to receive as little as 2/6 (12½p) per thousand. A system of limiting each fisherman to a fixed quota was introduced, but the market did not improve, and trade with the North of England was maintained only by agreeing to crippling discounts. By 1866, when the fleet was almost one hundred boats, the price per thousand ranged from 9/- to 16/-. Over-fishing, bad management and the inability of the fishermen to agree realistic quotas among themselves eventually led the industry into a decline from which it did not recover.

When other fish were plentiful and the price relatively stable, the Dock Commissioners invested £20,000 in the erection of a new fish market on the east side of the harbour. The market was opened on 5th December 1896, and shortly after 8 a.m. the Commissioners and salesmen proceeded to the Marine Hotel for a special breakfast. By 1932, 16,000 cwts of herring were landed annually and dealt with at Newhaven market along with a much larger quantity of white fish including halibut, plaice, hake, cod and haddock. Although new quick-freezing plant was installed in the early 1950s, by then the Newhaven fleet was in serious decline, and many men had gone to other boats on the east coast of Scotland and further afield.

The Society of Free Fishermen of Newhaven

From time 'immemorial' the affairs of the fishing industry and the provision of social benefits to the old and infirm people of Newhaven have been in the hands of the Society of Free Fishermen. Tradition has it that the Society is at least five hundred years old, but it was not until 1631 that meetings became more formal and records were kept. These meetings were usually held at the house of the retiring Boxmaster, when the accounts were checked and the financial statement was signed. Prior to 1817 membership was open to anyone, but when the Society grew to unmanageable proportions, a rule was passed confining membership to 'the lawful sons of fishermen whose names were clear on the books'. In its early years the Society's involvement in the community was almost equivalent to that of a small town council, with responsibility for welfare, burials, collection of fish tithes and control of the oyster beds.

Fish tithes were a particularly troublesome aspect of old Newhaven. The tithes were a tax based originally on the practice of giving a tenth part of stock or produce to the church. The church owned these tithes but let them out to tacksmen whose job it was to collect this unpopular tax. Collection was sporadic owing to strong resistance by the Society, and the fact that many people on the list simply could not afford to pay. In 1828 a scheme was suggested for collection of 3/- (15p) from each person liable, with one person acting as collector for a group of ten. The scheme was never fully implemented despite the tacksman offering to make a deduction for the expenses of collection. It eventually fell into disuse during Rev. William Buchanan's ministry at Newhaven.

The Society was also a considerable property owner in the old village. In 1766 it bought a piece of ground described as 'the fourth part of St. James Chapel Garden'. The Boxmaster, William Durham, was the highest bidder at £53 for the land, which included four houses with adjoining gardens. Although the property was acquired at a comparatively low price, the investment was marred by the high cost of subsequent legal wrangles over ownership. For a while the land was let to a Mr Waldie who used it as a coalyard, after which the site was cleared for the construction of Newhaven Free Church in 1852. The second major investment in the property market in 1794 was more successful. The transaction related to a piece of ground which was lying derelict to the south of the old pier. The dilapidated buildings were soon rebuilt and an income was received from the tenancy, but by 1867 the old barber's shop was closed, and the property was again in very poor condition. It was replaced by a new three-storey house on the face of which a clock was fitted, made by Ritchie & Son of Leith and set going on 10th April 1868.

The absence of clean shingle beaches at Newhaven deprived the fishermen of a convenient area on which to spread out their nets for drying and repairing. In 1848 the Society applied to the Board of Admiralty for permission to use a large area of cultivated ground to the south of the main street. This was later named the Fishermen's Park. Permission was granted to use the Park at a rent of £20 per year which included a small strip of land at New Lane. Although the agreement was entered into directly with the Society, the men who negotiated the deal appear to have collected the dues themselves for the first twenty years, before the Society took full control. The bushes which surrounded the Park were cleared away, and dykes were built round the perimeter, leaving a wide gateway for the passage of boats and equipment. Thus the Fishermen's Park was established as the centre of activity until the 1930s, when tenement buildings were erected on the site.

As far as the Society was concerned, its most important purchase was land on which to build its own hall. In 1878 a site became available at the west end of Main Street which had previously been used as a school. The site had been given *gratis* by Edinburgh Corporation for the school, but as the Fishermen's Hall could not be regarded as a building for public use, the same offer could not be repeated. The Corporation did, however, insert a stipulation that anyone buying the ground must provide accommodation for the

Reliance, the last boat made at Newhaven, and built at Allan and Brown's yard, Fishermen's Park, 1929, is hauled through the streets to the Harbour. Courtesy of Peter Carnie, Snr.

fishermen. When this had the effect of severely limiting the interest of prospective purchasers, the Society secured the land for a nominal feu duty. In April 1877 plans were drawn up for a main hall with two shops facing south in Main Street, and three houses at the back facing on to Pier Place. The Fishermen's Hall was opened at a grand soirée on Friday 18th January 1878, the leading dignitaries being Baillie Colston, the City Chamberlain, and Rev. Dr Fairbairn. The Hall cost £1,600, which involved the Society in substantial debt, but following a very successful bazaar in the Music Hall in George Street on 21st and 22nd October 1888, the profit of £741 was more than sufficient to pay off the outstanding sum.

The Newhaven fishermen's tenacity of spirit was more than once to the fore in times of national crisis. Among the Society's regalia are a silver medal and chain, and a silver cup commemorating moments of conflict. The medal and chain were presented by the Duke of Buccleuch and other prominent citizens to the Fishermen in 1796:

> In testimony of the brave and
> patriotic offer of the Fishermen
> of Newhaven to defend the coasts
> against the enemy this honorary mark
> of appreciation was voted by the County
> of Midlothian 21st November 1796.

162

On the other side of the medal there is a Scots thistle, with the words *Nemo me impune lacesset agmine remerum celeri.*

The silver cup was presented to the Boxmaster, James Noble, on 21st July 1807 by Captain Brodie, one of His Majesty's officers, in memory of the volunteers in Newhaven who went on board HMS *Texel* when called to the defence of their country against French men-of-war in the North Sea.

The regalia were completed by a medal and chain in 1888 to commemorate the Bazaar held in that year.

Churches

For many years prior to 1836 Newhaven did not have a church of its own. It came within the Parish of North Leith, whose minister held midweek services in the old school which stood on the site of the Fishermen's Hall. The services were so well attended that Rev. James Buchanan had to tell the younger members of the congregation to walk to North Leith Church in future and leave room at Newhaven for those less able for the journey.

In 1836 the architect John Henderson of Edinburgh designed a new church for Newhaven in the Gothic style on a site to the east of what is now Craighall Road. The vestibule with the gallery above was at the west end, and below the church there was hall accommodation. Seating was for four hundred, with the pulpit and the precentor's chair in the centre of the east wall. There was no organ and no chancel. The first service was taken by Rev. James Buchanan on Sunday 30th October 1836. During the first year Newhaven Church was administered by visiting preachers from North Leith, but on 25th January 1838 Rev. James Fairbairn was appointed as the first minister to the new Parish of Newhaven. His traditional background raised no eyebrows in Newhaven: he was born on 16th December 1804 the son of a Lauderdale farmer, and was educated at Lauder School and Edinburgh University. He also had strong leanings towards the idea of a free church in Scotland. To the surprise of some, and the jubilation of many others, including members of the Kirk Session, he 'came out' at the time of the Disruption on 18th May 1843 and formed a separate congregation as Newhaven Free Church. Such was Fairbairn's personal following in Newhaven that the Parish Church suffered greatly by his departure. In the years immediately after the Disruption, no one was appointed to Newhaven Parish Church, which was again brought under the control of North Leith. This rather unsatisfactory arrangement was, however, rectified in 1849 when Newhaven Church was re-opened for public worship. Rev. William Graham was appointed, but it was not until 20th July 1859 that Newhaven again became a Parish Church.

In 1870 Craighall Road was opened up and the front of the church was enclosed with railings. Attractive as they were, they must have provided scant comfort for the Trustees, who expressed 'great regret that such a roadway past the Church should exist at all'. Less opposition seems to have attended the installation of a two-manual pipe organ built in 1883 by Conacher & Co. of Huddersfield for £215. On the appointment of Rev. Thomas Pearson in 1887, the Parish Church entered a long period of prosperity and influence. The new minister was a man of considerable musical ability who was keen to appoint an organist of a sufficiently high calibre to do justice to the new church organ. Dr Robert McLeod, Musical Director at Moray House Training College, was chosen and led the congregation and the choir from 1894 to 1898. At the Diamond Jubilee in 1896 considerable interest was shown in a plan for enlarging the church. Unfortunately the first set of plans was too costly, but agreement was reached with another architect, William H. McLachlan, to complete the work within the budget. This entailed the removal of the east wall to lengthen the body of the church and create space for a chancel. The work was completed in 1899 for the sum of £1911.

When Rev. James Fairbairn and his followers broke away from Newhaven Parish Church in 1843, they did not have a permanent place for worship. However, in 1852 the new congregation had St. Andrew's Free Church built in Pier Place to designs by the architect F. Anderson Hamilton, and in 1883 the halls and steeple were added by Wallace and Flockhart of London. Thus, within a comparatively short time Newhaven moved from the position of having no church to having two good buildings with flourishing congregations in each. The large following at the Free Church was in no small way due to the charisma of Fairbairn himself. He was a man who understood the fisherfolk around him and was able to identify with their needs and their thoughts, especially at times when men were lost at sea. His spiritual comfort was matched by his practical ingenuity. At a time when the fishing fleet was lacking in prosperity and direction, Rev.

Rev. James Fairbairn, first Disruption minister of St. Andrew's Free Church, immortalised as the caring cleric by Charles Reade in his novel *Christie Johnstone*.
From Grant's *Old and New Edinburgh*.

James Fairbairn led a campaign for the rebuilding and modernisation of the entire fleet consisting of thirty-three large boats, each requiring an expenditure of £250, a sum utterly beyond the financial resources of families in a small fishing community. He died in 1879, leader of a very loyal congregation, and immortalised by Charles Reade as the caring cleric in his novel *Christie Johnstone*. Among Reade's other novels are *It is Never too Late to Mend* and *The Cloister and the Hearth*.

Schools

The first known school in Newhaven was in School Close or Lamb's Close in the early eighteenth century. No definite records survive, but it is generally supposed that its administration was undertaken by the Society of Free Fishermen. Much more definite records exist for the second school, the foundation stone of which was laid on 26th September 1817 on a site later used for the Fishermen's Hall. The cost of the school was met from public subscription and it was under the control of the Society until 1823. At £6 per annum the schoolmaster was by no means overpaid, especially when it was stipulated that the annual salary was not to be payable at all 'unless he remain a twelvemonth'. What he lacked in salary he gained in power and influence. Rule 5 of his contract of employment appears to have dispensed with the need for bureaucratic control of schoolmasters by providing 'that if any person shall be so rude as to come into school and challenge the Master for anything he is doing in school in the discharge of his duty the Master shall be at liberty to put him or them out'.

In 1822 Rev. Dr Ireland, minister at North Leith Church, was instrumental in forming the Hillhousefield, Bonnington and Newhaven Local Sabbath Evening School Society to promote religious instruction among young boys and girls. In the following year the Society of Free Fishermen relinquished control of their own school to this new body, which then concentrated on day schooling under its branch name Newhaven Education Society. A female section of the Society was formed in 1823, and in 1825 the whole school was reorganised by Miss Howell. In the first few years of development the committee agreed that their efforts were 'inferior to the House of Industry, St. John Street Canongate', but by 1827 the subjects taught were extended to reading, English grammar, writing and arithmetic. Later the male and female branches were amalgamated, and total attendances increased to around one hundred and fifty, with 'deserving pupils allowed to take a book home'.

In 1844 Dr James Buchanan of North Leith Church headed a committee which was to have a significant effect on education in Newhaven for many years to follow. The purpose of the committee was to secure the feu of ground to erect the first Victoria School building. When the school was taken over by Leith School Board in

1874, the number of places was one hundred and thirty. This was substantially increased when additional accommodation was provided in 1875, 1884 and again in 1897. In 1930 a one-storey extension designed by Reid and Forbes was built to house the infant department.

Unfortunately the log books for the original Newhaven School have not survived, but the first entry in September 1875 states that it was necessary for the Infant Department to meet in the old Free Fishermen's School because the new part of Victoria School was not quite ready for pupils. Other highlights in the history of the school are worth recording: 19th June 1902 — poorest children to be given a picnic in Victoria Park on Coronation Day — headmaster to select; 24th May 1915, Empire Day — all children went to the playground to sing 'Flag of Britain' and salute the flag; 3rd September 1937 — school to be wired for the installation of a wireless set. Newhaven's proximity to the Forth and to Leith Docks meant that 1939 was a time of great apprehension for everyone in the village. On 2nd September 1939 many pupils and parents were evacuated to Fort William, and arrangements were made for teaching the remaining pupils in various private houses: Mrs Morris, 38 Hawthornvale; Mrs Tweedie, 253 Newhaven Road; Mrs Gordon, 4 Ann Street etc. Despite, or perhaps because of, the increased workload involving air raid shelter practices, gas mask drill, fire watching and numerous alerts, the headmaster was able to record on 30th June 1944 a memorable centenary session. On 30th October 1944 a copy of the 'Armada' stone, presented by Henry Robb, Shipbuilders, was unveiled by the Lord Provost, Sir William Y. Darling, to mark the centenary of Victoria School. The carved wooden plaque was displayed on the ground floor of the school and is an exact copy of the very ancient stone which at one time was built into the post office building on the south side of Main Street. At the centenary service the girls of the school were dressed in striped petticoats and shawls, and the boys wore blue home-knitted jerseys. Ernest Brown, M.P., reminded the children that on the platform there were representatives of the three things that Hitler hated most — the Church, Parliament and Education. Happier days returned on 8th May 1945 when Victory in Europe was declared over the radio and the school closed for two days' holiday. In the post-war years Victoria School served its population well, and at the present time it is acutely aware of its responsibilities to keep alive the old traditions of Newhaven. The school maintains a small museum of old photographs of the village, old street signs, model ships, creels, nets and a ten-foot-high model of a lighthouse used during a Second World War fund-raising concert.

Newhaven had one other school, remembered now only by the sons and daughters of those who attended there. Madras School was built in 1862 for £1600 at the rear of Newhaven Parish Church, the name being derived from a specific stipulation accompanying a substantial grant by the Bell Trustees. Dr Andrew Bell was born in St. Andrews in 1753 and developed a pupil-teacher system of education while he was a chaplain at Madras: the system was widely adopted, particularly in the various schools in Edinburgh and St. Andrews which benefited from his bequests. In addition to the main school building at Newhaven a separate cottage was used as a schoolhouse. Being a parish school, Madras School's administration was in the hands of a Board consisting of four members of the Kirk Session, four subscribers and the minister as the chairman. The school was discontinued in 1888, although the accommodation was used for some years thereafter by Leith School Board, while alterations were being made at Victoria School. Eventually all the classes were moved out and the old Madras 'academy' became the church hall.

East to West through Newhaven

The 1759 plan of the Links of Newhaven by John Fergus and Robert Robinson shows Main Street with several closes running northwards towards the shore. Newhaven's oldest surviving hostelry, the Peacock Inn, is marked with the high water line coming up almost to the north wall of the building. Among the few other details shown is the line of Newhaven Road, appropriately named The Whale. It is clear, however, that the road systems were not well developed. For many years pedestrian access from the east was blocked, or severely restricted, by the Mantrap — a large area of deep coastal erosion which had claimed the life of more than one innocent traveller. By far the safest journey from Edinburgh was by the Newhaven stagecoach, which ran three times a day from William Bell's coach office opposite the Tron Church.

All that has gone, but not so very long ago Main Street was the arterial road of the old village, along which cable cars, coal lorries and half-finished boats jostled for position. Modern town planners, preoccupied with the idea of a traffic-free environment, have severed the artery at both ends, and wonder where the pulse has gone. On the other hand, the absence of heavy traffic gives a better opportunity to observe what remains of the old village.

At its east end old Newhaven begins at Annfield, a long terrace of three-storey houses started around 1800 but not finished until nearly fifty years later. Close to where the old village street is bypassed by the new section of Lindsay Road, a huge iron anchor straddles the pavement of whinstone setts. Whilst it is tempting to imagine that the anchor is all that remains of the *Great Michael*, the better opinion is that is was salvaged from a shipbreaker's yard at Inverkeithing. Annfield continues with modern flats constructed on the ground floor of setts taken from the old village street, and tenement buildings built in the 1930s on the site of the Fishermen's Park. Newhaven's War Memorial, to the memory of the men of the Newhaven churches who fell in the Great War 1914–1918, is set into the face of the tenement on the corner of Annfield and Newhaven Road. The inscriptions include the names of the men who belonged to the Parish Church and the Free Church, followed by the words 'Erected by John Pottinger 1935'. Immediately opposite, Victoria School boldly portrays the words '1843   Leith School Board 1885', below which is the corresponding War Memorial for the men and women of Newhaven who fell in the Second World War 1939–1945. The memorial was unveiled on 6th June 1948 by the Lady Provost, Miss Rodney Murray, in the company of the Lord Provost, Sir Andrew Murray, and James Hoy, Member of Parliament for Leith.

Behind Victoria School extensive land reclamation has 'moved' the old Peacock Hotel inland so that its stout north walls no longer sit out above the high spring tides. The Peacock is a hostelry of great antiquity which, for many years, has been a centre of local activity, as well as attracting visitors from much further afield to sample its gastronomic delights. The traditions of its first owner, Mr Peacock, are proudly maintained by the present proprietor, Peter Carnie, who comes from a very old-established Newhaven family. Originally the Peacock consisted of a few one-storey cottages facing the sea, but later a more substantial building was erected in Peacock's Court, with bar accommodation on the ground floor, and the dining room and bedrooms on the upper floor. Towards the end of the nineteenth century it was the established venue for a pay-off — the celebratory dinner held by members of a printing chapel to mark the occasion of

PEACOCK HOTEL, NEWHAVEN.

South-facing frontage of the old Peacock Hotel which belonged to Mrs Main, daughter and successor to the late Mrs Clark.
Courtesy of N.B. Traction Group Collection.

an apprentice becoming a journeyman. These evenings were usually on a Saturday, starting about 4.30 in the afternoon and going on until midnight. Reading between the lines, it would appear that around midnight the young journeyman was well and truly on his way to taking his first faltering steps in the company of his brothers. The Peacock has done much to keep the traditions of Newhaven alive. The present accommodation has been pleasingly refurbished in a style which befits the leading establishment of an old fishing village. A fireplace has recently been restored showing a magnificent peacock in coloured tiles, and there are numerous artefacts pertaining to boats and the fishing industry. Among these are a model of the *Great Michael*, large dolls wearing the traditional dress of the Newhaven fishwife, and a full set of photographs by David Octavius Hill and Robert Adamson showing life in Newhaven around 1844.

As with so many other small villages around Edinburgh, Newhaven's stock of houses was allowed to reach abysmal standards of maintenance in the 1950s and 1960s before any large-scale renovation was considered. By then much of the decay was so widespread that demolition was the only practical answer. In the 1970s almost £2 million was spent on the complete demolition and rebuilding of the south side of Main Street and the refurbishment of

New Lane bustling with activity in the days when Newhaven was in the forefront of the Scottish fishing industry.

many properties on the north side. Three-storey flats were designed for the south side by Ian G. Lindsay & Partners, who took the trouble to incorporate an ancient Newhaven stone in the gable wall of No. 6 Auchinleck Court. This stone has a most interesting history, recorded in the *Inventory of the Ancient and Historical Monuments of the City of Edinburgh* (1951). It has been moved on more than one occasion in the past. It consists of two carved panels which were built into the front of Newhaven Post Office, Main Street in 1914, after having been saved from an old cottage which stood previously on the same site. The upper triangular panel has a thistle on the top, the inscription NEMO ME IMPUNE LACESSET, the date 1588, and the words IN THE NEAM OF GOD. Between the date and the inscription there is a rigged ship with flags on all three masts displaying the St. Andrew's Cross. The lower square panel has a seventeenth-century moulding containing two globes in the lower part and a sextant, anchor and cross-staff in the upper part. The motto of Trinity House, PER (VIA) VERTVTI SYDERA TERRA MARE (Courage makes its way through heaven earth and sea), was recut in the stone, but a slight error was made with the word PERVIA. The details in these carved panels are reproduced in the iron plaque of the War Memorial on the front of Victoria School, and the wooden plaque inside the school.

To the north of Main Street several attractive closes remain, though greatly altered from the original layout. Fishmarket Square (formerly St. Andrew's Square) opens out, giving access to Pier Place and the harbour. Facing the harbour there is an interesting stone barometer case, first erected in 1775, then re-erected in 1900 with a ship cut into a square stone moulding, and round the base the words SOCIETY OF FREE FISHERMEN. The stone-fronted tenement nearby with the clock in the pediment was also erected by the Society. Immediately west of the barometer case is the old Newhaven Free Church (St. Andrew's), now in secular use, and a later addition greatly enhanced by small architectural features depicting crabs, starfish and other sea creatures. A small area on the harbour side of Pier Place has been developed in recent years to a group of seats in memory of various people closely connected with Newhaven.

Appropriately, Newhaven's most ancient building is in the centre of the old village, a few yards north of Main Street between Westmost Close and Lamb's Close. This is the ancient chapel of St. Mary and St. James, built around 1508 by James IV as a place of worship for the shipwrights who worked on the *Great Michael*. The chapel gradually fell into disuse, particularly after the Siege of Leith in 1544 and the Reformation in 1560, until in 1611 it was reported as being in ruins. The site was acquired by the Society of Free Fishermen in the middle of the eighteenth century and used by them as a place of burial until 1848. There is an interesting footnote in Alexander Campbell's *History of Leith* (1827) which states that an elegantly cut ornamental model of a cannon in stone, and a holy water font belonging to the ancient chapel, were in the possession of a gentleman living near Newhaven. Unfortunately no trace of these items has been found in recent years, but in 1972 a most important archaeological dig was undertaken at the chapel under the direction of the Department of Educational Studies at Edinburgh University. Several trenches were dug which revealed a mass of human skeletons in disarray, suggesting that they had been moved from some other area. At greater depths more skeletons were found, but in more ordered positions. Some skeletal remains were enclosed in wooden coffins, and the bodies were wrapped in shrouds. The team were also successful in locating the foundations of the outer walls, which suggested a rectangular building of internal length approximately sixty-three feet from west to east, and an internal breadth of approximately twenty-one feet. There were some traces of facing mortar on the inside, but there was

A horse bus and an open-topped electric car at the foot of Craighall Road, 1912. One of the shops in the background is the Buttercup Dairy Co.

no flooring apart from a few slabs, and there was no sign of an altar or other fitments. Small artefacts, found on the site, include medieval pottery, clay tobacco pipes and a two penny piece of the reign of Charles I minted in 1632.

To the west of the old chapel the brightly painted building with crowstepped stonework above the upper windows was built in 1878 as the Hall for the Society of Free Fishermen of Newhaven. The building, extending into Pier Place, has recently been acquired by the Port o' Leith Motor Boat Club who have maintained its traditions by remodelling the interior to resemble the *Great Michael* warship.

At the foot of Craighall Road the village street ends abruptly with a pavement and railing blocking vehicular access, but providing a useful site for the commemorative seat, presented by Charles Addison to mark the Golden Jubilee, 1927–1977, of the Newhaven Fisherwomen's Choir. Although the Fisherwomen's Choir is no longer in existence, an even older choir has been in continuous harmony for almost a century. The Newhaven Fisher Girls' Choir established in 1889 changed its name many years ago to Newhaven Fisher Lassies' Choir and continues under its conductor since 1938, Robert Allan, with a repertoire of Scottish folk and traditional fishing songs.

The Chain Pier, constructed in 1821 by Captain Brown for £4,000, was destroyed in a violent storm on 18th October 1898.
Courtesy of Edinburgh City Libraries.

A welcome piece of open ground at the west end of Newhaven is provided by Starbank Park, laid out at the end of last century on part of the garden ground of Starbank House. The central fountain, designed by George Simpson in 1910, was presented to the people of Newhaven by Thomas L. Devlin, J.P., of Newhaven. Early photographs show an ornamental fish at the fountain head and several Grecian urns around the peripheral stonework.

At the west end of the village the Chain Pier Bar marks the approximate location of the original Chain Pier constructed in 1821 by Captain Brown of the Royal Navy, as a private venture costing £4,000. The pier was five hundred feet long and four feet wide and was used by the steam packet companies operating to Stirling, Queensferry and other ports on the Forth. The pier was purchased in 1840 by the Alloa Steam Packet Company, but its popularity declined when bigger ships were unable to berth in the comparatively shallow water. Its early popularity with bathers and the Forth Swimming Club was of sufficient importance to justify inclusion in a property advertisement of 15th February 1832: '... that selfcontained house at the west end of the village of Newhaven lying on the south of the road leading to Cramond lately occupied as the Crown and Anchor Hotel,

The traditional style of architecture with pantiled roofs and outside stairs has been maintained in Wester Close, 1985.
Photograph by Phyllis Margaret Cant.

conveniently situated for Bathing Quarters'. After serving as a popular bathing resort for many years, the pier gradually fell into disrepair, and then suddenly into the sea during a violent storm on 18th October 1898.

The Chain Pier was intended to form part of a much more ambitious scheme to provide passenger and freight travel from the centre of Edinburgh to most towns and villages along the Firth of Forth. In 1846 the journey began at Canal Street Station, built on the site of what is now the polished glass and granite enclave of the new Waverley Market at the east end of Princes Street. Canal Street was so named in anticipation of a much bigger civic plan to extend the Union Canal from Port Hopetoun in Lothian Road, round the north side of the Castle rock, to Greenside. From Canal Street Station the Edinburgh Leith and Newhaven Railway Co. cut the Scotland Street Tunnel to the north giving direct access by rail from the city centre to Trinity Station perched on the hill above the Chain Pier. The line was later extended to Granton, but the original Trinity Station building still stands north west of York Road, where the cutting is supported by massive buttressed masonry. In keeping with its function to serve a busy fishing community, the station displayed practical ingenuity in providing for the comfort and convenience of its passengers. There was a small dial which showed the strength and direction of the wind, and there was a movable pane of glass in one of the windows through which the fisherwives could obtain their tickets without the need to enter the ticket office.

CHAPTER 8

Restalrig

Near the Fire Station at the foot of Smoky Brae, watchful eyes 'gaze' down upon the old village of Restalrig. Those eyes belong, not to the ever vigilant men of the fire service, but to Restalrig's own patron saint, St. Triduana. Perched high on the slated roof of Triduana's Well, a small statue depicts this saintly virgin holding the thorn branch on which her eyes were skewered.

According to legend, Triduana came to Scotland in the company of St. Rule and settled as a recluse at Rescobie in Angus. Her life of prayer and seclusion was not, however, sufficient protection from the amorous advances of Nectan, King of the Picts. Declaring himself mesmerised by the beauty of her eyes, he implored her to abandon her life of pious dedication and come to him. Instead, she fled to Athole 'at a place called Dunsallad' only to find that Nectan had sent word begging her to return. On learning from the King's ambassadors the reason for his great passion, Triduana plucked out her eyes, skewered them on a thorn, and handed them to the reluctant postilions for presentation to the King. With Nectan suitably discouraged, Triduana was free to lead her life as she had intended. She came to Lestalryk (Restalrig), where she spent her days healing and comforting the blind who journeyed from all parts of the country 'to mend their ene' in the special waters at Restalrig. She died sometime in the sixth century and was buried at Restalrig, her body being committed to the tomb from which the spring water originated. To this day on the 8th of October each year, a service of dedication is held at St. Triduana's Well at Restalrig Church in memory of a legend which has existed for more than a thousand years.

St. Triduana's Well; St. Margaret's Well

Although St. Triduana is of legendary origin, there is no doubt about the existence of St. Triduana's Well at Restalrig dating from the early fifteenth century. It is believed to have been erected by Sir Robert

Main Street of Restalrig village, now Restalrig Road South, with byres on the right and an unidentified hexagonal 'folly' to the left of the church. From Grant's *Old and New Edinburgh*.

Logan around 1438, when the family owned the Barony of Restalrig. Originally it consisted of a two-storey hexagonal building immediately adjacent to the south side of Restalrig Church. The upper storey was a chapel, whilst the lower vaulted area contained the well at which pilgrims bathed their eyes. At the Reformation in 1560 the building suffered considerable damage, the entire upper storey being demolished. Later, the lower area was used as a burial chamber, principally for the Logan family. For reasons which are now obscure, the lower chamber was covered with an earthen mound until the beginning of the twentieth century. It was realised in 1907 that the history and existence of St. Triduana's Well were in danger of being forgotten, but under the direction of the Earl of Moray plans were put in hand to renovate the ancient building. The earthen mound was removed to reveal the hexagonal lower chamber which was in a rather unpleasant condition from a combination of damp and the decomposition of human remains. Several stones were also found which proved beyond doubt that there had been a chapel built over the well, but unfortunately too many stones were missing for an accurate restoration to be done of the upper chapel. Several attempts were made to prevent water coming up through the floor before it was realised that the Logan family tomb was in fact St. Triduana's Well. Sympathetic restoration work revealed a most interesting vaulted chamber about thirty feet across with a centre pillar supporting a groined stone roof. The well still produces a fairly constant supply of water which is kept at a fixed level by an electric pump concealed below the heavy slabs of the perimeter seat.

In 1928 William Douglas, F.S.A. Scot., made a detailed study of the gravestones and inscriptions found in St. Triduana's Well and published his findings in the *Proceedings of the Society of Antiquaries of Scotland.* The main concern of his study was the armorial tombstone of Lady Jonet Ker of Restalrig, who was believed to be the wife of one of the seven Logan lairds. Identifying the laird concerned was no easy task, as a corner of the tombstone bearing part of the date had been broken off and lost many years previously. Hugo Arnot, writing in 1788, referred to the stone and gave the date of death as 17.5.1526, and Dr David Laing, writing in 1861, also gave the year as 1526 but the day as the 12th. After an exhaustive analysis of the quartering of the Logan Arms shown on the stone, William Douglas concluded that the date of death should read 1596 and that Lady Jonet was the second wife of the 7th laird, Sir Robert Logan. The conclusive proof for Douglas was that the stone carries heraldic details pertaining to the Home family which did not come to the Logans until after the Logan-Home marriage around 1580.

In the early part of the nineteenth century there was another well at Restalrig known as St. Margaret's, which has from time to time been confused with that of St. Triduana. To the south of the village a rough path meandered up the slope towards Abbeyhill, where the mossy roof of the old well was overhung by the branches of an alder tree. Beside the well there was a very small thatched cottage, the owner of which gained considerable commercial advantage from his situation by drawing off the water in barrels and taking it to Leith where he sold it 'to clarify the vision of the dwellers of that enlightened burgh'. Around 1850, however, the North British Railway Company began to build extensive workshops on their land close to St. Margaret's Well. As the well was considered to be of great antiquity and of interest to historians, the developers decided to retain it and build St. Margaret's Depot over the top of it. The depot was used for the repair and maintenance of railway engines on land later occupied by Meadowbank House, home of the Registers of Scotland. Access to the well was gained by a long narrow tunnel which suffered greatly from lack of light and proper ventilation. The situation came to the attention of the Society of Antiquaries of Scotland, who commissioned a report to establish the condition of the well and to suggest possibilities for its removal to another location. David Laing, born in 1793 the son of an Edinburgh bookseller, was appointed to prepare the report. He was considered the ideal choice, having been described at a very early stage in his career by John Gibson Lockhart as 'by far the most genuine specimen of a true old fashioned bibliopole that I ever saw exhibited in the person of a young man'. In 1855 David Laing submitted his report, indicating that the position of the well was so inappropriate and harmful to its stonework that there was no option but to move it, stone by stone. After considering several sites in Holyrood Park, H.M. Commissioners of Works organised its removal to an existing spring known as St. David's. Today it can still be seen in Holyrood Park not far from the gates of Holyrood Palace, tucked into a grassy bank and giving little indication that it has ever been anywhere else. It is listed and described in Billings' *Baronial and Ecclesiastical Antiquities of Scotland* (1852) under the heading 'St Margaret's Well, Restalrig'. It has a small round pillar rising out of the centre of the cistern, supporting a circle of ribbed vaultwork with ornamental bosses.

Restalrig Church

Restalrig Church has an ancient history extending from the twelfth century to the present day, reaching its zenith in the fifteenth century before being eclipsed and utterly cast down at the time of the Reformation in 1560. Early charters make interesting references to how the name evolved. The building of a new church in the Norman style of architecture was started in 1165 by Edward de Lestalric and completed in 1210 by Sir Thomas de Lestalric. In 1435 patronage of the church was transferred from the Bishop of St. Andrews to Thomas Logan of Restalrig, whose family held the Barony of Restalrig until 1609.

In addition to its being a place of pilgrimage, Restalrig Church benefited greatly from the influence and assistance of the Scottish

The original Restalrig Church dating from the twelfth century was destroyed at the Reformation, 1560, and restored by William Burn, 1828. Courtesy of Rev. W. Carmichael.

Kings, who were responsible for giving it collegiate status. In keeping with St Giles, Trinity College and St Mary's Kirk-o'-field, it assumed responsibility for the continuous worship of God rather than involvement in purely parochial matters. It was made collegiate by James III in 1487, and received continuous support from James IV, who ordained that it should have eight prebendaries in addition to the Dean. After James IV fell at Flodden in 1513, the foundation was completed by James V. In its heyday, Restalrig Church was a place of great religious importance, the prebendaries being actively involved in all aspects of the church. In return they were given a place in which to live and a piece of land for their own use as a garden. They had to be able to sing and be well versed in the protocol attached to the great festivals and processions, at which they would appear in their robes and scarlet hoods. The choir boys were in the nature of apprentices involved in cleaning the church, ringing the bells, carrying fuel and kindling the lights in the church for special services. But that way of life ended abruptly in 1560 at the Reformation. Restalrig was singled out for especially zealous treatment by the reformers, who were sent to ensure 'that the Kirk of Restalrig as a monument of idolatrie be raysit and utterly casten doun and destroyed'. Parts of the north and south walls and the east gable survived, but the west gable was lost along with the buildings of the Deanery on the east side. The parish was transferred to South Leith Church, and the stones of Restalrig Church were used to build part of the Netherbow Port in the Old Town. For almost three centuries it lay desolate until about 1828, when it was decided to restore the church. By then, however, the Restalrig Friendly Society had been operating for about a century, using the churchyard and ensuring that burials were conducted in a decent manner. The Society had come to assume ownership of the churchyard and the ruins, but the Minister and Kirk Session of South Leith had other ideas. The conflict ran in the Court of Session from 1828 to 1832, ending in a decision in favour of the Society. However, in 1836 the Society and the Minister and Kirk Session were able to adopt a restoration scheme acceptable to all parties. Plans were drawn up by William Burn the architect, and Restalrig was re-opened for worship on 20th August 1837. In 1868 the Restalrig Friendly Society relinquished all rights in the church, and in 1912 it was re-established as the Parish Church of Restalrig.

In more recent years several memorial windows have been added. In 1953 the east window of the chancel was dedicated 'To the Glory of God and in Loving Memory of Margaret Henderson who died on Easter Morning 1949 aged 17 years', and in 1966 another window depicting the theme Women of Faith was gifted by Adam Edward Shaw in memory of his wife Jane Morris Gibson Milligan Shaw. In 1984 the Logan window was dedicated in memory of the Logans of Restalrig. The window was gifted by Harry A. Logan and Marian Logan Wendell of Warren, Pennsylvania to mark the sexcentenary of the succession of the Logans to the Barony of Restalrig in 1382. The artist Miss Saidie F. McLellan, Fellow of the Society of British Master Glass Painters, took the Maltese Cross as the symbol for the window which depicts the Four Evangelists, the Logan heraldry, the crowns of James III, IV and V, and the healing waters of St. Triduana. Another interesting window, not intended as a memorial, was gifted to the church in 1980 by George Ferguson, a former organist at Restalrig. The design is based on Psalm 150, verse 6, 'Let everything that breathes praise the Lord'. Mr Sax Shaw took Mr and Mrs Ferguson's ideas and incorporated in the design a viol, a trumpet, a timbrel, a harp and an organ. The organ is taken from the Holy Trinity Church medieval altar panel by Hugo Van der Goes, which can be seen in the National Gallery of Scotland.

If stones could speak, the old graveyard around Restalrig Church would surely have an interesting story to tell. Although the church buildings were destroyed in 1560, the graveyard continued to be used by the Restalrig Friendly Society, and by the Episcopalians in Edinburgh who were prevented from using any other burial place in the city. During the nineteenth century several eminent figures were laid to rest at Restalrig including Henry Brougham of Brougham Hall, father of Lord Brougham, distinguished politician and law reformer whose name is perpetuated in Brougham Street near Tollcross. The family tomb of the Cauvin family is also at Restalrig, Louis Cauvin having left his fortune 'for the endowment of a hospital for the education of the sons of respectable people'. On the east wall there is a monument to Dr Thomas Murray (1792–1872), author of the *Literary History of Galloway* and *Biographical Annals of the Parish of Colinton.*

A few years ago Miss A.S. Cowper of Edinburgh made a special study of the graveyard, with particular reference to infant mortality. The children included many from the families of soldiers stationed at Piershill Barracks which stood to the south of Restalrig from 1793 to 1934. Of 405 child deaths from the barracks, recorded between 1800 and 1854, fourteen were stillborn, and 276 died within the first two years of life, from such complaints as consumption, fever and water on the brain.

The Barracks were built to form three sides of a quadrangle, the fourth side being completed by a high stone wall broken by two south-facing gateways. The cavalry regiments stationed there in the first half of the nineteenth century included the Dragoon Guards, the Hussars and the Scots Greys.

Restalrig Village

Although Restalrig village is now completely surrounded by urban development, there is still a distinctly different atmosphere in that part of Restalrig Road South which forms the old village street. In its day, as we saw, Restalrig was a place of pilgrimage for those with afflictions of the eye; it housed the Dean and the churchmen of the Collegiate Church; and later it was the unscheduled landing ground for James Tytler in the first-ever British hot-air balloon ascent of 1784; more recently it provided summer tea-gardens where visitors from Edinburgh could enjoy a day in the country. Although much has changed, there is still plenty of opportunity to inspect, to ponder, and to speculate on the meaning of what remains.

At the south end of the village near the Fire Station, the gates on the left give access to the churchyard beside the gatehouse or schoolhouse of 1770, a substantial two-storeyed building now used by the Model Railway Club. On the opposite side of the road the building used as the Church Hall has obviously had a domestic use in the past. It appears in many of the old prints as a row of two-storeyed houses with outside stairways, but the lower windows have now been built up and the upper storey has crowstepped brickwork added over the windows. Beyond the shops on the right, the picturesque building with the projecting crowstepped gable is probably the oldest house in the village. It has a date 1678 over the lintel, and it is said that for many years one of the stairway landings was made from a flat tombstone taken from the churchyard opposite. Immediately beside this building new iron gates lead through an open pend to Deanery Close. This recent development by Viewpoint Housing Association is built on the site of an old dairy. Although the byres were demolished some time ago, the house, which was used in conjunction with the dairy, is still there. The present owner, Mr Smith, a stonemason by trade, renovated the house, retaining many of the original features, and rediscovered its name: Dunira. The significance of the name Dunira in the village of Restalrig has not been established: the Ordnance Gazetteer of Scotland lists it in 1892 as a fine modern mansion in the parish of Comrie commanding a magnificent view of Strathearn and considered to be the favourite residence of Henry Dundas, Viscount Melville (1742–1811). Restalrig's Dunira has undergone many changes, but even at the present day it retains an uncanny association with the past. At one time it was used by an old Edinburgh church and became known as a place where the occasional travelling person could obtain hospitality. Whether it is a lost soul seeking refuge at Dunira or the return of a past owner is a matter of conjecture, but it is said the house has a presence which has been observed on several occasions in recent years.

Opposite Dunira a close look at the churchyard wall shows the original entrance now blocked up and lacking the embellishments intended for the left-hand stone pillar. At the time of the Church Bazaar in the Music Hall in George Street on 10th December 1908 one of the congregation drew up detailed plans of how the old entrance could be opened up and used again. It is here that the jougs

Restalrig Road South c.1900, showing the projecting gable of the oldest house in the village, 1678, and Dunira to the left.
Courtesy of Rev. W. Carmichael.

collar hung, but it was stolen some years ago and has not been replaced. In any case modern traffic conditions through the village at this corner would make a gate or the attraction of the jougs collar rather dangerous.

Immediately north of Dunira the old walls and gateway to the Deanery of Restalrig now give access to trade premises. Although badly worn, the gate piers on each side are still visible with the tops set out on corbels, and there are traces of an old door and window now filled in. At this point the roadway widens with modern housing on the left, and on the right there is a neat whitewashed house with black railings believed to be close to the site of the legendary Habb's Castle. One of the few references to it is by John Russell in *The Story of Leith*, in which he suggests that the name may be a corruption of Abbot's Castle. This is also the site of one of the dairies owned by John Wood of Restalrig. The last house, before the corner block, is the doctor's surgery, appropriately named St. Triduana.

The south corner of Restalrig Road South and Loaning Road has recently been developed by George Wimpey & Co. into flats built of an attractive bronze-coloured brick. There is an interesting feature on the corner incorporating the gate of the house, St. Margaret's, which stood on this site until 1982. In earlier years the outbuildings around St. Margaret's were used as a dairy by John Wood and later by J.M. & M. Henderson Ltd., the makers of world-famous Capital Oatcakes 'As Grannie Baked Them'. To this day the older residents of Restalrig refer to this part of the village as Scone John's Corner, a fitting tribute to the Henderson family who pioneered factory 'home baking' at the end of the First World War. At the present day Simmers of Hatton include reference to J.M. & M. Henderson of Restalrig in their attractive colour brochure, *A Century of Excellence.*

Opposite the mouth of Loaning Road there is yet another property with a world-famous name, Brooklyn House. It has an impressive portico over the front door, a tall castellated tower to the rear, and a date 1879. The old maps of Edinburgh, however, show the property at least as early as 1860, with the plan of the house showing neither the portico, nor the tower. It has always been suggested that the house was named by a gentleman who made his fortune in America and retired to Restalrig. If this was around 1879, as suggested by the date on the house, then it is possible that the owner, James Buchanan, was responsible for adding the refinements to the house on his return from America. On the other side of the lane, the small house with the shutters was called Brooklyn Cottage and must have been associated with Brooklyn House at one time, along with the stables and outbuildings to the rear. However, Brooklyn Cottage has had a separate existence for many years, being owned by the old Restalrig family of Dods when it was the Old Inn, Restalrig. The Dods family later moved the licensed premises into the tenement building next door where the business still flourishes. The choice of name, 'The Bunch of Roses', is said to originate from the days when many of its clientèle were employed at St. Margaret's Railway Works, to the south of the village. From time to time the men would take the opportunity of a light refreshment when, strictly speaking, they should have been working. Unknown to them, of course, the same characteristic was frequently shared by the bosses, which meant that there was a very real risk of entering the pub during working hours and coming face to face with the gaffer. The publican, never wanting in diplomacy, placed a bunch of roses in the pub window to warn the men that it was not safe to enter.

Headquarters of Kinloch Anderson Ltd, Royal Appointment Holders, world-famous for tartans and tweeds, established 1868 in George Street, Edinburgh.
Courtesy of Kinloch Anderson Ltd. Photograph by Andrew Wilson.

Opposite the pub a large area of ground has been given over to industrial use. Munrospun, famous for the manufacture of knitwear and clothing, operated here for many years. Part of their extensive premises to the south is now used by several small workshop businesses under the control of the Scottish Development Agency. The main part of the building, however, with its characteristic red brick tower, has been transformed into the headquarters of Kinloch Anderson Ltd., known the world over for their high-quality clothing in tartans and tweeds. Since 1972 the Restalrig premises have included the main administrative block and the departments of sales, dispatch, production and warehousing. Much of the manufacturing side is done at a fine modern factory at Muirkirk, Ayrshire, and the retail department is at John Knox's House in the High Street. When Kinloch Anderson came to Restalrig they were, of course, already a long-established family business, started in 1868 by William Anderson at 14/16 George Street, Edinburgh. Coinciding with their move to Restalrig, the manufacturing activities of the company grew rapidly, its export performance being recognised by a Queen's Award for Export Achievement in 1979. Thus Restalrig, and the

Kemp's Corner, showing Charles Arthur Kemp Snr. and his staff outside the shop c.1935.
Courtesy of Charles Arthur Kemp Jnr.

world, can look forward to another century of service from one of Edinburgh's great family businesses, Holders of Royal Appointments to H.M. the Queen, to H.R.H. the Duke of Edinburgh, and to H.R.H. the Prince of Wales.

Kemp's Corner is not listed in the city's street directories, nor is it shown on any old map of Edinburgh. To anyone living in Restalrig, however, Kemp's Corner has long been associated with the licensed grocer on the corner of Restalrig Road South and Marionville Road. Charles Arthur Kemp Snr. came to Edinburgh from Orkney in 1906, and in 1908 he bought the Restalrig premises. When he opened for business on 21st December 1908, his first day's takings amounted to 16/- (80p). With a keen sense of business acumen, long hours, and an intimate knowledge of the Orkney markets for butter, eggs, cheese and rabbits, he built up a very active trade, both at the retail shop and as a wholesaler of Orkney products in Edinburgh. The shop also stocked a wide variety of wines and spirits under trade names related to every corner of the globe: Southalia White Wine — Produce of Australia; Pluto Fine Golden South African Sherry — Empire Produce; and Fine Old Tawny Port. There was also Kemp's blended

Finest Old Scotch Whisky, Barslay Perkins Imperial Stout, and Bass bottled and corked on the premises. In 1934 Charles Arthur Kemp Jnr. joined his father in the business after a short apprenticeship with J. & J. Tod of Edinburgh, and maintained the family business until 1982 when he retired.

Lochend Castle

On the west side of Lochend Road South, part of the old estate of the Logans is now laid out as a public park around what remains of Lochend Loch. Near the north entrance the sixteenth-century dovecot stands, on ground once known as Logan Lea. The east-facing entrance has been built up and replaced by a new doorway facing south, and there are traces of a window above the string course. The most unusual feature is, however, the raised collar of stonework round the top. The dovecot was designed so that the birds would reach the stone nesting boxes through an opening in the roof, but some historians believe that the collar was added in the mid-seventeenth century when the dovecot was used as a kiln for disinfection during the plague of 1645. It is known that the ground near Marionville Road was described in old title deeds as Kilnacre.

At the south end of the park, high on the precipitous rock face, are the remnants of a very old building variously described as Lochend Castle, Lochend House or Restalrig Castle, ancestral seat of the Logans of Restalrig, whose baronetcy can be traced back to the fourteenth century. The dominance of the Logan family endured until the fifteenth century, after which there was a gradual dissipation of their wealth and influence, culminating in the disastrous Gowrie Conspiracy of 1600. A temporary respite from misfortune occurred in 1580 when Sir Robert Logan secured ownership of Fast Castle near St. Abb's Head on his marriage to the daughter of Sir Patrick Home. At the end of the century, however, the whole country was rife with speculation about the attempt on the life of the King. In 1600 John the Third Earl of Gowrie and his brother Alexander, Master of Ruthven, conspired to assassinate King James VI, but the plot was unsuccessful and they were overpowered and killed in Gowrie House at Perth. To reinforce the sense of public outrage and to give due weight to the seriousness of the offence their bodies were brought to Edinburgh where they were 'hanged quartered and beheaded'. Sir

Lochend Castle, ancestral seat of the Logans of Restalrig whose baronetcy can be traced back to the fourteenth century.
From Grant's *Old and New Edinburgh.*

Robert Logan lived out his life in peace and on his death in 1606 was buried in the family tomb probably at South Leith Church. Although Sir Robert was dead and gone, the rumours were not so easily buried. In 1608 George Sprott, a notary from Eyemouth, who had worked on various transactions with Sir Robert Logan, began to talk. His idle gossip linked the name of Sir Robert with the Gowrie Conspiracy. Sprott maintained that he had proof of lengthy correspondence between Sir Robert Logan and the Earl of Gowrie immediately prior to the Perth incident. Sprott was arrested and charged with concealing treason. Under cross-examination and no doubt influenced by the unexpected threat to his own life, he changed his evidence on more than one occasion, but he was eventually found guilty and hanged on 12th August 1608. An interesting story is told of how Sprott protested his innocence to the end and warned the assembled crowd that in his dying moments he would give them a signal to show that they had condemned an innocent man. On mounting the scaffold, the execution was carried out without significant departure from the usual procedure. But as the spectators began to murmur their approval, Sprott was heard to clap his hands loudly three times before collapsing inert. The story does not, of course, explain how a man claps his hands with his neck broken and his limbs secured by manacles.

Even after Sprott was hanged, his suspect evidence was examined again and again until five letters allegedly written by Sir Robert Logan confirming his involvement in the Conspiracy were produced in court and attested by witnesses. In 1609 Sir Robert was 'summoned' to appear before the court. His remains were exhumed, the body was laid before the court and on a finding of guilty, sentence of forfeiture was passed on his title, lands and property. The case must surely be unique in legal history, the accused having spent many hours in the box without speaking a single word in his own defence! It is generally considered that Sir Robert Logan was convicted on evidence which, to say the least, was tenuous and inconclusive, but that did not prevent his estates being passed to Lord Balmerino who held them until he, too, was dispossessed for being on the losing side at the time of the '45 Rebellion.

Although Lochend Castle was destroyed many years ago, the commanding site above the water is now occupied by another interesting old house owned by Lothian Regional Council and used as Lochend Children's Centre. The remaining part of the Castle with the distinctive stepped chimney is incorporated in the caretaker's house to the west of the main building.

Hawkhill House

Hawkhill House stood near what is now Hawkhill Recreation Ground in the days when Lochend Road had only a handful of houses built near the Leith end. The house was built in 1759 for Lord Alemore to designs drawn in 1757 by John Adam, eldest son of William Adam. Although it had a rather plain exterior, the overall plan was considered to be excellent, with two large rooms on the east side, one square and one oblong, opening into one another to create a very large area for the entertainment of guests. With the possible exception of an ugly glass porch built over the original classical front doorway, the house 'married diversity with dignity' — that is to say until the mid-1960s. By that time, the use to which the house was put was certainly diverse, but there was little dignity left, with the furniture gone and the landscape paintings abandoned, flaking and falling to bits in their original gilt frames. In 1966 the Education

Committee of Edinburgh Corporation petitioned to have Hawkhill House demolished, as they wished to use the ground for the extension of recreational facilities. The petition was challenged by the Scottish Georgian Society, who spent considerable time and effort trying to convince the Corporation that the house could be saved without incurring disproportionate costs. It was generally agreed that the house contained some very attractive plasterwork, chimneypieces and original woodwork, and that it would be possible to remove it, stone by stone, to another site for about £100,000. Unfortunately no suitable buyer could be found, despite widespread advertising. On the evening of 7th February 1971 Hawkhill House was extensively damaged by fire and was demolished shortly thereafter. Fortunately the Scottish Georgian Society had already removed from the building and put into store a marble fireplace, a plaster centrepiece from the octagonal hall, and some pieces of fine wood carving.

Marionville House

Closer to Restalrig on the south side of Marionville Road, the solid square building of Marionville House stands behind high stone walls in which can still be detected the original gateway and supporting stonework. Marionville has long since thrown off 'the air of depression and melancholy' referred to by Robert Chambers in his *Traditions of Edinburgh*. It was built in the middle of the eighteenth century for two spinster ladies, the Misses Ramsay, who amassed a reasonable fortune from their successful business as milliners near Old Lyon Close in the High Street. The sisters' affected and pretentious involvement with the upper classes incurred the wrath of the everyday people of Restalrig, who sought to redress the imbalance with a measure of derisory wit. Using the old Scots word for a patch of material, they nicknamed the house Lappet Ha', a name which might well have gone down in history but for the much more compelling story of Captain Macrae.

Around 1790 Marionville was the home of Captain Macrae, head of one of Edinburgh's most fashionable families of the day, and owner of estates in Dumfriesshire. He had been retired for some years from the Irish Carabiniers and was considered to be of a generous and friendly disposition. On the debit side he had an overdeveloped sense of the respect due to a gentleman, and a fiery temper, which on more than one occasion had put him on a diet of humble pie. One such occasion was during a visit to Drumsheugh House when he threw a messenger of the law over the bannister for having had the audacity to serve a summons for debt on Rev. Mr Cunningham as he was going into the dining room of the house. When Macrae later discovered that payment of the debt had been requested many times and that the messenger had been seriously injured, he apologised and paid him three hundred guineas in compensation.

During their ownership of Marionville the Macraes arranged private theatrical performances for the entertainment of their guests. Among those who attended regularly were Sir George Ramsay of Banff and Lady Ramsay, who were on very close terms with the Macraes. At the end of a production one evening at the Old Theatre Royal, Macrae was escorting a lady from the theatre and arranging transport to take her home. He ordered 'a chair' and was about to help the lady into it when a footman stepped forward and claimed that he had already ordered the chair for his employer. In fact the footman was so drunk that he had forgotten that his employer had gone home earlier in the evening. Macrae, in his characteristic manner, took up the challenge, struck the footman several times and created a fracas in which the guests and onlookers were inclined to take sides. When Macrae discovered the next day that the drunken footman was in the employment of Lady Ramsay, he went to her house and apologised. Unfortunately the footman, James Merry, had already decided to have his revenge and had issued a writ for damages against the Captain. This incensed Macrae so much that he wrote to Sir George Ramsay demanding either that the writ be withdrawn or, alternatively, that James Merry be dismissed from his post. To Macrae's astonishment Sir George wrote back to say that he could not intervene. The ensuing correspondence grew more and more acrimonious until the two gentlemen, hell bent on proving that they were each men of honour, met at 12 noon at Ward's Inn near Musselburgh Links — complete with guns, seconds, and Benjamin Bell the surgeon. Captain Macrae expressed the wish that the matter be settled amicably. There were proposals and counter-proposals culminating in Sir George's second suggesting that if Macrae would apologise to Sir George for the style of his letters, then Sir George would immediately dismiss the servant. Macrae replied that he was prepared to settle on that basis but that he would require to be guided by the advice of his second. The question was put to his second, who

Captain Macrae of Marionville, the fiery-tempered duellist with an inset
showing him at target practice.
From Kay's *Original Portraits.*

replied, 'It is altogether impossible; Sir George must in the first place
turn off his servant and Mr Macrae will then apologise'. On hearing
this, Macrae collapsed in tears, knowing full well the impossible
position in which he was placed. The parties proceeded to the Links
and measured off twelve paces. On the signal being given, Sir George
fired first, the bullet passing through the collar of Macrae's coat and
slightly grazing his neck. At that, Captain Macrae, who had always
maintained that he would fire in the air, took deliberate aim and
brought Sir George to the ground with a shot from which he did not
recover. Public feeling ran high against Macrae, who was accused of
having had extensive pistol practice before the duel. He fled to

France. A summons was issued for his arrest but he did not appear, and sentence of outlawry was passed. He died in obscurity on 16th January 1820, the victim of his own fiery temper.

Restalrig House

A few hundred yards to the north of Restalrig village there is a modern high-rise block known as Restalrig House, built by James Miller & Partners Ltd. in 1965. The high stone perimeter wall on the north side and one or two mature trees are the only remnants of the original Restalrig House which stood on the site until a warrant for its demolition was issued on 20th September 1963. It is a house which has not been given detailed attention by writers on Restalrig, but there is a short account of its history in John Small's *Castles and Mansions of the Lothians* (1883). Apparently it was built for Alexander Duncan, W.S., between 1815 and 1817 and enlarged a few years later by Sir Henry Duncan, second son of the first Lord Duncan. The main entrance was at the lodge house which stood on the corner of Restalrig Drive and Restalrig Road South. Imposing pillars flanked the main gateway and a smaller pedestrian gateway to the left-hand side. A long curving tree-lined avenue led to the main house which was positioned close to the north boundary of the estate. The policies extended to fifteen acres of mature trees and ornamental gardens studded with sundials and statuettes, with a well-equipped stable block in the north-east corner. The house was a substantial square building of two storeys and basement, with numerous dummy windows, all contributing to its self-assured Georgian symmetry.

Craigentinny House

Perhaps the most ancient and picturesque of the Restalrig houses still remaining is Craigentinny House in Loaning Road, only a few hundred yards from the old village street. It has been used as a Community Centre for the district since the 1940s, but its history goes back to the end of the sixteenth century. The original house, belonging to the Nisbets of Dean, was skilfully altered in 1849 by the architect David Rhind in such a way that it is now difficult to distinguish the original house from the later additions. There is an

Craigentinny House, Loaning Road, sixteenth-century baronial mansion of
the Nisbets of Dean, used as a Community Centre since the 1940s.
From Grant's *Old and New Edinburgh*.

armorial shield over the south-facing entrance, but unfortunately it is
so weathered as to be indecipherable.

In the middle of the eighteenth century the house and a large part
of the estate were bought by William Miller, a prosperous seed
merchant in Edinburgh. Later the property passed to his son, also
named William. Fairly late in life the younger William Miller
married Miss Rawson, the couple living in London and Paris, and
producing a son, William Henry Miller, born in 1789. He spent most
of his life in England; he never married and was something of a
recluse by nature; but he became Member of Parliament for
Newcastle-under-Lyme in 1830. In the latter part of his life he
developed a great interest in collecting books for his library at his
Buckinghamshire home, Britwell Court. He earned himself the

Restalrig Village, 1985, looking south with the old walls of the Deanery on the left and on the right a small iron gate leading to Restalrig Parish Church and the Churchyard.
Photograph by Phyllis Margaret Cant.

nickname 'Measure Miller' from his eccentric habit of visiting various book sales and measuring precisely the size of each volume before deciding if it would enhance his existing collection. When he died in Edinburgh in 1848 he bequeathed his library, 'containing for rarity and condition an unrivalled collection of books', to his old college at Cambridge, but the conditions attached to the gift were so complicated that the bequest was not taken up. By then the public were perhaps beginning to get some idea of just how eccentric Miller had been. In the words of Daniel Wilson, the Edinburgh historian, Miller 'was notable for his spare figure, thin treble voice and total absence of beard', characteristics which led the villagers of Restalrig to assert that he was either a woman or 'a fairy changeling'. Whatever he was, he took his secret to the grave and made sure that it would not be lightly uncovered. Some six weeks after his death, the cortège left Craigentinny House for a remote spot on his own estate where he was interred at a depth of forty feet below the curious onlookers. A squad of workmen laboured long and hard to fill the grave, which was later capped by a huge mausoleum-type structure, now known locally as the Craigentinny Marbles. The tomb stands high above the modern bungalows in Craigentinny Crescent, but it has kept its secret well:

197

THIS MONUMENT WAS ERECTED TO THE MEMORY OF
WILLIAM HENRY MILLER
AND HIS PARENTS
WILLIAM MILLER AND MARTHA RAWSON OR MILLER

HERE ARE INTERRED
MARTHA MILLER
DIED 11th JANUARY 1827
WILLIAM HENRY MILLER
M.P. FOR NEWCASTLE-UNDER-LYME
BORN 13th FEBRUARY 1789 DIED 31st OCTOBER 1848
SARAH MARSH
BORN 20th APRIL 1792 DIED 6th AUGUST 1860
ELLEN MARSH
BORN 29th AUGUST 1801 DIED 4th NOVEMBER 1861

ALL OF CRAIGENTINNY AND BRITWELL
BUCKINGHAMSHIRE
THE SITE WAS CONSECRATED ON 13th SEPTEMBER 1860
THE SCULPTURES WERE ADDED IN 1866

ARCHITECT   SCULPTOR
DAVID RHIND   ALFRED GATLEY
EDINBURGH   ROME

The Craigentinny Marbles, burial place of the eccentric William Henry Miller, 1789 — 1848. The marble panels carved in low relief by Alfred Gatley depict 'The Overthrow of Pharaoh in the Red Sea' and 'The Song of Moses and Miriam'.

CHAPTER 9

Stockbridge

Stockbridge is Edinburgh's New Town village, straddling the Water of Leith between the older communities of Dean to the west, and Canonmills to the east. Although Stockbridge cannot claim great antiquity, its two centuries of recorded history provide abundant evidence of its contribution to the character of Edinburgh. Its principal claim to fame is undoubtedly that inexhaustible list of artists, historians and men of letters, who were either born in the village, or lived there at a significant time in their careers. In the early nineteenth century its proximity to the New Town brought it further acclaim as a convenient and spacious area in which to establish several of the great new educational institutions of the day. Later, the Victorian era brought the Colonies, tenement buildings, Board Schools and more reliable transport.

Today, Stockbridge has the bustle and confidence of a prosperous community of fashionable housing, restaurants, shops and businesses, sitting side by side with the earliest relics of the old village.

Old Stockbridge and its Distinguished Residents

A little more than two hundred years ago Stockbridge was a quiet backwater, almost exclusively dependent upon a rural economy. There were one or two big houses set in substantial grounds, but development was retarded by the absence of adequate communication across the Water of Leith. An old wooden bridge for pedestrians only (which may well have been the origin of the name Stoke-bridge) had been in existence for many years, but carts and horses were required to use the ford, reached by a fairly steep incline from each bank. Not only were travellers and local people inconvenienced by the absence of a proper bridge, but they were also required to pay dues at the toll, erected about 1760 at the south end of what is now Kerr Street. To pay bridge tolls would have been bad enough, but the idea of paying to cross a dangerous ford met with

Stock Bridge, Water of Leith, from Thomas H. Shepherd, *Modern Athens*.
Courtesy of Mr & Mrs A. Mitchell.

determined opposition from the local landowners. On 12th
November 1784 they petitioned the Trustees for the Bridges and
Highways in the County of Edinburgh in the following terms:

> Your petitioners therefore pray the Honourable Meeting to order the
> sum of £400 sterling at least to be applied out of the first and readiest of
> the tolls collected at Kirk braehead, to the making the road, and erecting
> a bridge at the foot of Stockbridge...

Their pleas were heard and a bridge was built sometime between
1785 and 1786. It was a stone structure of one arch, raised in the
centre, which was later levelled and widened around 1830. Its
existence was no doubt an important factor in the rate of development
of the village in the early nineteenth century. Ainslie's Map of 1804
shows Stockbridge still dominated by estates and open ground.
Raeburn Place is formed, but referred to as the *Road from
Queensferry* and Dean Street is described as the *Road from the Dean*
meaning, of course, from Village of Dean. The early maps refer to
two other old roads variously described at different times: the first
was Kirk Road or Church Street (now Gloucester Street and Lane)
which ran from St. Cuthbert's Church at the West End to
Stockbridge; and the other was Gabriel's Road which started near

Register House and ran, generally north-west to Silvermills and along the line of present-day Saxe Coburg Street and Place, to what is now the Colonies. By 1817 Kirkwood's Map shows the Stock Bridge as the focal point of the village with much of the basic street layout already formed, though with some notable omissions. To the east of the Stock Bridge, Hamilton Place is formed but not named, and leads to Dean Bank on the left, and to the village of Silvermills farther on, to the right. The mill lade follows approximately the line of the proposed north side of Brunswick Street (later renamed St. Stephen Street). Raeburn Place is named and flanked by handsome detached properties on each side. Between Dean Street and the Water of Leith, Henry Raeburn's property is developed on the west side to form the parallel streets around Ann Street. Upper Dean Terrace is referred to as Mineral Street on account of its proximity to the mineral wells of St. Bernard and St. George. The east side of Raeburn's property is still undeveloped, containing the old houses of St. Bernard's and Deanhaugh.

Deanhaugh House at the beginning of the nineteenth century was one of the most important houses in Stockbridge. It survived until 1880 when it was swept away for the construction of tenement buildings on the south side of Leslie Place. By then it had been divided into separate flats and probably had little in common with the early description given by Cumberland Hill:

> Deanhaugh House was a plain unpretentious building of three storeys, with its out-offices, in no way distinguished for its architectural beauty or dimensions; but its situation was both pleasant and picturesque standing back a little from the sloping bank of the Water of Leith, sheltered on the east by the fine old beeches on its own grounds, and on the west by the lofty elms of the western avenue to St. Bernard's. The entrance to the house was by a gateway supported by two massive stone pillars. A short avenue led up to the front entrance.

Deanhaugh House was purchased in 1777 by James Leslie, 'Count' of Deanhaugh, whose widow Ann Leslie (already the mother of three children) married Henry Raeburn, the celebrated portrait painter. Raeburn was born on 4th March 1756 in a modest cottage to the west of what is now Kerr Street, the younger son of William Raeburn, yarn-boiler at Stockbridge. Having lost both parents by the time he was six years old, he attended Heriot's Hospital until age sixteen when he commenced an apprenticeship with James Gilliland, goldsmith in Parliament Close. His artistic ability was recognised at a fairly young age, when he concentrated on miniature paintings, which were very much in demand. After touring in London and Rome he returned to Edinburgh, setting up a studio in George Street in 1787 and moving to York Place in 1795. He moved from Deanhaugh House to the much grander property of St. Bernard's House shortly after 1789. He became Scotland's foremost portrait painter, being elected an Associate of the Royal Academy in 1814 and an Academician the following year. During King George IV's visit to Edinburgh in 1822 Henry Raeburn was knighted at a ceremony at Hopetoun House. After a short sudden illness, he died on 8th July 1823 at the age of sixty-seven. In addition to being remembered as a distinguished artist, it has been suggested that Raeburn spent much of his time planning the lay-out of streets in the development of his own estate, from around 1813. Whilst it is very likely that he would have taken a keen interest in design, the better opinion appears to be that Ann Street, named after the artist's wife, was designed by the architect James Milne.

St. Bernard's, the principal mansion of old Stockbridge, had earned itself a place in history even before the arrival of Henry Raeburn. It stood to the south-west of Deanhaugh House and was also described by Cumberland Hill:

> It was a large, irregular pile — the centre, a plain three storeyed dwelling house. Two square castellated projections came out upon each side in front so that the entrance was from three sides of a square. Some curious old stones were built into the house — these were chiefly from houses that had been taken down in the Old Town. Into the front of one of the castellated projections was built a very fine Gothic window, and on the front of the other castellated projection was also to appearance a Gothic window, but it was really a painted imitation. Under the former was a beautifully executed 'Triumph of Bacchus' cut in white marble. One of the stones built into the opposite projection was broad and circular-topped: it had evidently been used as the lintel of a door having this inscription upon it —

The Lord is my Protector
Alexandrus Clark

Prior to Raeburn's occupation, St. Bernard's was owned by the humorous and eccentric Walter Ross, Writer to the Signet and Registrar of Distillery Licences in Scotland. He was a great collector of antiquities and spent much of his time pursuing his absorbing hobby of ornamental gardening. The story is told of how he dealt with unwelcome intruders on his estate after the hours of darkness. He let it be known in the village that his grounds were protected by an array of spring-guns and mantraps, but unfortunately no one believed him, and vandalism continued at its previous level. In a last attempt to convince the villagers that he was not just *pulling* their leg, old Ross drew upon his macabre sense of humour. He acquired a human leg from the Royal Infirmary, dressed it up in a stocking, shoe and buckle and sent it round the village, with the town crier, who held it aloft, proclaiming that it had been found the previous night in Mr Ross's estate, and offering to restore it to anyone who could make up the matching pair. With the intruders suitably discouraged, Ross returned to improving his estate.

His crowning achievement was undoubtedly his own Folly, erected on the highest point of ground in the north-west corner of his estate. It was about forty feet high, by about twenty feet square, consisting of two rooms one above the other, the upper floor being reached by an outside stairway which wound round three sides of the tower. The upper apartment was well decorated, and the roof contained numerous ornamentations around a painting of some incident in heathen mythology. The ground-floor entrance was by a large gate facing east. From a distance, it gave the impression of an old, rusticated Border peel or tower-house: from closer range it gave inquisitive strangers a chilling reminder that Ross was not far away. When he died suddenly and mysteriously on 11th March 1789 his body, at his own request, was kept eight days and then interred in the under part of the tower with the top of his coffin left open. Several years later, in 1818, when the surrounding area was being redeveloped, he was re-interred in St. Cuthbert's Churchyard, and Ross's Folly was eventually demolished in 1825.

Although Raeburn was probably the most renowned artist to come from Stockbridge, he was by no means the only one. David Roberts was born in the village on 24th October 1796, by which time Raeburn had already established his York Place studio and was living at St. Bernard's House. Roberts' parents, when they were first married, lived in Gavin's Land, Haugh Street in what was then one of the oldest parts of the village. The house was of two storeys with an outside staircase, part of the accommodation being used as a house, and part as a workshop for Roberts' father, who was a shoemaker. Shortly afterwards they moved to Duncan's Land in Church Street

The house where David Roberts was born on 24th October 1796, now Duncan's Land Restaurant.
From Grant's *Old and New Edinburgh.*

(now Gloucester Street), one of the most interesting old houses in Stockbridge, built from stones which were taken from houses in the Lawnmarket, demolished to allow the opening up of Bank Street at the top of the Mound. Across the lintel of Duncan's Land, in which David Roberts was born, is the inscription

FEAR GOD ONLYE
1.6.0.5.I.R.

Young David began to show artistic ability at about ten years of age and was later apprenticed to Gavin Beugo, a house painter who lived near Silvermills and who ran his business from West Register Street. After completion of his apprenticeship, Roberts became interested in painting theatrical scenery, and later toured in England and in the north of Scotland. On returning to Edinburgh in 1818 he formed a business arrangement with John Jackson, the decorative painter, but left Edinburgh again without completing the contract. His first exhibition of paintings was at the Exhibition of the Works of Living Artists at Edinburgh in 1822, after which he travelled extensively in

Spain, Syria and Egypt. He was admitted as an Associate of the Royal Academy in 1839 and as an Academician in 1841. Although absent from Edinburgh for much of his career, he maintained close links with the city, and especially Stockbridge. Edinburgh honoured him in 1842 at a special dinner on 19th October in the Hopetoun Rooms, and on 29th September 1858 he was presented with the freedom of the city. He died suddenly in London on 25th November 1864 and was buried in Norwood Cemetery. In 1984, lithographs dated 1842 to 1845 made from Roberts' drawings of *The Holy Land* were sold at Sotheby's in London for £51,000.

Many other prominent figures in various walks of life lived at some time in Stockbridge. Each is a study on his own, but the list includes such distinguished names as Professor Sir James Young Simpson at Deanhaugh Street and Dean Terrace; Robert Scott Lauder R.S.A., born at Silvermills in 1803; Professor John Wilson ('Christopher North'), who lived in Ann Street for several years; Robert Chambers L.L.D., publisher of *Traditions of Edinburgh* (1824), at India Place and Ann Street; and George Meikle Kemp, architect of the Scott Monument, who lived at Saunders Street in the latter part of his life.

Churches and Church Schools

Stockbridge is a microcosm of church history. Although many of the early churches and church schools have disappeared, nevertheless it is possible to trace the history of their development from what remains. Some of the buildings have been demolished, in whole or in part, some are in secular use, others lie empty and nearly ruinous, and a few are as majestic now as on the day they were first opened.

The oldest existing church is the former St. Bernard's Parish Church, now St. Bernard's Stockbridge, in Saxe Coburg Street. It has a distinctive classical facade by James Milne, with pairs of Ionic pillars supporting a pediment and square clock tower. When the church was opened on 16th November 1823, it took the name West Claremont Street Chapel of Ease, as it was built by the Kirk Session of the parish of St. Cuthbert's. The first incumbent was Rev. James Henderson, an Evangelical minister from Berwick-upon-Tweed, later a Moderator of the General Assembly. During the time of Rev.

James MacFarlane (who later went to Duddingston) the Chapel of Ease was made a parish church by the General Assembly of 1834, with a kirk session elected in July 1835, but after the Disruption in 1843 this arrangement was cancelled and it was not until 1851 that the name was changed to St. Bernard's Parish Church. Perhaps the most famous minister was the Rev. George Matheson, the 'Blind Seer' who wrote many hymns and books.

As early as 1826 a parochial school, known as the Sessional School of St. Cuthbert's Parish Church, was established in Dean Street. For almost half a century before the existence of Board Schools under the Education Act of 1872, the parish school taught a wide range of subjects including English, reading, grammar, writing, arithmetic, history, geography and scripture knowledge from 9 a.m. to 11.30 a.m. and 12.30 p.m. to 3 p.m. for a fee of 2/6d. for juniors and 3/6d. for seniors. When the school closed after the 1872 Act, the building continued to be used as a Mission Hall. To combat at least some of the social evils of the day, volunteers organised sewing classes, reading classes and the Penny Savings Bank. By all accounts Dean Street Mission Hall soon established itself as a centre of activity in the parish, with the Band of Hope, and the Sabbath Morning Fellowship Association. From around 1880 St. Bernard's Literary Society held programmes of songs and readings under the title *Penny Reading* at which Miss Wilkie rendered *The Bird's Lullaby* followed by *Complaints* by Mr R. Morgan, though presumably not directed at Miss Wilkie's earlier efforts. By 1888 the title *Penny Reading* had been dropped, and tickets ranged from 3d to 1/ – .

At the present day the Mission Hall is used as St. Bernard's Parish Church Hall, although there are plans to turn it into a Church Centre for Stockbridge. The main church building in Saxe Coburg Street has recently undergone extensive renovation to create a community and cultural centre, in addition to its primary function as a place of worship. During the alterations in 1983, a narthex was created by the removal of pews under the gallery, and the large Victorian pulpit was taken out of the apse, thus opening up the raised area at the front of the church, to give more room for staged events like concerts or drama presentations.

In common with many Scottish churches, the Chapel of Ease suffered badly at the time of the Disruption. Rev. Alexander W. Brown had been minister for less than a year when he 'came out' with

The distinctive classical facade of St. Bernard's Stockbridge Church, Saxe Coburg Street, by James Milne, 1823.
From Smith's *Sketch of St. Bernard's.*

the Kirk Session and joined the historic procession from St. Andrew's Church in George Street to Tanfield Hall on 18th May 1843. As no church building was available for St. Bernard's Free Church congregation, they worshipped for a while at Tanfield Hall. A site was later acquired at Silvermills (Henderson Row) and the foundation stone was laid on 7th August 1843. The congregation planned an unpretentious brick building with a felt roof so that they might help poorer churches in country areas. Unfortunately the low, felt roof did not succeed in keeping the rain out in the winter, nor the dripping tar in the hot summer. Although hundreds of pounds were spent on repairs, the church was demolished and a new one built on the same site in 1856, designed by the architect John Milne as a replica of the Martyrs' Free Church in St. Andrews, also by Milne.

Like the Established Church, the Free Church of St. Bernard's set up its own school in a building immediately to the west of the church with almost four hundred children in attendance. Following the Education Act of 1872, St. Bernard's Free Church offered their school building to the new Education Board but instead, Stockbridge School was begun in 1874 and opened in 1877.

In 1900 St. Bernard's Free Church became St. Bernard's United Free Church. In 1929, at the reunion with the Established Church, it became St. Bernard's South; and in 1945 it formed a union with Davidson Church in Eyre Place and became St. Bernard's Davidson Church. Its centenary service was held in 1956 when Rev. Frederick Levison traced the history of the church based on earlier work done by Rev. George Steven. Other roots were also traced. Dean Street Church was originally established in Dean Street in 1828. It became a Secession Church in 1829 and United Presbyterian in 1847. In 1861 the congregation moved to Queen Street and in 1881 to Eyre Place, calling the church Davidson. However, part of the congregation remained at Dean Street and became a United Presbyterian congregation which became United Free in 1900. It united with St. Bernard's U.F. Church in 1915.

Following a union with the Parish Church in 1980, under the present minister, Rev. John R. Munro, St. Bernard's Davidson lies vacant and neglected, its buttressed and pinnacled stonework blackened and lifeless. Beside it, the old brick-built school has fared no better, with broken windows and blocked up doorways.

St. Stephen's Church is probably the most significant landmark in the district, built between 1827 and 1828 for £18,975 to designs by William H. Playfair. It was a most difficult site to develop, the natural contours of the ground falling away steeply to the north, yet presenting an uninterrupted vista southwards, to George Street. These factors undoubtedly influenced Playfair in his final design, which is basically a square, diagonally sited, with the north and south corners cut off. The imposing south doorway, at the head of a huge flight of steps, entered the church at gallery level, while entry to the main body of the church was by two side doors. At first sight, the main entrance appears to face exactly south to the statue of William Pitt at the junction of Frederick Street and George Street, but, in fact, the whole church is set slightly askew to the west. That does not, however, detract significantly from the boldness of its design or from the majesty of its great tower 162 feet in height, said to contain the longest pendulum in Europe. Though generally considered to meet most of the challenges of this awkward site, the absence of lateral support on each side of the yawning entrance prompted Professor Blackie to voice the opinion that it was like 'a mouth without cheeks'. In the mid-1950s extensive reorganisation of the interior of the church was undertaken by the architect Gilbert H. Jenkins of London. A reinforced concrete floor was put in at gallery level to create the main body of the church, leaving the lower area for hall accommodation and a small theatre. The fine 'Old Father Willis' organ of 1880 was re-erected on the new church level.

St. Stephen's was dedicated as one of the Burgh Churches of Edinburgh on Sunday 21st December 1828 in the presence of the Lord Provost and magistrates, the first minister being Rev. Dr. William Muir. Owing to the personal following of Dr. Muir, St. Stephen's was not affected at the time of the Disruption. In the following year, however, advocates of the Free Church formed a new congregation at the Straiton Gallery in Wemyss Place where they remained until 1901 when the congregation moved to Fettes Avenue.

When Dr Muir came to St. Stephen's, he discovered that many of his adult parishioners were illiterate. Evening school was started in one of the cellars below the church, and in 1835 St. Stephen's School was opened with the assistance of a Government grant, in Brunswick Street (now renamed St. Stephen Street). The school continued independently after the introduction of School Boards in 1872, until about 1890 when it was unable to meet the more exacting standards of equipment required to maintain its grant. By that time St. Stephen's Church had already established their Mission Hall, also in Brunswick Street, the foundation stone of which was laid on 19th May 1883 by Lord Mure. The Mission Hall was sold in 1956 when the new halls were created under the reconstructed church. St. Stephen's School still stands, with an open Bible carved in stone high up on the front of the building. The inscription on the pages reads:

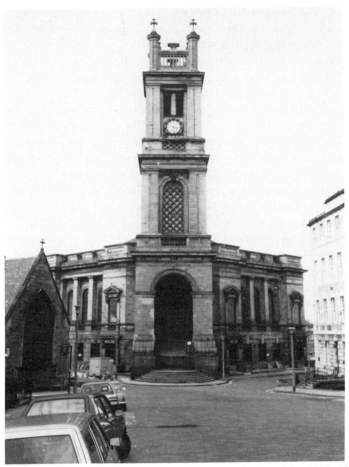

The massive tower of St. Stephen's Church by W.H. Playfair, 1827–1828, with the much smaller proportions of St. Vincent's Episcopal Church 1857, on the left.
Photograph by A.C. Robson.

HOLY BIBLE

THOSE	EARLY
THAT SEEK	SHALL FIND
ME	ME

St. Vincent's Episcopal Church, designed in English Gothic by J., W. H. and J. M. Hay of Liverpool, was built in 1857 as an English Episcopal church on the corner of St. Stephen Street and St. Vincent

Street. The north aisle, entrance porch and shortened spire face towards St. Stephen Street while the chancel gable faces St. Vincent Street. The original organ was by William Townsend in 1872, rebuilt by Blackett and Howden in 1897, and replaced in 1981 by the organ from Christ Church in Trinity Road. There are also several interesting stained glass windows depicting heraldic subjects in keeping with the heraldic shields on the gallery balustrade and the ceiling.

The church was purchased in 1874 by William Forbes Skene W.S., who gifted it to the Scottish Episcopal Church in memory of his parents, James Skene of Rubislaw and Jane Forbes. Its position in the New Town resulted in its being attended by several members of the legal profession but by 1961 the congregation had reduced to such an extent that St. Vincent's became a Mission under St. Paul and St. George's in York Place. On St. Lazarus' Day, 17th December, 1967 St. Vincent's was inaugurated as a Chapel of the Commandery of Lochore in the Military and Hospitaller Order of St. Lazarus of Jerusalem. The service was attended by the Prince Grand Master and His Beatitude Maximos V, Catholic Patriarch of Antioch and all the Orient and of Jerusalem and Alexandria, Spiritual Protector of the Order of St. Lazarus. Also present were the Moderator of the General Assembly of the Church of Scotland, the Dean of the Thistle and Chapel Royal, and a representative of the Archbishop of St. Andrews and Edinburgh. In 1971 the church was purchased by Lt. Colonel Robert Gayre of Gayre and Nigg, Hereditary Grand Commander of Lochore. As a Collegiate Church, St. Vincent's is ecumenical, with a Chapter of Canons drawn from the Anglican and Roman Catholic Churches, and the Church of Scotland.

The church hall was built of red and yellow bricks in the early 1860s to the east of St. Stephen's School in Brunswick Street (now St. Stephen Street).

In Deanhaugh Street all that remains of Stockbridge Church is its square stone and slated tower forming part of the brick-built flats of 1980 by Matthew, Hamilton and Maclean. Although the church ended its days in the heart of Stockbridge, it cannot claim to have originated there. In fact, it was born in Lothian Road opposite St. Cuthbert's Church in 1844 and was named St. George's Free Church. In 1868 when the railway required more land, the shell of St. George's Free Church was bought and transferred, stone by stone, to its new position at Stockbridge, and the tower was added. The foundation stone was laid (for the second time) on 1st January 1868 and the church was opened on 8th November 1868, the first minister being Dr. Bruce, who refused the honour of having the church named after him.

A Free Church School was started for boys and girls in a small building beside the church, on the corner of Dean Street. When this was closed in September 1880, the pupils were transferred to Stockbridge School.

There was at least one other church in Stockbridge in comparatively recent years, albeit with a much smaller congregation. In Hamilton Place,

> We hev a kirk, a dear wee kirk,
> It's ca'd the Wesley Hall,
> Of a' the kirks that's in the toon,
> Tae us it's best of all.

The building used by the Wesleyan Methodist Church is now occupied by Theatre Workshop.

Other Schools and Institutions

In addition to the various church schools, Stockbridge attracted several other educational establishments, some of which pioneered specialist training in Edinburgh, and beyond.

For many years Edinburgh has been closely involved in the education of deaf and dumb children. Indeed the district of Dumbiedykes, on the south side of the city, takes its name from a house beside Holyrood Park in which Mr Braidwood, an instructor of the deaf and dumb, resided with his pupils. Better facilities and training in this specialised form of teaching were provided in June 1810 on the founding of the Institution for the Education of Deaf and Dumb Children. Although this new Institution was almost completely dependent upon charitable contributions, it was able to acquire a much more spacious site in 1823 for the erection of a new building, designed by James Gillespie Graham, in Distillery Park, on the north side of Henderson Row. The foundation stone was laid by one of the senior pupils on 22nd May 1823 in the silent company of his classmates, 'whose looks', according to the *Edinburgh Advertiser*, 'bespoke the feelings of their minds, and which would have been a sufficient recompense to the contributors for the building, had they been witnesses of the scene'.

When the Institute opened its doors to pupils in 1824, little did they know that the education of deaf and dumb children was soon to receive another substantial impetus from charitable sources. James Donaldson, publisher and printer of West Bow, was already the head of a very successful business, and when he died at Broughton Hall on 19th October 1830, he directed that a sum of £210,000 should be made available

> to build and found an hospital for boys and girls to be called Donaldson's Hospital preferring those of the name of Donaldson and Marshall to be after the plan of the Orphan Hospital in Edinburgh and John Watson's Hospital.

Donaldson's Trustees obtained competitive plans from Gillespie Graham, W. H. Playfair and David Hamilton before instructing the work on Playfair's magnificently ornate quadrangle at West Coates, commenced in 1841 but not finished until 1851. Pupils were admitted on 16th October 1850, and for almost a century Donaldson's Hospital at West Coates, and the Institution for the Education of Deaf and Dumb Children, maintained separate identities, albeit engaged in the same type of work. In 1939 the two schools combined to form Donaldson's School for the Deaf, senior pupils being taught at West Coates and junior pupils (up to age twelve) at Henderson Row. In the late 1950s the Henderson Row building was closed temporarily for modernisation.

A brief but memorable event occurred on 20th July 1968 when 20th Century Fox arrived to film *The Prime of Miss Jean Brodie*, starring Maggie Smith as Miss Brodie. The solid stone gate piers acquired additional finials, and a decorative iron over-gate temporarily converted Donaldson's School to the Marcia Blaine School for Girls.

In 1977, following reorganisation of Donaldson's at West Coates, the Henderson Row building was sold to its worthy neighbour, the Edinburgh Academy.

The gate pillars of Donaldson's School for the Deaf, temporarily renamed Marcia Blaine School for Girls, for *The Prime of Miss Jean Brodie,* filmed in July 1968. Courtesy of Mrs Barbara A. Cant.
Photograph by the late John K. Cant M.A., former headmaster at Donaldson's School.

In the early 1820s the area around what is now Henderson Row was changing rapidly as the New Town spread northwards in a series of elegant terraces and crescents. Building work had already reached as far as Saxe Coburg Place, and soon the construction of the Institution for the Education of Deaf and Dumb Children would be surpassed by another great educational challenge, the Edinburgh Academy. The Academy, perhaps more so than any other school in Edinburgh, was forged on the anvil of discontent at the educational philosophy of the day. In Edinburgh, at the beginning of the nineteenth century, classical education was mainly in the hands of the Town Council's own High School, but several factors were operating in favour of a new classical school situated in the New Town. This vision was enthusiastically taken up and brought to fruition by two leading Whigs of the day (both of whom had been educated at the High School), namely Henry Cockburn (later Lord Cockburn) and Leonard Horner. When they shrewdly crossed the political divide by asking John Russel W.S. to complete the triumvirate, and so to make the project acceptable to the influential high Tory, Sir Walter Scott, success appeared to be within their grasp. Unfortunately, opposition was encountered from members of Edinburgh Town Council. The Council had come under pressure from the masters at the High School, who saw a new academy as a definite threat to their status, and indeed to their livelihood. A long series of meetings took place between the Subscribers to the new school and the Town Council who even proposed, perhaps in desperation, to build a new High School on a site to the east of the Mound. This proposal was rejected by the Subscribers, who resolved, at a meeting on 16th May 1823 in the Waterloo Hotel, to go it alone.

The site in Henderson Row, previously proposed by Cockburn and Horner, was acquired, and William Burn the architect was asked to make modifications to his drawings to bring costs within the budget of £13,000, yet maintaining the most stringent specifications:

> The whole stone of whatever description used in the building must be laid upon their natural beds, and the lime will be mixed up with clean sharp pit sand and pure fresh water .... The plaster lime must all be mixed up with hair of the best quality, and be prepared at least six weeks before it is laid on the walls...
> The whole roofs of all the buildings will be covered with the best Welsh Queen slates, hung with malleable iron nails, steeped in linseed oil when hot and laid on a shouldering of haired lime...

The first Rector was appointed — Dr John Williams, formerly of Winchester and of Lampeter College in Wales — and the school was opened on 1st October 1824. The initial enrolment of 372 boys sat through the lengthy opening orations by Sir Walter Scott and Henry Mackenzie, the famous author of *The Man of Feeling*.

The new Edinburgh Academy adopted a system of instruction based generally on the High School system, with a Rector and four Classical Masters, but there were important differences written into the first syllabus. In particular, there was to be more emphasis on Greek, a separate master was to be employed for English, and greater attention was to be paid to Geography and Arithmetic.

The Rector, perhaps hopeful that he was writing the first page of a long history, requested one boon from an enlightened public — that they would not be hasty in their censure, nor premature in their applause. A century and a half later after the Academy had produced a long line of distinguished leaders in every walk of life, Magnus Magnusson, in *The Clacken and the Slate*, told the fascinating story

The Edinburgh Academy, Henderson Row, designed by William Burn, and opened on 1st October 1824.
From Thomas H. Shepherd, *Modern Athens*.

of the Edinburgh Academy from 1824 to 1974 'in its context of time and place, in Edinburgh, in Scotland, in the development of education'.

The 1851 Ordnance Survey map provides interesting information concerning the development of the triangular piece of ground bounded by present-day Hamilton Place, Saxe Coburg Street and Dean Bank Lane. Dean Bank House is shown in the north corner with Dean Bank Cottage close by, both buildings dating from the late eighteenth century and still extant. A more complicated range of buildings, Dean Bank Institution and Dean Bank Lodge, is situated in ornamental gardens and shrubberies, now occupied by Stockbridge Primary School and Stockbridge Public Library. Dean Bank Lodge, although immediately adjoining Dean Bank Institution, was in the private occupation of William J. Renny W.S., of Webster and Renny, Solicitors, 74 Queen Street, Edinburgh.

Dean Bank Institution for the Reformation of Juvenile Female Delinquents was founded in 1832 with the following expression of intent:

> The parties whose good is contemplated are young female delinquents whether legally convicted of crime or not, who have no home, or worse than no home to go to, and who manifest a wish to return to better ways.

217

An endless succession of young girls was referred there, many after release from the Bridewell which was founded in 1791 in Waterloo Place, as Edinburgh's new House of Correction. Case histories for the year 1840 suggest that, for some, confinement to Dean Bank Institution could follow from comparatively minor deviation from 'acceptable' standards of behaviour:

> Case 1 — Her fault was stealing from her mistress — she is seemingly friendless — had never attended a place of worship — two years in Dean Bank Institution.

> Case 2 — Well educated but wholly ignorant of religion — had never received religious instruction — her fault was selling a book which had been stolen by her brother.

The ages of the twenty-four inmates ranged from ten to fifteen years, and all were equally subjected to the rigours of 'moral restraint, religious influence and training in branches of female industry'. A well-organised tariff of charges for work done by the girls gave prices for sewing: Chemises 10d, Drawers (per pair) 6d, Pinafores 3d; and for washing only, 2d, 1d, 1d respectively. An early photograph, taken in the garden of the Institution, shows a group of about twenty-six girls all apparently well dressed and well nourished in the charge of four or five mature staff.

At the time of the 37th Report in 1869 the name was changed to Dean Bank Institution for the Religious, Moral and Industrial Training of Girls. Extensive alterations were made to the premises in 1890, and the work of the Institution continued well into the twentieth century, by which time Stockbridge Primary School had been in existence for at least thirty years.

Stockbridge Public School in Hamilton Place was designed in 1874 in the Gothic style by R. Rowand Anderson, as one of the earliest Board Schools. It was designed for six hundred pupils, most of whom lived locally and had formerly attended one of the small parochial schools attached to the various churches. Stockbridge School immediately absorbed the pupils from St. Bernard's Free Church School and St. Mary's Public School, to which were added those from Deanhaugh Street School a few years later. Although it was considered, architecturally, one of the best Board Schools of that era, subsequent generations of staff and pupils have been constantly harassed by the inconvenient internal lay-out, which does not provide orthodox corridors between different parts of the building.

The school was opened on 12th January 1877 with 537 children and a large crowd of parents and friends in attendance. Members of the Board, Professor Calderwood, Rev. Dr Begg and Rev. Williamson, were joined by several Bailies and Councillors representing the City. Most of the first week was spent classifying the children into different groups, as their academic attainment was not uniform by age, and the janitor was sent to locate the truanters, 'many of whom were beyond all control of parents'.

Various references in the school logs, meticulously kept since 1877, highlight periods of extreme austerity during each of the two World Wars, and a general increase over the years in extra-curricular activities. Large-scale reorganisation of classes was required in 1915 when Flora Stevenson's School was made into a military hospital, and the pupils were transferred to Stockbridge. The extra hands were, however, put to good use in Miss Murray's class, which collected 13/– for British soldiers interned in Germany, and followed this donation with an assortment of home comforts: twenty pairs of socks, three knitted face cloths, two pyjama cords and a knitted bed rug. After 1919 the school extended its activities in a number of ways: in 1923 the pupils performed *Grand Humorous Operetta Babette* in the Wesley Hall in Hamilton Place; in 1926 swimming classes were started at Glenogle Road Baths, but were temporarily discontinued as only cold water was available owing to coal shortages during the miners' strike; and in 1929 an unusual holiday was celebrated to mark the Union of the Church of Scotland and the United Free Church. At the outbreak of war in 1939 many parents and children were evacuated to Speyside only a few weeks before the first air raid over the Edinburgh area was recorded by the school, on 16th October 1939. Post-war events included a Coronation Service held at St. Bernard's Davidson Church, and a visit to the Ritz Cinema on 12th June 1953 to see *Elizabeth is Queen*.

At the present day Stockbridge Primary, in common with many Edinburgh schools, is closely involved with the community around it and is conscious of its long history. The old Dean Bank Institution building immediately adjacent to the school has been used for many years as an Annexe to provide accommodation for various organisations.

St. Bernard's Public School, formerly George Heriot's Hospital School, now used by Lothian Regional Council as St. Bernard's Education Centre. Photograph by A.C. Robson.

While Rowand Anderson was designing Stockbridge Public School, another able architect, John Chesser, was drawing up plans for George Heriot's Hospital School at the south end of Dean Park Street. This building, with a marginal similarity to its parent institution at Lauriston Place, was also designed in 1874 but was not opened until a few months after Stockbridge, on 17th December 1877. To begin with, the ratio of teachers to pupils was very good, with a headteacher and three assistants to forty-three children, but this desirable state of affairs did not apply to all aspects of the school. Work was frequently hindered by an acute shortage of slate pencils, and from time to time clothing was sent down from Heriot's Hospital for distribution among the poorer children. But the far-sighted generosity of Jinglin' Geordie, goldsmith and banker, was not forgotten: on the anniversary of George Heriot's birth, celebrated on 8th June 1882, the children marched to the Hospital grounds at Lauriston Place to sing the usual songs, and to be rewarded on their return with a bun and an orange.

In 1887 a large extension, designed by the Edinburgh School Board's architect Robert Wilson, was erected to the east of the main building, and the whole complex was renamed St. Bernard's Public School. At the same time the School Board entered into a new arrangement with the Heriot Trust with regard to the payment of fees for pupils sent by the Trust to the school. A sum of 4d. per week per child was established. A tight grip was always kept on the public purse strings to ensure that money invested in education provided a worthwhile dividend. On 22nd October 1889 the Inspector of the City Parochial Board wrote to the headmaster asking to be informed before a pauper child belonging to the City Parish was transferred to Standard VI, to enable the Board to judge whether it was expedient that the child be kept on. On the subject of discipline, the Children Act of 1908 produced several interesting cases in the years immediately after it became law: 1912 — one boy, convicted of theft for the third time, sentenced to nine stripes; 1916 — one boy, convicted at the Police Court for begging, sent to Mars Training Ship; 1917 — two boys, convicted of hanging on cable cars, fined 1/- each.

Like other schools in Edinburgh, St. Bernard's was disrupted during the Second World War by constant reorganisation caused by evacuations. When the school closed on 28th June 1957 with a roll of only 256 pupils, the headmaster faithfully concluded the school log with a complete list of all staff employed on the last day:

Headmaster: J. D. Crawford.
Infants: Miss McKenzie (Infant Mistress); Mrs Flora Wilson.
Primary: Mrs Anna Stewart; Miss Elizabeth Tanner; Mrs Ada Robertson; Mrs June Niven; Mrs Neilina Scott; Miss Elizabeth Mitchell; Mr Edmund Donald.
Visiting staff: Mrs Risse Sharpton, Sewing;
Miss Elspeth Cameron, Singing; Miss Isobel Henderson,
Physical training; Miss Margaret Glass, Art;
Miss Joan Rogers, Speech Therapy.
Janitor: Mr John Forrest.
Clerical Assistant: Miss Anne Duffus.

At the present day, St. Bernard's is used by Lothian Regional Council as St. Bernard's Education Centre and the Schools' Library Service. The only visible outward signs of its original function are the weathered mouldings above the window pediments with the initials G.H.

In and Around Stockbridge at the Present Day

In geographical terms, Stockbridge is one of Edinburgh's largest villages, requiring a fairly long walk to encompass all its places of interest. Although it is two hundred years since the first stone bridge was built, the Stock Bridge at Deanhaugh Street is still the focal point of the district, and the obvious place to begin any tour of the district. The bridge has a plaque on each parapet confirming that it was first erected in 1786, and widened and improved in 1900–01 by David C. Proudfoot, Engineer, when the Right Honourable James Steel was Lord Provost of Edinburgh. The distinctive pointed stones which form part of the parapet are shown quite clearly at each corner of the bridge in a picture of Stockbridge and St. Bernard's House dated 1790. From the bridge now, two famous towers are clearly visible. Adjacent to the north-east parapet is the slender, rounded tower now part of the Trustee Savings Bank, the original building dating from about 1840, but greatly enhanced by the addition of the balustrades and the corbelled clock-tower by MacGibbon and Ross in 1900. On the left, the other tower, square and much taller, is all that remains of Stockbridge Free Church, demolished in 1980.

At the north end of Deanhaugh Street, traffic lights at Dean Street and Raeburn Place mark the approximate site of the weighing machine which was set into the middle of the roadway. Tucked round to the right in St. Bernard's Row, the modern flats with V-shaped balconies were built in 1982 on the site of an old cinema, opened in 1911 as the Palace, and renamed St. Bernard's Picture Palace the following year. In 1921 the name was changed to the Savoy and again in 1960 to the Tudor. By then, many of Edinburgh's smaller cinemas were in financial difficulties and the Tudor lost the fight on 23rd April 1966 with Gregory Peck in *The Guns of Navarone*.

Raeburn Place was built between 1814 and 1825 with several villas on each side of the road, still clearly visible as private houses at the back of the shop frontages built, much later, in the gardens. About halfway along, on the left-hand side, a curious narrow street built as Hermitage Place, but recently renamed Raeburn Street, leads to a single terrace of houses with classical frontages, once protected at night by locked gates. Dean Street lies at the south end, beyond the remaining stone pillars. The building on the opposite pavement, occupied by the National Trust for Scotland, was erected in 1828 as a Relief Congregation Church and taken over around 1917 as the

Pavilion cinema. Following the introduction of sound, the cinema was reopened as the Dean Picture House on 12th May 1930 with Jack Holt in *Submarine* and Audrey Ferris in *Beware of Bachelors*, but it appears to have closed before the beginning of the Second World War. Immediately to the east are St. Bernard's Church Halls, built as St. Cuthbert's Church School in 1826, and opposite, at No. 31, a door pediment reads:

18 MORNING LIGHT 84
DEAN STREET U.F. CHURCH
MISSION HALL

The octagonal-shaped harled building at the south end of Cheyne Street is Stockbridge House Day Centre used as a club for old people, and at the head of Dean Street is the former St. Bernard's School. To the south-east, lying between Dean Street and the Water of Leith, are the beautifully elegant streets of the Raeburn estate: the double arcs of St. Bernard's Crescent, with Ann Street, Danube Street and Carlton Street running parallel to meet Upper Dean Terrace and Dean Terrace perched above the water. Almost opposite Danube Street, St. Bernard's Bridge, built in 1824, crosses the Water of Leith to a heavy but ornate flight of steps, added in the late nineteenth century. The riverside walk to the right leads to Dean village, past St. Bernard's Well and St. George's Well.

St. Bernard's Well is by far the grander of the two ancient wells on the south bank. Originally a much smaller well-house dated from 1760, but in 1788 Lord Gardenstone, a senator of the College of Justice, believing that he had benefited from the medicinal properties in the water, commissioned Alexander Nasmyth to design a much grander structure. This is substantially the well which is seen today, built against the water's edge in the dank atmosphere of overhanging trees. The base is constructed of very large, roughly hewn stones, supporting a circular, domed temple of ten plain Doric columns, within which stands a statue of Hygeia. The statue is not the original, having been replaced in 1888 when the well was restored, at the expense of William Nelson. Beside the well, on its east side, a stone tablet encircles a low relief medallion of William Nelson by the sculptor John Rhind, above which are the words THE LIBERAL DEVISETH LIBERAL THINGS, and the ontwined initials W.N. The lower part of the tablet records, for posterity, the generosity of William Nelson:

ERECTED BY THE
LORD PROVOST, MAGISTRATES AND COUNCIL
OF THE CITY OF EDINBURGH
TO COMMEMORATE
THE PUBLIC SPIRIT AND GENEROSITY OF THE LATE
WILLIAM NELSON
OF SALISBURY GREEN
WHO HAVING PURCHASED, RESTORED AND
EMBELLISHED ST. BERNARD'S WELL AND
THE SURROUNDING GROUNDS
GIFTED THEM TO THE CORPORATION
FOR THE BENEFIT OF THE CITIZENS OF EDINBURGH
IN ALL TIME COMING
JANUARY 1888

THE RIGHT HON. SIR THOMAS CLARK BART.
LORD PROVOST

When Lord Gardenstone first opened the well to the public, he appointed George Murdoch of Stockbridge as the custodian, and drew up a long list of rules and regulations concerning its proper use. Glasses and cups for drinking were to be provided by Mr Murdoch who was required to be in attendance from 6 a.m. to 9 a.m. each morning as well as at other times of the day. Subscribers paid five shillings per season, and non-subscribers 1d per day for adults and ½d per day for children. Water, drawn off to be consumed away from the well, was charged at ½d per Scots pint and, in order to maintain strict standards of hygiene, there was an absolute ban on bathing limbs or sores. After partaking of the water, persons were required to 'retire immediately and walk about, or take other exercise for an interval of at least five minutes, both as a benefit to themselves, and to make way for other water drinkers'.

A few hundred yards upstream from St. Bernard's is the much less impressive St. George's Well with a pedimented gable containing the date 1810 at the front, and a round-nosed gable end to the rear built high above the water's edge. At this point the pathway is within a few hundred yards of Dean Bridge, but turning back to St. Bernard's Bridge, the walkway leads on to Saunders Street and back to the Stock Bridge.

A walk round the paths and streets to the east of the Stock Bridge is equally instructive. A small iron gate at the north end of the Stock Bridge leads down a flight of iron steps to the Deanhaugh Path section

The former interior of St. Bernard's Well, originally built in 1788, and restored in 1888 by William Nelson of Salisbury Green.

of the Water of Leith Walkway. On the right bank an array of masonry walls and buttresses supports the rear of premises in Hamilton Place and Dean Bank Lane. On the left of the footpath, near Malta House, interesting new housing occupies the site of Veitch's Court, and ahead the Falshaw Bridge carries Bridge Place across the Water of Leith. The bridge, designed by David C.

A view c. 1950, looking north across the Stock Bridge towards Raeburn Place with the tower of Stockbridge Church on the left and the Edinburgh Savings Bank on the right.
Courtesy of Mrs Barbara A. Cant.

Proudfoot, engineer, and built by Peter Shaw, the contractor, was opened in May 1877 by the Right Hon. Sir James Falshaw Bart., Lord Provost. Almost eighty years later, in 1956, it was strengthened with prestressed concrete beams to designs prepared by the City Architect. On the far side of the bridge the road divides: to the left, through the pillars, to Arboretum Road, and to the right into Glenogle Road and the Colonies.

The history and development of the Colonies is a most interesting story, ably written and illustrated in 1984 by Rosemary J. Pipes in *The Colonies of Stockbridge*. The houses, constructed from 1861 by the Edinburgh Co-operative Building Company Limited, were intended to provide low-priced housing for working people, an aim admirably achieved in the early days of the Co-operative. The names of the various terraces follow those of the principal participants in the original company: Hugh Miller, stonemason, writer, journalist and geologist; Hugh Gilzean Reid, journalist and later Liberal M.P., and James Colville, stonemason and first manager of the Co-operative.

On the south side of Glenogle Road, facing the Colonies, are the large castellated, red sandstone towers of Glenogle Baths designed by

226

The opposite view to the foregoing looking south across the Stock Bridge from Deanhaugh Street to Kerr Street.
Courtesy of Mrs Barbara A. Cant.

Robert Morham in 1897. A meandering pathway to the side of the baths leads up to an awkward gap in the elegant frontages of Saxe Coburg Place, and so to St. Bernard's Parish Church and into Henderson Row. The Edinburgh Academy maintains its dignified presence in its original building, beside the building of Donaldson's School for the Deaf which it later acquired. The gate pillars remain, but without the finials and the ironwork fleetingly acquired when it donned the mantle of Marcia Blaine School for Girls. On the south side of Henderson Row, St. Bernard's Free Church and the Church School are in almost derelict condition, sad reminders of their original ideals. Lying between that church and St. Stephen's Church the old hamlet of Silvermills has all but gone, except the name, and a few remnants of old buildings, arranged along the lade. The only jewel in the crown is Silvermills House, recently restored for Strathearn Advertising Ltd.

Returning to the Stock Bridge by Hamilton Place reveals further evidence of Stockbridge's varied history. On the right are Stockbridge Primary School, and Stockbridge Library designed by

H. Ramsay Taylor in 1898. The Salvation Army Hall, built in 1937 on the site of a former sweetie factory, is now the headquarters for the Edinburgh Division. The Hall was used by the Stockbridge Corps of the Salvation Army until 1979 when it amalgamated with the Leith Corps. Immediately opposite the library, a wide pend gives access to Patriothall, a housing development, in coloured brick, arranged around three sides of a cobbled square, the houses on the south side being reached from balconies supported by ornamental iron brackets.

Opposite the mouth of Dean Park Lane the former Wesley Hall is now the headquarters of Theatre Workshop Edinburgh. This thriving theatre and community arts resources centre operates throughout Scotland, mounting in-house productions, art classes and other community work. In addition to its own professional theatre company there is a Theatre-in-Education programme in conjunction with the Scottish Health Education Group and a Drama with the Handicapped project. It is also a popular venue for national and international companies visiting Edinburgh.

Two similar buildings on the north side of Hamilton Place, backing onto the Water of Leith, have been put to contrasting uses. No. 5, a fashionable restaurant, was the village police station, and the public toilets were once the fire station. Just before the traffic lights, the north entrance to Stockbridge Market curves in on each side of an 'island' tenement stairway. Nothing remains of the Market itself, designed in 1824 by Archibald Scott to include stalls for fish, poultry, fruit and vegetables, similar to the Liverpool Market. Round the corner at Glanville Place and Bakers Place the extensive Stockbridge Mills were wrecked by a violent explosion at Todd's Mill in 1901 when six persons died and several others were injured. Modern housing now occupies most of the ground area previously used as mills. Beyond the open ground to the west is Duncan's Land Restaurant, Gloucester Place, occupying the building in which David Roberts R.A. was born in 1796.

St. Stephen Street, perhaps more than any other, typifies the changing face of Stockbridge. The three brass balls of the Equitable Loan Office established in 1845 adorn the south-west corner, but farther in, the mood changes and the range of shops and restaurants speaks of a different age: prints, gramophone horns, guitars, sweaters, jewellery, 'Tommy Rot' and much more besides, combine with cafes, coiffure and candlesticks to create a feeling of general

Deanhaugh Path, from the Falshaw Bridge, part of the intended Water of
Leith Walkway, which will extend from Balerno to Leith.
Photograph, 1985, by Phyllis Margaret Cant.

laissez-faire. The arched entrance to Stockbridge Market provides a
unique backcloth in the short cul-de-sac of St. Stephen Place, and
near the junction with Clarence Street a group of old Stockbridge
buildings has taken on a new lease of life: St. Stephen's School, with
the open Bible on the roof line, has been owned since 1945 by J.
Shepherd & Son Ltd., manufacturing stationers; the red brick St.
Vincent's Church Hall is home to the Theatre School of Dance and
Drama; and the former St. Stephen's Church Halls lie empty
awaiting a new tenant. Beyond Clarence Street, the last section is
dominated by Cinderella's Rockerfella's cacophonous 'mecca' of the
young at heart, one-time skating rink, music hall, theatre, horse
repository and cinema.

Suggestions for Further Reading

General

Author	Title	Year of Publication
Birrell, J.F.	An Edinburgh Alphabet	1980
	Book of the Old Edinburgh Club	1908 to date
Fothergill, George A.	Stones & Curiosities of Edinburgh and Neighbourhood	1910
Geddie, John	The Fringes of Edinburgh	1926
Gifford, John, McWilliam, Colin & Walker, David	The Buildings of Scotland: Edinburgh	1984
Grant, James	Old and New Edinburgh	1882
Gray, W. Forbes	Historic Churches of Edinburgh	1940
McKean, Charles	Edinburgh: An Illustrated Architectural Guide	1982
Royal Commission on the Ancient Monuments of Scotland	The City of Edinburgh	1951
Shepherd, Thomas H.	Modern Athens	1831
Thomas, Brendon	The Last Picture Shows: Edinburgh	1984

Corstorphine

Beveridge, A.	Some Corstorphine Street Names	1983
Corstorphine Trust	Corstorphine Notes	1975
Cowper, A.S.	Various Corstorphine Papers	1968 on
Dey, William G.	St. Anne's, Corstorphine	1966
Milligan, Oswald B.	Corstorphine and its Parish Church	1929
Scottish Arts Council	Dovecot Tapestries Jubilee Exhibition 1912–1962	1962
Scottish Arts Council	Small Tapestries	1976

Author	Title	Year of Publica-tion
Scottish Arts Council	*Master Weavers: Tapestry from the Dovecot Studios 1912–1980*	1980
Selway, G. Upton	*A Mid-Lothian Village*	1890
Thomson, D.M.	*The Corstorphine Heirloom*	1946

Cramond

Breeze, David J.	*The Northern Frontiers of Roman Britain*	1982
Cadell, Patrick	*The Iron Mills at Cramond*	1973
Cramond Association	*Cramond*	1979
Cramond Heritage Trust	*Cramond Heritage Park*	n.d.
Sidgwick, Frank (editor)	*The Complete Marjory Fleming*	1934
Small, John	*Castles & Mansions of the Lothians*	1883
Wood, John P.	*The Antient and Modern State of the Parish of Cramond*	1794

Davidson's Mains

Brown, Robin & McCallum, Ian	*The History of Davidson's Mains*	1968
Fairley, John A.	*Lauriston Castle*	1925
Gray, W. Forbes	*Some Old Scots Judges*	1914
Philip, Rev. Adam	*The Ancestry of Randall Thomas Davidson D.D., Archbishop of Canterbury*	1903
Rowan, Martha	*Lauriston Castle*	1974
Taylor, James	*Lord Jeffrey and Craigcrook*	1892

Dean

Ballantine, James	*The Miller of Deanhaugh*	1844
Environmental Resource Centre	*The Water of Leith Trail: Dean to Stockbridge*	1982
Geddie, John	*The Home Country of R.L. Stevenson*	1898

Author	Title	Year of Publication
Hill, Cumberland	*Historic Memorials & Reminiscences of Stockbridge & Water of Leith*	1887
Jamieson, Stanley (editor)	*The Water of Leith*	1984
Sanderson, Kenneth W.	*Belgrave Crescent Gardens*	1983
Skinner, Basil	*The House on the Bridge*	1982

Duddingston

Author	Title	Year of Publication
Baird, William	*Annals of Duddingston and Portobello*	1898
Bell, A.S. (editor)	*The Scottish Antiquarian Tradition*	1981
Cameron, Charles W.	*Curiosities of Old Edinburgh*	1975
Chambers, Robert	*The Innocent Railway*	1847
Cruikshank, W.G.	*Duddingston Kirk and Village*	1979
MacDonald, Ross	*Famous Edinburgh Crimes*	1953
Napier, Robert W.	*John Thomson of Duddingston*	1919
Smith, David B.	*Curling: an Illustrated History*	1981
Speedy, Tom	*Craigmillar and its Environs*	1892
Warrender, Margaret	*Walks near Edinburgh*	1895

Newcraighall

Author	Title	Year of Publication
Arnot, R. Page	*A History of the Scottish Miners*	1955
Brister, Charles	*This is my Kingdom*	1972
Gray, W. Forbes	*Some Old Scots Judges*	1914
Hannan, Thomas	*Famous Scottish Houses — The Lowlands*	1928
McNeill, Peter	*Blawearie*	1887
McWilliam, Colin	*The Buildings of Scotland: Lothian*	1978
National Coal Board	*A Short History of the Scottish Coal-mining Industry*	1958

Newhaven

Author	Title	Year of Publication
Anderson, James	*Report on ship canal from Newhaven to Leith*	1834

Author	Title	Year of Publication
Burnett, Rev. A. Ian	*The Church of Newhaven-on-Forth, 1836–1936*	1936
Campbell, Alex.	*The History of Leith*	1827
Colston, James	*The Town & Port of Leith*	1892
Cupples, Mrs George	*Newhaven: Its origin and history*	1888
McGowran, Tom	*Newhaven on Forth*	1985
Marshall, James Scott	*The Life and Times of Leith*	1986
Russell, John	*The Story of Leith*	1922
Wallace, J.C.	*Chapel of St. Mary & St. James: Book of the Old Edinburgh Club* xxxiv	1979
Wallace, Joyce M.	*Traditions of Trinity and Leith*	1985
Wilson, James (edited by Robin M. Black)	*Society of Free Fishermen of Newhaven*	1951

Restalrig

Barnett, T. Ratcliffe	*Border By-ways & Lothian Lore*	1950
Cowper, A. S.	*Restalrig Churchyard & Piershill Barracks*	1977
Gray, W. Forbes	*An Edinburgh Miscellany*	1925
Notman, Rev. Robert Black	*Restalrig Parish Church*	1961
Russell, John	*The Story of Leith*	1922
Smith, James	*The Story of Craigentinny: Book of the Old Edinburgh Club* xxii	1938
Stirton, E.G.K.	*The Tragedy of Marionville*	1930

Stockbridge

Allan, Norman	*The Stockbridge Scouts, 1908–1983*	1983
Environmental Resource Centre	*The Water of Leith Trail: Dean to Stockbridge*	1982
Environmental Resource Centre	*The Water of Leith Trail: Stockbridge to Canonmills*	1982
Hill, Cumberland	*Historic Memorials of Stockbridge*	1887

Author	Title	Year of Publica-tion
Jamieson, Stanley (editor)	*The Water of Leith*	1984
Kerr, Andrew	*A History of Ann Street*	1982
McWilliam, Colin	*Edinburgh New Town Guide*	1984
Magnusson, Magnus	*The Clacken and the Slate*	1974
Pipes, Rosemary J.	*The Colonies of Stockbridge*	1984
Sands, The Hon. Lord	*The Story of St. Stephen's Edinburgh, 1828–1928*	1927
Smith, John Turnbull	*Sketch of St. Bernard's*	1907
Young, George A.	*St. Bernard's Parish Church, 1823–1973*	1973

Index

235